RELEVANCE AND APPLICATION OF HERITAGE IN CONTEMPORARY SOCIETY

In the contemporary world, unprecedented global events are challenging our ability to protect and enhance cultural heritage for future generations. *Relevance and Application of Heritage in Contemporary Society* examines innovative and flexible approaches to cultural heritage protection.

Bringing together cultural heritage scholars and activists from across the world, the volume showcases a spectrum of exciting new approaches to heritage protection, community involvement, and strategic utilization of expertise. The contributions deal with a range of highly topical issues, including armed conflict and non-state actors, as well as broad questions of public heritage, museum roles in society, heritage tourism, disputed ownership, and indigenous and local approaches. In so doing, the volume builds upon, and introduces readers to, a new cultural heritage declaration codified during a 2016 workshop at the Royal Ontario Museum, Canada.

Offering a clarion call for an enduring spirit of innovation, collaboration, education, and outreach, *Relevance and Application of Heritage in Contemporary Society* will be important reading for scholars, students, cultural heritage managers, and local community stakeholders.

Pei-Lin Yu is Associate Professor of Anthropology at Boise State University, Idaho, USA, with twenty years of experience in federal cultural heritage management. She has conducted ethnoarchaeological research in both Venezuela and Taiwan.

Chen Shen is a Senior Curator of Chinese Art and Archaeology at Royal Ontario Museum, Toronto, Canada, where he currently serves as Vice President of World Cultures. He is cross-appointed as Professor in the East Asian Studies Department at the University of Toronto.

George S. Smith was formerly the associate director of the National Park Service's Southeast Archaeological Center (USA) and currently holds an appointment in the Department of Anthropology at Florida State University, Florida, USA.

RELEVANCE AND APPLICATION OF HERITAGE IN CONTEMPORARY SOCIETY

Edited by Pei-Lin Yu, Chen Shen, and George S. Smith

NEW YORK AND LONDON

First published 2018
by Routledge
711 Third Avenue, New York, NY 10017

and by Routledge
2 Park Square, Milton Park, Abingdon, Oxon, OX14 4RN

Routledge is an imprint of the Taylor & Francis Group, an informa business

© 2018 Taylor & Francis

The right of Pei-Lin Yu, Chen Shen, and George S. Smith to be identified as the authors of the editorial material, and of the authors for their individual chapters, has been asserted in accordance with sections 77 and 78 of the Copyright, Designs and Patents Act 1988.

All rights reserved. No part of this book may be reprinted or reproduced or utilised in any form or by any electronic, mechanical, or other means, now known or hereafter invented, including photocopying and recording, or in any information storage or retrieval system, without permission in writing from the publishers.

Trademark notice: Product or corporate names may be trademarks or registered trademarks, and are used only for identification and explanation without intent to infringe.

Library of Congress Cataloging-in-Publication Data
A catalog record for this title has been requested

ISBN: 978-1-62958-388-4 (hbk)
ISBN: 978-1-62958-389-1 (pbk)
ISBN: 978-0-203-70227-7 (ebk)

Typeset in Bembo
by Apex CoVantage, LLC

CONTENTS

List of Illustrations	*viii*
List of Contributors	*x*

1 Balancing the Past with the Needs and Concerns of Contemporary Society   1
  George S. Smith, Pei-Lin Yu, and Chen Shen

2 Lessons Since 2003: Protecting Cultural Heritage during Conflict   11
  Peter Stone

3 Online Public Opinion and Archaeological Heritage Conservation: A Case Study from Western Canada   21
  David Pokotylo

4 Objects of the Past: Relevance of Cultural Heritage in 21st-Century Museums   35
  Chen Shen

5 What's a Museum to Do? The Global Trade in Illegal Antiquities   44
  L. Eden Burgess

6 Public Perception and Policy Changes of Cultural Heritage Management in China   56
  Jigen Tang

7 Value and Values in Heritage Tourism from the Grand Tour
to the Experience Economy 66
Uzi Baram

8 Heritage in a Changing World and Higher Education for
Heritage Managers: A Pilot Program from Egypt 79
Fekri Hassan

9 Higher Education and Cultural Heritage Management
Programs: A Personal Perspective 91
George S. Smith

10 Engaging "the Public" in Heritage: Which Public and
Whose Heritage? 96
Elizabeth S. Chilton

11 Regulating Indigenous Heritage: Impacts of Governmental
Policies and Procedures on Indigenous Heritage 105
Joe Watkins

12 The New Data Makers: Indigenous Innovations in Cultural
Heritage Management 115
Pei-Lin Yu

13 Cultural Heritage Management in Developing Countries:
Challenges and Opportunities 125
Jeffrey H. Altschul

14 Heritage in the Global Economy: Protecting Cultural
Heritage through Nongovernmental and Voluntary Practices 135
Marion Werkheiser, Trace Brooks, and Ellen Chapman

15 Heritage, Climate Change, and Adaptation Planning 146
Diane L. Douglas

16 The Fusion of Law and Ethics in Cultural Heritage
Management: The 21st Century Confronts Archaeology 160
Hilary A. Soderland and Ian A. Lilley

17 Cultural Heritage Stewardship: Global Challenges and
New Approaches for an Uncertain Future 186
Arlene K. Fleming

*Appendix A: The Toronto Declaration on the Relevance and
Application of Heritage in Contemporary Society, Full English Version*   *199*
Appendix B: Spanish-Language 'Pocket' Version of the Toronto Declaration   *203*
*Appendix C: Chinese- (Simplified) Language 'Pocket' Version of the
Toronto Declaration*   *205*
Appendix D: French-Language 'Pocket' Version of the Toronto Declaration   *207*
Appendix E: Arabic-Language 'Pocket' Version of the Toronto Declaration   *209*
Index   *210*

ILLUSTRATIONS

Figures

3.1	Gulf Islands Residents and First Nations Protesting House Construction on Grace Islet, August 26, 2014	24
3.2	Distribution of Number of Reader Comments to a Discussion Thread	27
3.3	Distribution of Number of Comments Contributed by Reader	28
3.4	Distribution of Online Commenter 'Types'	29
3.5	Distribution of Online Commenter Types by Controversy Phase	29
4.1a-b	Chinese Jade *bi* Disc Dated to 4,000 Years Ago, a Ritual Jade Object of Liangzhu Culture in Eastern China, Once in the Collection of China's Famed Wu Dacheng, Is Now the Latest Addition to the ROM	39
4.2	The Africa Program at the ROM	42
6.1	A Shang Dynasty Chariot under Excavation at Yinxu	59
6.2	The National Archaeological Park of Yinxu, Created in 2010	62
6.3	A Questionnaire Used to Survey the Attitude of Local Residents at Yinxu	64
7.1	Tourists Disembarking from Cruise Ship at Cozumel	68
7.2	Theming for Disney World Begins on the Highway	69
7.3	Venice at Disney World	72
7.4	Tables and Tourists at Piazza San Marco	73
12.1	Ira Matt, left, and Don Sam, right, of the Confederated Salish and Kootenai Tribal Cultural Preservation Program Document Items Found Melting out of an Ice Patch	121
17.1	Flooding and Wind in Jacksonville, Florida, during Hurricane Irma in 2017	189

Tables

3.1	Online Newspaper Reader Comments Database.	25
3.2	Online Reader Comment Types and Characteristics	26
13.1	CHP Risk Analysis (Threats and Opportunities) Results	132
15.1	Climate Change Impacts on Heritage Resources	149
15.2	Cultural Adaptive Strategies to Climate Change	152

CONTRIBUTORS

Jeffrey H. Altschul is President of the SRI Foundation and has served as President of the Society for American Archaeology, President of the Register of Professional Archaeologists, and as Principal in two cultural heritage consultancies. His research centers on sustainable cultural heritage frameworks in developing countries including North and Latin America, Europe, West Africa, and Central Asia.

Uzi Baram is Professor of Anthropology at New College of Florida and founding director of the New College of Public Archaeology. His teaching and research includes the archaeology of the Ottoman Empire, historic landscapes in North America, studies of race and inequalities, the intersection of archaeology and tourism, and the dynamics of heritage.

Trace Brooks is an attorney with the Balch Law Group in Atlanta, Georgia, and a student in the Tax LL.M. program at the University of Florida. Trace is a graduate of the Georgia State University College of Law and the Department of Anthropology.

L. Eden Burgess is an attorney and lobbyist with Cultural Heritage Partners, PLLC. She has represented nonprofits, tribes, foreign states, museums, and collectors and has litigated complex claims involving Nazi seizures, wartime looting, forced sales, and thefts. She also advises the Gas and Preservation Partnership (GAPP), a nonprofit approach to multiparty solutions involving the gas industry and the preservation community.

Ellen Chapman is a doctoral candidate in the Department of Anthropology at the College of William & Mary and recently defended her dissertation proposal, "Hidden under the River City: The Archaeological Landscape and Concepts of Archaeological Value in Richmond, Virginia".

Contributors xi

Elizabeth S. Chilton is Dean of the Harpur College of Arts and Sciences at Binghamton University in New York. She has served as a Professor of Anthropology and founder and director of the Center for Heritage & Society. Her work focuses on heritage studies, the archaeology of New England, Native American maize horticulture, social complexity, and the analysis of material culture.

Diane L. Douglas is Senior Archaeologist and Principal Investigator at Applied EarthWorks, Inc. She has more than twenty-five years of experience managing large-scale, multidisciplinary environmental assessments (EAs), environmental impact statements (EISs), and environmental social impact assessments (ESIAs), and her work focuses on climate change adaptation and disaster risk reduction planning. She has provided these services for FEMA and the UN ISDR among other global partners.

Arlene K. Fleming is a Cultural Resource and Development Specialist at the World Bank Group. She has worked in investment for cultural heritage development in Turkey, Lebanon, Tunisia, Morocco, China, and Eritrea, where she was team leader for the Cultural Assets Rehabilitation Project. She has reformulated policy for safeguarding physical cultural resources in bank-financed projects and directed the Physical Cultural Resources Country Profiles project and advises UNESCO, U.S. government agencies, and nongovernmental agencies on the protection and management of cultural resources.

Fekri Hassan is the director of Egypt's first higher education program in cultural heritage management at the French University in Egypt. He is also professor emeritus and former chair of Petrie Professor of Archaeology of the Institute of Archaeology and Department of Egyptology of University College London, editor of the *African Archaeological Review* journal, contributory editor of *The Review of Archaeology*, and Honorary President of the Egyptian Cultural Heritage Organisation.

Ian A. Lilley is Professor in Aboriginal and Torres Strait Islander Studies at the University of Queensland in Australia. He has worked in Australasian and Indo-Pacific archaeology and cultural heritage for forty years and has served as Secretary-General of the ICOMOS International Scientific Committee on Archaeological Heritage Management and on the IUCN World Commissions on Protected Areas and Environmental, Economic and Social Policy. In addition, he served as Secretary of the World Archaeological Congress and as President of the Australian Archaeological Association.

David Pokotylo is Associate Professor of anthropology at the University of British Columbia and past President of the Canadian Archaeological Association. He has worked on the Statement of Principles for Ethical Conduct Pertaining to Aboriginal Peoples, and his research involves public perceptions of archaeological preservation in contemporary society and its economic implications.

Chen Shen is a Senior Curator of Chinese Art and Archaeology, currently serves as Vice President of World Cultures at Royal Ontario Museum, Toronto, Canada, and is cross-appointed as Professor at the East Asian Studies Department, University of Toronto.

George S. Smith retired as the associate director of the National Park Service's Southeast Archaeological Center and currently holds an appointment in the Department of Anthropology at Florida State University.

Hilary A. Soderland has directed the PhD in Law Program at the University of Washington School of Law and teaches interdisciplinary courses to law, social science, and humanities graduate students. A registered professional Archaeologist, her publications include articles, commissioned works, and coedited books on archaeology legislation, cultural heritage law, repatriation, and archaeological resource protection and heritage management on three continents.

Peter Stone, OBE, is UNESCO Chair in Cultural Property Protection and Peace Professor of Heritage Studies and Head of School of Arts and Cultures at Newcastle University. He is also Secretary General of the Association of National Committees of the Blue Shield, Chairman of the UK National Committee of the Blue Shield, and a member of the UK National Commission for UNESCO's Expert Network.

Jigen Tang is the Chair Professor at Southern University of Science and Technology in Shenzhen, China. His research includes cultural heritage management, public archaeology, Bronze Age China, and mortuary archaeology. He has worked with ICOMOS on exhibits including the South to North Water Project; Treasures of the Capital of the Shang Dynasty; History of Chinese Writing; Archaeological Work at Yinxu; and the 40th Anniversary of the Institute of Archaeology, Chinese Academy of Social Sciences for the Palace Museum at the Forbidden City in Beijing.

Joe Watkins is a member of the Choctaw Nation of Oklahoma, has been involved in anthropology for more than forty-five years. He is currently serving as supervisory anthropologist and the chief of the Tribal Relations and American Cultures Program of the National Park Service in Washington, DC. His research focuses on impacts of national policy guidelines on the heritage of communities across the United States and worldwide.

Marion Werkheiser is cofounder and managing member of Cultural Heritage Partners, PLLC. She is a strategic advisor to clients throughout the cultural heritage and preservation communities and cofounded the Lawyers' Committee for Cultural Heritage Preservation, serving as vice president. Marion is also an expert member of the International Council on Monuments and Sites (ICOMOS) Committee on Legal, Administrative, and Financial Issues.

Pei-Lin Yu is Associate Professor at Boise State University, has more than twenty years of experience in federal cultural heritage management and indigenous cultural heritage partnerships in the American West. She has also conducted ethnoarchaeological research with Venezuelan hunting and gathering peoples and recently worked under a Senior Fulbright Fellowship with Taiwan's indigenous farmers.

1

BALANCING THE PAST WITH THE NEEDS AND CONCERNS OF CONTEMPORARY SOCIETY

George S. Smith, Pei-Lin Yu, and Chen Shen

Introduction

Balancing the past with the needs and concerns of contemporary society is essential to maintaining relevance to contemporary societies. This balance requires applying legal, ethical, management, and scientific perspectives in a manner that is accountable and sustainable and includes the ethical responsibility to interact, consult, and work with stakeholders to advocate for the quality of life for future generations. This builds capacity for the past to compete with other agendas, allows different ways of viewing the past to coexist, and maintains adaptive options to keep cultural heritage relevant in contemporary society during times of rapid change.

The lives of people are rich with the past remembered. Knowing and connecting to the past gives insight to who we are, how we live our lives, how we view and treat others, and how we treat the past. Because the past is examined and explained within the context of contemporary society, it is continually influenced by social, political, religious, and/or scientific factors. This is why the heritage community needs to be aware of how the past is understood within the context of various agendas and how those agendas influence the way heritage is valued, protected, studied, and used. The heritage community is diverse, including not only those who study, manage, and protect the past but those who engage with descendants and other stakeholders—and stakeholders themselves. The community as a whole benefits from an understanding of the past in the modern world in order to be relevant and to contribute effectively to understanding and appreciation of public benefits of our collective cultural patrimony.

Being aware that there is not just one way of knowing about the past and making sure that the past is not dominated by only a few voices are critical to telling our collective story. It is important that the past be studied in a way that provides creditable accounts of how old things are, where they came from, and how they were used (Biehl and Prescott 2012; Lipe 2002). This contributes significantly to our understanding and empowers the public to make informed decisions about multiple and often competing explanations and agendas regarding the past. Remembering the past has been a vital part of the human experience for millennia, first as oral tradition and later with additions of pictorial representations including art and writing. Memories—whether individual or collective or held by dominant or subordinate groups—serve to validate the past (Shackel 2001). However, this does not mean that competing ideas about the past cannot exist. In fact, it is not unusual to have different versions of the same past operating at the same time and be equally valid even if not consistent (Ibid.). The main requirement for a common past to be relevant, and therefore transferred and perpetuated, is that there be collective remembering.

There are many ways of looking at the past (Hutt et al. 1999; Shackel 2001; Tsosie 1997), all of which define who talks and who listens. The heritage community must make a commitment to understanding various perspectives relating to the past, which may work at cross-purposes. The dialogue must not only be about the past itself but also about those whose past is studied. As long as the majority of antiquity laws treat the past under the concept of property law and not human rights (Silverman and Ruggles 2007a, b), there will be questions of ownership, which defines who owns and controls the past and for what purpose. Efforts to protect and understand the past must not separate the past from the people, because all people have the right to cultural survival, even within the context of assimilation policies and concepts of 'common good', 'public resource', or 'public trust' (Knudson 1991; Silverman and Ruggles 2007a, b; Tsosie 1997). After years of exclusion, many groups around the world are finding their voices, demanding inclusion to tell the story of their past.

This is resulting in universal declarations regarding people's inalienable right to have a meaningful connection to their past. Numerous international documents include but are not limited to the Universal Declaration of Human Rights (1948), the Convention for the Protection of Cultural Resources in the Event of Armed Conflict (1954), the Declaration of Principles of International Cultural Cooperation (1966), the International Covenant of Civil and Political Rights (1966), the International Covenant of Economic, Social and Cultural Rights (1966), the Convention on the Means of Prohibiting and Preventing the Illicit Import, Export and Transfer of Ownership of Cultural Property (1970), the Convention Concerning the Protection of the World Cultural and Natural Heritage (1972), the UNIDROIT (International Institute for the Unification of Private Law) Convention on Stolen or Illegally Exported Cultural Objects (1995), and the Convention on the Protection of the Underwater Cultural Heritage (2001). These declarations clearly demonstrate that having a meaningful connection to one's own past is a fundamental human right and that damage to any nation's past (tangible and intangible) is damage to all of humankind. Furthermore, these documents assert that the dignity and value of culture must be respected as a fundamental right because the past is a basic element of civilization and understanding between peoples and well-being of humanity and the progress of civilization.

An integral part of these documents is that the past is an important element in the history of peoples, nations, and their relations with each other concerning their common past (Elia 2014; Gerstenblith 2014; Labadi 2014; Messenger and Smith 2010; O'Keefe 2014; Willems 2014). Currently, all countries have established national laws dealing with the protection of the past, demonstrating its universal value and importance in modern society (Messenger and Smith 2010).

What Gets Valued

Any discussion of what gets valued, including the past, begins in the realm of ethics and morals. This has been examined and discussed from both Western and non-Western perspectives (Lipe 1974; Lowenthal 2004; Lynott and Wylie 1995; Scarre and Scarre 2006; Soderland 2013; Zimmerman et al. 2003). Values, in no small part, are also based on memory (Silverman and Ruggles 2007a, b). In exploring the concept of values, a number of common themes emerge that have direct application to what gets valued and why. These include the belief that value is assigned and has something to do with the quality of life for individuals, communities, and nations and that choosing to value the past—or not choosing to value it—has consequences (Clark 2006; Guyer 1993; Smith et al. 2010; Tessitore 1996). As such, the question of valuing the past could be discussed in terms of freedom and responsibility as expressed within the realm of duty, honor, personal responsibility, fairness, inclusiveness, stewardship, social obligations, quality of life, and a broad range of similar considerations. The question will always be: whose values to include? This forms the basis for the assertion that information about the public's preferences can only improve decision making.

Although the heritage community is beginning to address how to define and apply valuing the past in contemporary society, efforts to connect to the past in meaningful ways are nothing new (Fowler 1992; Hewison 1987; Lowenthal 1985; Messenger and Smith 2010). However, this process has not always been smooth and equitable, because valuing the past worldwide can be influenced by many factors. Geopolitical changes such as those in government and governance, some through an electoral process, others through social change or armed conflict, can have significant impacts on valuing the past and whose past takes priority. This, no doubt, influences who speaks and who listens.

Many if not all governments have struggled with balancing the past with the needs of contemporary society (Clark 2010; de Blasi 2010; Fleming 2010; Fleming and Campbell 2010; Jansen 2010; Lizama Aranda 2010; Morgan et al. 2010; Smith and Messenger 2010). These efforts have not all been successful. There has been a long-established history of using the past to establish rights to the land. This has been demonstrated worldwide through colonialism and efforts to establish national identities and pride, even at the expense of other claims. This can bring about complex issues dealing with land tenure, social conflict, indigenous rights, and economic development. Careful attention to terminology is part of the solution. Terms used in the establishment of laws, regulations, policies, and guidelines can influence how the past is studied, managed, and used (Willem 2010). For example, the widely used term 'cultural resource management' suggests to some use and exploitation, while the term 'cultural heritage management' suggests conservation and acknowledgment of other ways of knowing and dealing with the past (Burke and Smith 2010). This seems to be more of an issue in countries with large extant indigenous populations. This is not a generally accepted concept worldwide; thus discussion and debate will likely continue for some time.

When incorporated into mainstream planning, our understanding of the past can not only contribute to economic development but provide impacts to the quality of life. As such demonstrating the relevance, application, and incorporation of cultural patrimony can enhance overall sustainable economic growth. The heritage community is awaking to the power of the past for empowering economic development and not just being a consumer of budgetary resources. The past has values that can be defined and discussed in many ways. Because the past deals with many aspects of cultural, moral, spiritual, political, and economic aspects of communities and nations, it can be a powerful engine for economic development if and only if it is incorporated into development projects along with sociocultural knowledge, thus maximizing patrimony's vast economic and educational value. But first and foremost, it is critical to know the extent of those resources in such a way as to preserve commonalities and diversity, neither at the expense of the other (Cernea 2001).

Using inclusive terminology that brings stakeholders into the development of management philosophies allows non-Western and Western concepts of time and authenticity to be accommodated and successfully coexist with practices that see renewing sites as a means of showing respect while still maintaining integrity. This can impact an array of important issues and the decision-making process regarding the past at the local, national, and global levels, including but not limited to public education, economic development, indigenous claims and rights, multiethnic heritage, political agendas and ideologies, armed conflict, international agreements and organizations, collection management, tourism, poverty reduction, sustainable development, principles of the market economy and business practices including impact assessment and contracting, the law and legal and legislative systems, private land issues, religious and political issues, historic preservation, consultation requirements, ownership issues, lobbying and advocacy, management principles, best practices based on internationally accepted principles, the international problems revolving around the illegal international antiquities market, and the need for public accountability. Where this is embraced, it strengthens our ability to protect our dwindling global patrimony, give voice to those who cannot speak for themselves, see our commonalities and respect our differences, and work together for harmony and peace (Bender and Smith 2000).

Stakeholders and Inclusiveness

In defining values relating to the past, it is critical that we find ways to achieve greater inclusiveness in the decision-making process. The lack of accountability has been a major problem for the heritage community. We call for a broader definition of values relating to the past that includes not only the built environment but remnants of the past embedded in the ground or underwater along with a people's history and culture, all of which contribute to a collective memory that guides the present, impacts the future, and connects the past with the present.

What is it that compels us to make a connection with our past? Answers to the fundamental questions of what the past is and why it is important must be sought within a larger anthropological framework. All cultures have some means of relating to the past. It is clear that an accurate representation of the past is a critical element of all social life. No matter how the past is structured, understanding the past and protecting it are an integral part of the collective human experience. The question, then, is, how can we deal effectively with the past in contemporary society in a way that is clear and accountable and based on a decision process that includes stakeholders in an effort to help advance local conditions while at the same time not compromising the quality of life for future generations? It is critical that we first understand the nature of the community (Gould 2014).

The inclusion of many different stakeholders has emerged as one of the important themes in defining, applying, and valuing the past (Lowenthal 2004; Watkins et al. 2000; Meskell and Pels 2005). The stakeholder theme is inextricably entwined with parallel discussions of codes of conduct and ethics. At its core, ethical responsibility involves interaction and consultation with those who have a stake in the past under consideration. There should be robust and meaningful dialogue between the stakeholders and those who seek to use, investigate, or preserve the past in question. This statement brings up several fundamental questions:

- Whose past are we concerned about preserving?
- Who has the right to be a steward?
- Who is allowed to have a voice, and who has the authority to make such a choice?
- How do you balance Western epistemologies against alternate epistemologies?
- How do you interpret and present a resource when stakeholders' voices are in conflict?
- Does the past belong to everyone, or do some stakeholders have a stronger claim to particular pieces than others? Who has the authority to decide?

All these questions have a common theme: who owns the past? This important question must be framed not just in reference to current and past geopolitical boundaries or homelands. It must in some way reflect the human family. In our distant past when human populations were small and less dispersed, communities were tight knit. Through separation and time, we have developed differences that now must be considered in our global village. Protecting the past may be a function of location, but its basis is founded on a shared common past. We must act locally but think globally. We must consider and weigh the past with respect to current and future needs. For nations to exist, they must have a connection to a past, and to grow and fully participate as global partners, nations must find the balance between past, present, and future. Today with the technology available to us, we can regain functionality as a community—a global community. The book you are holding springs from this concept.

About This Volume

To apply the latest knowledge from archaeology, history, anthropology, and legal studies to emerging global situations that call for new adaptive strategies for broad definition and fair application of cultural heritage, a workshop was convened at the Royal Ontario Museum in Toronto in October 2016. An international team of experts explored heritage themes in contemporary society and identified key actions to ensure that heritage is inclusive and has a place now and in the future.

The contributions in this volume reflect an iterative process in which subject matter experts prepared papers, participated in a workshop of focused discussion and scoping of recommended actions, then revised papers using new data and syncretic results achieved during the workshop. The result is a cohesive treatment of the many ways to ensure relevance of cultural heritage and apply it in contemporary society. In a culminating and multilingual Declaration (see Appendices A–E), participants codified issues and concerns; affirmed and clarified our shared commitment to diverse, inclusive, and relevant heritage; explored ways to improve the relevance and application of heritage values; and made specific recommendations regarding methods for accomplishment.

The topic of relevancy to contemporary society covers a broad conceptual, spatial, and temporal span. The papers in the volume are organized in a conceptual arc that begins with the urgency of global threats posed to cultural heritage by warfare and nonstate armed conflict. Stone describes the history behind cooperative international solutions and features the operations of Blue Shield to address these threats proactively. Public support of cultural heritage begins at home, and learning and analyzing the attitudes of local communities toward cultural heritage protection are the subject of Pokotylo's analysis of a fascinating case study from British Columbia.

For families and other community members seeking cultural heritage experiences through culturally meaningful objects, Shen's chapter celebrates the unique role of museums in public life, shared heritage, and story making. The mission of museums can be complicated by the effects of the global illegal antiquities sector, which are elucidated by Burgess along with international cooperative efforts to mitigate those impacts. The influence of cultural heritage preservation and interpretation can have profound effects on local communities, many unintended. Tang describes the challenges faced by communities that are located literally atop one of the world's most significant heritage cultural landscapes: the State of Yin at Anyang, China.

Tourism is the lifeblood of heritage destinations and is evolving in new directions worldwide. The rapidly expanding experience economy is the subject of Baram's thorough treatment of 19th century roots in 'grand tours' and how that impulse continues to transform the ways that tourists seek out and experience cultural heritage in Europe and Florida. Stewardship of heritage tourism locations and the broad array of cultural heritage increasingly calls for a multidisciplinary skillset, and Smith describes the rapid evolution of cultural heritage education toward meeting that goal over the past three decades. Hassan's perspective from the heritage education sector in Egypt highlights international directions involving multiple partners including local community members in the heritage education enterprise.

Reexamining definitions of cultural heritage stakeholders, especially what is meant by the 'public', is key to enhancing the relevance of heritage to contemporary society. Chilton takes a close look at prior assumptions about publics and exploring methods for redefining this crucial concept and terminology. In colonized countries, indigenous perspectives and interests related to cultural heritage stewardship face unique challenges. Watkins synthesizes the accomplishments of U.S. policy and trust relationships toward Native cultural heritage stewardship with critical unmet needs that point toward increasing self-determination in heritage management. We must keep in mind that a sense of identity and place is also an important part of our heritage and that when assessing the public interest in the past it is important to have reliable data about what the public thinks is critical to long-term studies (EFTEC 2005). Yu continues with Watkins's theme by celebrating indigenous data creation, analysis, and management with case studies from Pacific Northwest interior tribal programs.

Managing the past and the potential economic rewards is contingent upon valuing and protecting them. As such studying, managing and protecting the past can be considered a public good, not only at the local level but at the national and global levels as well. This justifies the use of public funds. Capturing the public value of the past is critical to sustainable economic development (Clark 2006). Flexibility in form and function of cultural heritage infrastructure is the subject of Altschul's discussion of developing countries, which must balance stewardship of cultural heritage with the basic needs of contemporary societies such as economic growth. Expanding cultural heritage partnerships with an extragovernmental approach that emphasizes voluntary practices is one method outlined by Werkheiser et al., which brings the corporate sector into the heritage 'tent' through strategic incentives. On the local end of the scale, small traditional communities are highly adapted to their home environments through time-tested cultural knowledge. Douglas makes the case that this knowledge is worthy of preservation in its own right as cultural heritage and also an important source of tactics to offset impacts from one of the biggest challenges to face contemporary societies today: climate change.

The mutual influence of cultural heritage upon contemporary ethics and morals is the focus of the final two chapters. Soderland and Lilley's discussion of the effect of law and ethics on professional practice and engagement of archaeologists spotlights the ways that ethics are interwoven into every aspect of archaeology, including day-to-day planning and fieldwork. The stakes are high, as are opportunities for cultural heritage to make a difference. Bringing the arc of this volume to closure with another look at the upheavals of the early 21st century, Fleming makes a powerful case for the importance of cultural heritage in tackling global crises that transcend boundaries (e.g., climate change, the refugee crisis) and offering hope for resilient and healthy societies and ecosystems.

Conclusion

It is clear that there is a tremendous opportunity to draw upon our collective patrimony and national and international policies on a worldwide scale in order to articulate the need for effective, sustainable, and responsive policies and practices regarding the past. This is critical if we are to develop and continually adapt best practices; be responsive to crisis or conflict situations on a global scale; ensure adequate funding at the local, national, and international levels; and create new models, tools, and partnerships to help protect, manage, and enjoy our collective cultural patrimony.

The relevance of the past must be demonstrated to 21st-century communities, and it is up to the cultural heritage community to take the lead in this endeavor. In order to effectively address the relevance of the past and its application in contemporary society as a global community, we need to undertake the following:

- Understand the full extent of collective past and quantify those values so that they can be taken into consideration with respect to local, national, and international policies, strategies, and financing and how to enlist the fiscal and human resources of developers, national and local governments, local communities, nongovernmental agencies, professional and international organizations, funding agencies, regulators, researchers, educators, and the public to ensure that heritage is defined broadly and applied fairly.
- Overcome isolation of the global heritage community with respect to development, tourism, international partnerships, and networks in order to build reciprocal cooperative bridges.
- Develop and promote a heritage community as an advocate for our cultural patrimony that could help integrate institutional and financial support and ensure input at the level where policy crafting, resource allocation, and actual planning of government assistance and collaboration take place. And finally
- Intensify efforts at education and training at local, regional, and global levels with respect to the past.

We hope that this volume and its accompanying Declaration will play a part in advancing the relevance and application of heritage in contemporary society worldwide. This effort has received generous support from the Wenner-Gren Foundation, the Royal Ontario Museum, and Boise State University. Editor royalties from its sale will be donated to the World Archaeological Congress.

References

Bender, S. J., and G. S. Smith, editors 2000 *Teaching Archaeology in the 21st Century*. Society for American Archaeology, Washington, DC.

Biehl, P. F., and C. Prescott, editors 2012 *Heritage in the Context of Globalization Europe and the Americas*. Springer, New York.

Burke, H., and C. Smith 2010 Vestiges of Colonialism: Manifestations of the Culture/Nature Divide in Australian Heritage Management. In *Cultural Heritage Management: A Global Perspective*, edited by P. Mauch Messenger and G. S. Smith, pp. 21–37. University Press of Florida, Gainesville.

Cernea, M. M. 2001 At the Cutting Edge: Cultural Patrimony Protection Through Development Projects. In *Historic Cities and Sacred Sites: Cultural Roots for Urban Futures*, edited by I. Serageldin, E. Shluger, and J. Martin-Brown, pp. 67–88. The World Bank, Washington, DC.

Clark, K. 2010 Values in Cultural Resource Management. In *Heritage Values in Contemporary Society*, edited by G. S. Smith, P. Mauch Messenger and H. A. Soderland, pp. 89–99. Left Coast Press, Walnut Creek, California.

———. 2006 *Capturing the Public Value of Heritage: The Proceedings of the London Conference 25–26, January 2006*. English Heritage, Swindon, England.

deBlasi, P. 2010 Twenty Years of Cultural/Heritage Resources Management in Brazil: A Short Evaluation (1986–2006). In *Cultural Heritage Management: A Global Perspective*, edited by P. Mauch Messenger and G. S. Smith, pp. 38–47. University Press of Florida, Gainesville.

EFTEC 2005 *Valuation of Historic Environment: The Scope of Using Results of Valuation Studies in the Appraisal and Assessment of Heritage Related Projects and Programs, Executive Summary*. Report to the English Heritage, the Heritage Lottery Fund, The Department for Culture, Media, and Sports, and the Department of Transportation, London.

Elia, R. J. 2014 International Conventions Pertaining to Heritage Policy. In *Encyclopedia of Global Archaeology*, edited by C. Smith, pp. 3954–3961. Springer, New York.

Fleming, A. K. 2010 Heritage Values, Public Policy, and Development. In *Heritage Values in Contemporary Society*, edited by G. S. Smith, P. Mauch Messenger and H. A. Soderland, pp. 101–112. Left Coast Press, Walnut Creek, California.

Fleming, A. K., and I. L. Campbell 2010 Cultural Heritage and the Development Process: Policies and Performance Standards of the World Bank. In *Cultural Heritage Management: A Global Perspective*, edited by P. Mauch Messenger and G. S. Smith, pp. 243–250. University Press of Florida, Gainesville.

Fowler, P. J. 1992 *The Past in Contemporary Society: Then, Now*. Routledge, London.

Gerstenblith, P. 2014 UNESCO (1970) and UNIDROIT (1995) Conventions. In *Encyclopedia of Global Archaeology*, edited by C. Smith, pp. 7428–7434 Springer, New York.

Gould, P. G. 2014 *Putting the Past to Work: Archaeology, Community and Economic Development*. Unpublished PhD dissertation, Institute of Archaeology, University College London, London.

Guyer, P. 1993 *Kant and the Experience of Freedom: Essays on Aesthetics and Morality*. Cambridge University Press, Cambridge.

Hewison, R. 1987 *The Heritage Industry*. Oxford University Press, Oxford.

Hutt, S., C. M. Blanco, and O. Varmer 1999 *Heritage Resources Law: Protecting the Archeological and Cultural Environment*. John Wiley and Sons, Inc., New York.

Jansen II, W. H. 2010 Issues, Intuitions, and Resources in the Policy Mix. In *Cultural Heritage Management: A Global Perspective*, edited by P. Mauch Messenger and G. S. Smith, pp. 230–242. University Press of Florida, Gainesville.

Knudson, R. 1991 The Archaeological Public Trust in Context. In *Protecting the Past*, edited by G. S. Smith and J. E. Ehrenhard, pp. 3–7. CRC Press, Boca Raton.

Labadi, S. 2014 UNESCO World Heritage Convention (1972). In *Encyclopedia of Global Archaeology*, edited by C. Smith, pp. 7434–739. Springer, New York.

Lipe, W. D 2002 Public Benefits of Archaeological Research. In *Public Benefits of Archaeology*, edited by B. J. Little, pp. 20–28. University Press of Florida, Gainesville.

———. 1974 A Conservation Model for American Archaeology. *The Kiva* (39):213–245.
Lizama Aranda, L. 2010 Heritage Values and Mexican Cultural Policies: Dispossession of the "Other's" Culture by the Mexican Archaeological System. In *Heritage Values in Contemporary Society*, edited by P. Mauch Messenger, G. S. Smith, and H. A. Soderland, pp. 225–238. Left Coast Press, Walnut Creek.
Lowenthal, D. 2004 Heritage Ethics. In *Interpreting the Past 1. Presenting Archaeological Sites to the Public*, edited by N. Silberman, D. Callebaur and A. E. Killebrew, pp. 23–31. Flemish Heritage Institute, Brussels.
———. 1985 *The Past Is a Foreign Country*. Cambridge University Press, Cambridge.
Lynott, M. J., and A. Wylie 1995 *Ethics in American Archaeology: Challenges for the 1990s*. Special Report. Society for American Archaeology, Washington, DC.
Meskell, L., and P. Pels 2005 *Embedding Ethics*. Berg, Oxford
Messenger, P. Mauch., and G. S. Smith, editors 2010 *Cultural Heritage Management: A Global Perspective*. University Press of Florida, Gainesville.
Morgan, D. W., N. I. M. Morgan, B. Barrett, and S. Coping 2010 From National to Local: Intangible Values and the Decentralization of Heritage Management in the United States. In *Heritage Values in Contemporary Society*, edited by P. Mauch Messenger, G. S. Smith, and H. A. Soderland, pp. 113–128. Left Coast Press, Walnut Creek.
O'Keefe, P. J. 2014 UNIDROIT Convention on Stolen or Illegally Exported Cultural Objects (1995). In *Encyclopedia of Global Archaeology*, edited by C. Smith, pp. 7450–7455. Springer, New York.
Scarre, C., and G. Scarre 2006 *The Ethics of Archaeology. Philosophical Perspectives on Archaeological Practice*. Cambridge University Press, Cambridge.
Shackel, P. 2001 Public Memory and the Search for the Power in American Historical Archaeology. *American Anthropologist* 103(3):655–670.
Silverman, H., and D. F. Ruggles, editors 2007a *Cultural Heritage and Human Rights*. Springer, New York
———. 2007b Cultural Heritage and Human Rights. In *Heritage and Human Rights*, edited by H. Silverman and D. F. Ruggles, pp. 3–22. Springer, New York.
Smith, G. S., P. Mauch Messenger, and H. A. Soderland, editors 2010 *Heritage Values in Contemporary Society*. Left Coast Press, Walnut Creek.
Soderland, H. A. 2013 Heritage Values, Jurisprudence, and Globalization. In *Heritage in the Context of Globalization Europe and the Americas*, edited by P. F. Biehl and C. Prescott, pp. 11–17. Springer, New York.
Tessitore, A. 1996 *Reading Aristotle's Ethics: Virtue, Rhetoric and Political Philosophy*. State University of New York Press, Albany.
Tsosie, R. 1997 Indigenous Rights and Archaeology. In *Native Americans and Archaeologists: Stepping Stones to Common Ground*, edited by N. Swindler, K. E. Dongoske, R. Anyon, and A. S. Downer, pp. 64–76. AltaMira Press, Walnut Creek.
Watkins, J., K. A. Pyburn, and P. Cressey 2000 Community Relations: What the Practicing Archaeologists Needs to Know to Work Effectively with Local and/or Descendant Communities. In *Teaching Archaeology in the Twenty-First Century*, edited by S. J. Bender and G. S. Smith, pp. 73–82. Society for American Archaeology, Washington, DC.
Willems, W. J. H. 2014 UNESCO (1970) and Malta (1992). In *Encyclopedia of Global Archaeology*, edited by C. Smith, pp. 7433–7434. Springer, New York.
———. 2010 Laws, Language, and Learning: Managing Archaeological Heritage Resources in Europe. In *Cultural Heritage Management: A Global Perspective*, edited by P. Mauch Messenger and G. S. Smith, pp. 2212–229. University Press of Florida, Gainesville.
Zimmerman, L., K. Vitelli, and J. Hollowell-Zimmer, editors 2003 *Ethical Issues in Archaeology*. AltaMira Press, Walnut Creek.

2

LESSONS SINCE 2003

Protecting Cultural Heritage during Conflict

Peter Stone

In war, things get damaged and destroyed; people, military and civilian, get killed. That's war, and there is nothing you can do about it. To think that we might be able, or even think it legitimate, to attempt to protect a sub-set of 'things' is surely ludicrous and naive. And yet that is exactly what a group of heritage experts, encouraged by media, public, and political outcry—over, for example, the looting of the National Museum of Iraq or the destruction of parts of the ancient city of Palmyra—have been doing since 2003. Referring to the 1954 Hague Convention on the Protection of Cultural Property in the Event of Armed Conflict and its two Protocols of 1954 and 1999 (hereafter the 1954 Convention), this group has been trying to encourage armed combatants that the protection of cultural property is not only a good thing to do but also an important thing to do for a whole variety of different and compelling reasons.

This chapter outlines some of the arguments as to why cultural property should be protected, some of the protective framework that has been put into place, and activities that have been undertaken to help protect cultural property during armed conflict. These activities were begun by working with mainly European and American forces to limit the damage to the cultural property of the countries to which the forces were deployed and then developed to include the proactive protection of cultural property before and in the aftermath of conflict. Such work is undertaken with the belief that the heritage community must accept some of the responsibility for the damage and destruction done during recent conflicts as we communally failed to provide politicians and the military with the rationale for, and information to, protect cultural property before, during, and after these conflicts.

Historical Context

Interestingly, while cultural property is frequently a casualty of conflict, numerous military theorists and strategists, from Sun Tzu in 6th-century BC China to von Clausewitz in 19th-century Europe, have argued that allowing the cultural property of your enemy to be destroyed (or, worse, destroying it yourself) is bad military practice, as it can lead to resentment, make subjugated populations difficult to govern, and become the first reason for the next conflict (Sun Tzu 1998; von Clausewitz 1997).

Admittedly, it is only relatively recently that such advice has been acted upon. The restitution of cultural property removed as 'spoils of war' and for display and scientific study was introduced in the Treaty of Vienna following the Napoleonic wars (Miles 2011), and protection of cultural property during war was first enshrined in law in the 1863 *Instructions for the Government of Armies of the United States in the Field* (the 'Lieber Code'), which stated "Classical works of art, libraries, scientific collections ... must be secured against all avoidable injury ..." (Adjutant General's Office 1863, Article 35). A number of international treaties, for example the Hague Conventions of 1899 and 1907 and the 1935 Roerich Pact, developed this approach, and despite and because of the enormous damage to European heritage in the First World War, the international community was still debating how better to protect cultural property during war on the eve of the Second World War.

The First World War had also seen positive action. Upon the capture of Jerusalem in 1917, the British commander Allenby instructed that "every sacred building, monument, holy spot, shrine, traditional site ... of the three religions will be maintained and protected" (http://firstworldwar.com/source/jerusalem_allenbyprocl.htm, accessed August 17, 2017) and, showing a nuanced understanding of cultural sensitivities, ensured that Muslim troops from the Indian Army were deployed to protect important Islamic sites. In the Second World War, the protection of cultural property was seen clearly as part of the responsibility of the combatants, and the Allies and some elements of Axis forces took this responsibility seriously. The 'Monuments, Fine Arts, and Archives' unit was created in Allied forces, and these 'Monuments Men' made enormous efforts to protect cultural property in all theatres of the war (see Woolley 1947; Nicholas 1995; Edsel 2013). The unit had the full backing of the Supreme Allied Commander Eisenhower, who wrote immediately before the Normandy landings reminding troops that "Inevitably, in the path of our advance will be found historical monuments and cultural centres which symbolise to the world all that we are fighting to preserve. It is the responsibility of every commander to protect and respect these symbols wherever possible ..." (Instruction from Supreme Allied Commander, May 26, 1944). Many cultural sites, buildings, and collections were, of course, destroyed—but as much as possible was done to limit the destruction.

After the war, the international community came together to produce the 1954 Convention and its 1st Protocol (that mainly related to postconflict reparation of cultural property). However, sadly, little was done afterward to continue the work of these conscript-soldiers (although limited elements of their work were retained within some military 'civil affairs' units). Despite the addition of the 2nd (1999) Protocol (that provided for a new category of 'enhanced' protection for particularly important sites and that included the opportunity to treat the deliberate targeting of cultural property as a war crime), by the 2003 invasion of Iraq, few military forces retained anything other than a superficial expertise or commitment to the protection of cultural property. Unfortunately, despite numerous efforts on the part of some archaeologists in 2002 and early 2003, there was negligible planning for the protection of cultural property prior to the 2003 invasion of Iraq (Stone and Farchakh Bajjaly 2008).

What Cultural Property Is Protected?

The 1954 Convention defines cultural property (Article 1) as:

"(a) Movable or immovable property of great importance to the cultural heritage of every people, such as monuments of architecture, art or history, whether religious or secular; archaeological sites; groups of buildings which, as a whole, are of historical or artistic interest; works of art; manuscripts, books and other objects of artistic, historical or archaeological interest; as well as scientific collections and important collections of books or archives or of reproductions of the property defined above;
(b) Buildings whose main and effective purpose is to preserve or exhibit the movable cultural property defined in sub-paragraph (a) such as museums, large libraries and depositories of archives, and refuges intended to shelter, in the event of armed conflict, the movable cultural property defined in sub-paragraph (a);
(c) Centres containing a large amount of cultural property as defined in sub-paragraphs (a) and (b), to be known as 'centres containing monuments'".

This has to be our starting point. Article 16 states that the distinctive emblem of the Convention will be a Blue Shield.

The Blue Shield

In anticipation of the 2nd Protocol, and echoing Article 16, four of the major heritage organizations (the International Council of Archives, the International Council of Museums, the International Council on Monuments and Sites, and the International Federation of Library Associations and Institutions) combined in 1996 to create the International Committee of the Blue Shield. While the Blue Shield is frequently referred to as the 'cultural equivalent' of the Red Cross, there are three minor differences: the Red Cross/Red Crescent has an unparalleled international profile, whereas the Blue Shield is almost unknown; the Red Cross has a multimillion-pound annual budget, whereas the Blue Shield has no annual budget; and the Red Cross employs some 12,000 paid professional staff in eighty-plus countries, whereas the Blue Shield has no paid staff.

It is obviously correct that a greater priority is given to the protection of people (and, with people, intangible cultural heritage) than to cultural property. However, for the international community to fail to fund the Blue Shield at all shows an underestimation of the importance and value people ascribe to their cultural property. The Blue Shield is, therefore, essentially a network of willing volunteers—with some thirty national committees—working to protect cultural property during armed conflict and, as many of the major actors are the same, following environmental disaster. It "respects the principles of joint action, independence, neutrality, professionalism, respect for cultural identity and diversity, and works on a not-for-profit basis" (Statutes Article 2.2). Much of the work described in what follows has been instigated by the Blue Shield.

Why Is the Protection of Cultural Property Important?

While most cultural property is, of course, threatened, damaged, and destroyed through urban and agricultural developments, damage during conflict can seriously diminish a country's cultural property. There are numerous arguments, pertinent for the military and their political masters, why all reasonable measures should be taken to protect cultural property generically—not least that historic sites, buildings, and objects are finite resources that, once destroyed in combat, cannot be retrieved. History may not look kindly on those responsible for such destruction. Space precludes any detailed analysis of these arguments, and it is acknowledged that the following comments are overly simplistic and gloss over complex debates, but, from a political and military perspective, at the very least, a combination of academic, cultural/social, economic, medical, political, and specifically military arguments have been identified that must be considered by those with the responsibility of waging war.

This must be put into some context. The nature of war has changed dramatically since 1945, and a military that has won a war now frequently finds itself being tasked to be responsible for helping to deliver an economically viable and stable postconflict country before it can withdraw—in other words, the victor(s) must also win the peace (Hammes 2004). It is suggested that if the protection of cultural property can help in this, then military planners would be negligent if they did not consider cultural property protection as part of their responsibility.

At the most fundamental 'academic' level, the past and its physical manifestations are critical to our understanding of what it means to be human. We study the past to understand the present to help create the future. Without the tangible evidence of that past, this process is significantly more difficult. The ability to interact with the past in this way is frequently seen as an attribute of a modern, civilized, stable society. Cultural property is also central to the cultural and social life of communities and, at a national level, is frequently used as the 'stage' for the performance of intangible cultural heritage such as the pomp and ceremony surrounding state openings of parliaments, or their equivalents, around the world (also see Altschul, Hassan this volume). This can, of course, also be a negative association, as in the use of the Theatre at Palmyra for mass executions (and for the use of the Internet and social media, see chapters by Pokotylo this volume). More frequently, cultural property helps to preserve national and local traditions and culture and to build community pride in its heritage (Chilton this volume). An increasing body of research also testifies to the relationship between historic environments and individuals' well-being (see for example Fujiwara et al. 2014). People who live in historic environments appear to have higher 'social capital'—"a term which refers to benefits in terms of wellbeing, good health and civil engagement" (Graham et al. 2009:4). This all goes back to Sun Tzu's argument that destruction of cultural property is poor military practice. For an occupying—or 'stabilizing'—force, a community that can retain its pride and stability is an easier community to govern or support.

Perhaps more pragmatically, the UN's World Tourism Organisation notes that in 2015, tourism accounted for 9% of global GNP and one in eleven jobs (www.e-unwto.org/doi/pdf/10.18111/9789284416899 accessed May 4, 2016, and see Baram this volume). In 2007, some 40% of tourists cited culture as the prime reason for travel (OECD 2009, p. 21). Cultural heritage tourism benefits communities and countries by creating jobs and businesses, diversifying local economies, attracting visitors interested in history and preservation (who tend to have a higher daily expenditure than general tourists), and generating local investment in historic resources. With respect to the Middle East and North Africa (MENA) region specifically, a 2001 World Bank report noted the "highly valuable cultural endowments in all the region's countries" that opened up "major opportunities for development, providing a major source of employment, and thereby contributing to the reduction of poverty and the decrease of chronic joblessness" (World Bank 2001:vii). In other words, cultural heritage and its exploitation is (or at least was) perceived to be at the heart of the economic development of the MENA region. Once again, from a military perspective, allowing cultural property to be destroyed has the potential to undermine the economic recovery of a postconflict country and may therefore lead to longer military deployments and, potentially, greater friction between the military and host community.

The political use, manipulation, and abuse of heritage is now accepted as an ever-present issue. From a military perspective, political interest in heritage may have a direct relationship with the reasons for the conflict and may therefore have a direct impact on required military action. For example, in the civil war in the former Yugoslavia, heritage and religious sites were specifically targeted by troops on all sides as politicians, and no doubt some elements within the armed forces, strove to remove all evidence of other communities ever having lived in particular geographical areas (see, e.g., Chapman 1994). No military planner should ignore the political agenda relating to heritage. An astute military might have questioned why the cultural implications of the removal of Saddam Hussein played no part in the political planning of the 2003 invasion (see Ricks 2006).

While some in the military have queried me as to whether any of these arguments are really military concerns, the final two arguments are unequivocally firmly in the military domain. First, the protection of cultural property is now accepted as an obligation codified as part of international humanitarian law (IHL). In addition to the 1954 Convention, cultural property protection is an integral part of the 1977 Additional Protocol I to the 1949 Geneva Conventions (Articles 53 and 85[4][d])

and the 1998 Rome Statute of the International Criminal Court (Articles 8[2][b]
[ix] and 8[2][e][iv]) (and see Toman 1996; Hensel 2007; Gerstenblith 2009). IHL
stresses that occupying forces should not withdraw until there are competent and
effective authorities to whom governance can be handed over.

No one implies that protecting cultural property in times of armed conflict is
easy (e.g., see Bevan 2006; Yahya 2008), but the responsibility of the military to
include it in their planning and actions, under IHL, is unequivocal. Finally, there are
clear *military* arguments for protecting cultural property. A key consideration for all
officers is to get those troops for whom they have responsibility in and out of 'theatre' as quickly and with as few casualties as possible. Any activity or approach that
can help with this is frequently referred to as a 'force multiplier'. There are, unfortunately, too many recent examples of when failure to protect cultural property led
directly or indirectly to military problems, bad publicity, and, in some instances, to
an escalation of hostilities and casualties (see, e.g., Corn 2005; Curtis 2004; Phillips
2009). The military are, however, increasingly aware of these mistakes and, as outlined in what follows, in some instances, are taking steps to address previous failures.

The Four Tier Approach

With these arguments in mind, in conjunction with colleagues (and we must regard
them as such) in the UK Ministry of Defence, the U.S. Department of Defense,
various European militaries, and NATO, efforts have been made to develop what
has become known as the 'Four Tier Approach' (Stone 2013a) that provides a policy
outline and practical framework for the inclusion of cultural property protection
into military training, doctrine, and long-term planning. These 'tiers' are essentially the four times when there needs to be a close relationship between heritage
experts and the military if the latter are to protect cultural property during conflict
effectively.

Tier 1 requires the integration of cultural property protection training within
basic training for all military personnel. This does not mean a massive increase
in training—an unrealistic and probably unnecessary aspiration. Rather, it means
developing a level of training appropriate to rank and responsibility. For junior
ranks, this may be delivered, for example, through posters, packs of playing cards,
and short films. Senior ranks and, when identified, those with particular responsibility for cultural property protection, will need progressively more detailed training. However, as a fundamental message, all those in uniform should realize that,
in extremis, protecting cultural property may save their lives. Tier 2 is introduced as
soon as deployment becomes a possibility, and the military needs an understanding of the cultural property they will encounter in a particular location. This is
the time to provide or review specific information about cultural property to be
protected in a particular theatre of operations. A number of countries have developed specific materials for this tier, including the packs of country-focused playing
cards produced by the U.S., Dutch, and Norwegian armed forces, the latter with
the support of the Norwegian Blue Shield. Tier 3 is activity during conflict and

Tier 4 postconflict activity during what the military refers to as 'stabilization'. This approach (see Stone 2013a for more detail) provides a framework for future collaboration with the intention that cultural property protection will be integrated as a core element of military planning into the future. It takes as axiomatic that the heritage community cannot sit back and wait for the next catastrophe but rather must plan to mitigate the impact of the next war.

Why Is Cultural Property Damaged and Destroyed?

If the military are to take the protection of cultural property seriously, they need to understand why and how it is damaged and destroyed during conflict. I have identified elsewhere (2016) seven reasons for such damage and destruction: (i) protection of cultural property is not regarded as important enough to include in pre-conflict planning; (ii) cultural property is regarded as legitimate 'spoils of war'; (iii) it becomes collateral damage; (iv) through lack of military awareness; (v) through looting (Burgess this volume); (vi) through 'enforced neglect'; and (vii) as the result of specific targeting. Again, space precludes a detailed analysis of these reasons, but the Blue Shield is beginning to address these issues within the overall framework of the Four Tier Approach in the hope that action relating to as many reasons as possible will lead to an overall reduction in damage.

Recent Activity

A central focus of the Blue Shield is to encourage all countries to ratify the 1954 Convention and its Protocols and to establish supporting national legislation. In 2003, when the United States and the UK led the invasion of Iraq, neither had ratified either the Convention or its Protocols. Partly as the result of pressure from the United States Blue Shield national committee, the United States ratified the 1954 Convention but not the Protocols in 2009. Recently, the U.S. Senate passed to the president for signing H.R.1493—the Protect and Preserve International Cultural Property Act. This Act was signed into law in May of 2016. Following pressure from the UK Blue Shield national committee and others, the UK finally introduced the Cultural Property (Armed Conflicts) Bill in Parliament in May 2016 that, together with the ratification of the 1954 Convention and both Protocols, passed into UK Law on 12 December 2017.

A separate focus has been the development of the Four Tier Approach policy framework and identifying the seven reasons that cultural property is damaged. Both have required close liaison, long negotiation, and slow confidence building with both the heritage sector and the military. If we are to succeed in the protection of cultural property during conflict, the military need to understand that we (cultural heritage experts) are willing not only to help them understand why they should protect cultural property but also to devise appropriate mechanisms for doing so. We also need the heritage community to step up to the mark and help with the identification of cultural property that needs protection as well as training the military about the importance and relevance of protection. It was as a direct consequence of the republication of the Four Tier Approach in the *British Army Review* in 2013 that the British Army set up a Cultural Property Protection Working Group. It is anticipated that this group will lead to the establishment of a formal cultural property protection capability within UK armed forces that will be fully operational by 2020 (and see Purbrick 2016). The United States is actively considering reestablishing a similar unit.

Such liaison is not necessarily speedy. Discussions began in 2006 that finally led to the publication of *Cultural Property Protection Makes Sense* by the NATO-affiliated civilian/military Centre of Excellence in 2015 (CIMIC 2015). European militaries have met annually over the last seven years at Coping with Culture conferences. Cultural property protection has been a constant topic for discussion, and the British have held their own international Culture in Conflict symposia for the past nine years. The issue is increasingly on the military agenda, and NATO instigated an internal review regarding cultural property protection that recommended that NATO should:

> create a cultural property protection policy featuring the commitment of the Alliance to protect cultural property, definitions of cultural property and cultural property protection and designation of roles and responsibilities inside NATO, including the creation of a cultural property advocate responsible for maintaining contact with internal and external cultural property protection sources of information and provide the flow of that information to the operational planners in the event of a crisis.
>
> *(NATO 2012:iv)*

Unfortunately, at the time of writing in early 2017, this recommendation has not yet been implemented. It appears that senior internal NATO military thinking is that such responsibility should be incorporated in the doctrine of individual constituent members of NATO and not as overarching NATO doctrine. This is a view that Blue Shield hopes can be modified.

Blue Shield national committees and international teams have been involved in numerous training programmes for the military in countries as diverse as Austria, the United States, Lebanon, New Zealand, and Cambodia. We have also helped to train UN deployments in Mali and Lebanon. The UK Blue Shield national committee supported Newcastle University in the development, on behalf of UNESCO, of a three-day training program for company commander–level officers. These materials will be available on the UNESCO website, and Blue Shield, where possible, will be available to work with any military to modify and adapt the materials as necessary.

The Blue Shield has also been involved in the production of lists of cultural property not to be damaged if at all possible for areas affected by conflict. Such lists have been compiled for Libya, Mali, Syria, Yemen, and Iraq. They are not without contention (Stone 2013b). Four major issues need to be addressed: First, the process of compilation of the lists is contentious: who produces the list and to what standard? Second, the scope of such lists continues to be debated. Third, the size of different lists has prompted a variety of responses from different militaries, with some seeking as much information as possible and others requesting more 'manageable' lists. Finally, while the Convention stipulates that all types of cultural property should be protected, it has proved to be extremely difficult to produce reliable lists of sufficient detail for libraries, archives, art museums, and galleries. Again, much more work must be done before there is an effective, efficient, and acceptable process for the development of such lists. However, there is good evidence that at least some of these lists have been used by NATO to minimize damage to cultural property, and action taken in Libya led directly to the establishment of the internal NATO review mentioned earlier. We have also carried out a series of during-/postconflict assessment missions—to Egypt, Libya, and Mali and most recently to Palmyra.

Legal action has also taken place. Two Serbian officers were imprisoned in 2004 for the militarily unjustified shelling of the World Heritage site of Dubrovnik, and Ahmad Al Mahdi, a member of Ansar Dine, was sentenced in 2016 to nine years' imprisonment by the International Criminal Court for the destruction of cultural property in Timbuktu in 2012. Much more is being done. The military are beginning to understand the strategic importance of protecting cultural property during conflict; the heritage community must understand that the military can only do this with our help. International attention ensures this issue will be of key relevance to contemporary society as long as armed conflict exists.

References

Adjutant General's Office 1863 *Instructions for the Government of Armies of the United States in the Field* (General Orders No. 100—The Lieber Code), Electronic document, http://avalon.law.yale.edu/19th_century/lieber.asp#sec1, accessed May 3, 2016.

Bevan, R. 2006 *The Destruction of Memory: Architecture at War*. Reaktion, London.

Chapman, J. 1994 Destruction of a Common Heritage: The Archaeology of War in Croatia, Bosnia and Herzegovina. *Antiquity* 68:120–126.

CIMIC Centre of Excellence 2015 *Cultural Property Protection Makes Sense*. Electronic document, www.cimic-coe.org/products/conceptual-design/downloads/ccoe-publications/, accessed May 3, 2016.

Corn, G. 2005 "Snipers in the Minaret: What is the Rule?" The Law of War and the Protection of Cultural Property: A Complex Equation. *The Army Lawyer*, July 2005, 28–40.

Curtis, J. 2004 Report on Meeting at Babylon 11th–13th December 2004. Electronic document, www.britishmuseum.org/PDF/BabylonReport04.pdf, accessed May 6, 2016.

Edsel, R. M. 2013 *Saving Italy: The Race to Rescue a Nation's Treasures from the Nazis*, W. W. Norton & Company, New York.

Fujiwara, D, T. Cornwall, and P. Dolan 2014 *Heritage and Wellbeing*. Historic England, London. Electronic document, http://hc.historicengland.org.uk/content/pub/2190644/heritage-and-wellbeing.pdf, accessed May 6, 2016.

Gerstenblith, P. 2009 Archaeology in the Context of War: Legal Frameworks for Protecting Cultural Heritage During Armed Conflict. *Archaeologies* 5:18–31.

Graham, H, R. Mason, and A. Newman 2009 *Historic Environment, Sense of Place, and Social Capital: A Literature Review*, English Heritage, London. Electronic document, http://eprints.soton.ac.uk/182155/1/Historic_Environment,_Sense_of_Place_and_Social_Capital_Lit_Review.pdf, accessed May 6, 2016.

Hammes, T. X. 2004 *The Sling and The Stone: On War in the 21st Century*. Zenith Press, St Paul, Minnesota.

Hensel, H. M. 2007 The Protection of Cultural Objects During Armed Conflicts, In *The Law of Armed Conflict: Constraints on the Contemporary use of Military Force*, edited by H. M. Hensel, pp. 39–104. Aldershot, Ashgate.

Miles, M. 2011 Still in the Aftermath of Waterloo: A Brief History of Decisions About Restitution. In *Cultural Heritage, Ethics and the Military*, edited by P. Stone, pp. 29–42. Boydell, Woodbridge.

NATO (North Atlantic Treaty Organization) 2012 *Cultural Property Protection in the Operations Planning Process*, Unclassified Report by NATO's Joint Analysis and Lessons Learned Centre, Lisbon, Portugal.

Nicholas, L. 1995 *The Rape of Europa: the Fate of Europe's Treasures in the Third Reich and the Second World War*. Vintage Books, New York.

OECD (Organisation for Economic Cooperation and Development) 2009 *The Impact of Culture on Tourism*. OECD, Paris.

Phillips, M. 2009 Learning a Hard History Lesson in Talibanistan. *The Wall Street Journal*, May 13, 2009. Electronic document, http://online.wsj.com/article/SB124224652409516525.html#articleTabs_slideshow%26articleTabs%3Darticle, accessed May 6, 2016.

Purbrick, T. 2016 Monuments Men: Part One, British Army Blog. Electronic document, https://britisharmyblog.wordpress.com/2016/10/21/monuments-men-part-one/, accessed May 6, 2016.

Ricks, T. E. 2006 *Fiasco: The American Military Adventure in Iraq*. Penguin, London.

Stone, P. G. 2016 The Challenge of Protecting Heritage in Times of Armed Conflict. *Museum International*, 1–15.

———. 2013a A Four-Tier Approach to the Protection of Cultural Property in the Event of Armed Conflict. *Antiquity*, 87(335):166–177

———. 2013b War and Heritage: Using Inventories to Protect Cultural Property. In *Conservation Perspectives*, The GCI Newsletter, Fall 2013, Heritage Inventories. Electronic document, www.getty.edu/conservation/publications_resources/newsletters/28_2/war_heritage.html.

Stone, P. G., and J. Farchakh Bajjaly, editors 2008 *The Destruction of Cultural Heritage in Iraq*. Boydell Press, Woodbridge.

Sun Tzu 1998 *The Art of War*, translated by T. Cleary. Shambhala, London.

Toman, J. 1996 *The Protection of Cultural Property in the Event of Armed Conflict*. UNESCO, Paris.

von Clausewitz, C. 1997[1832] *On War (Vom Kriege)*. Ferdinand Dümmler, Berlin. 1997 facsimile, Wordsworth Editions, Ware, England. Woolley, L. 1947 *A Record of the Work Done By the Military Authorities for the Protection of the Treasures of Art and History in War Areas*. HMSO, London.

World Bank 2001 *Cultural Heritage and Development: A Framework for Action in the Middle East and North Africa*. World Bank, Washington, DC.

Yahya, A. H. 2008 Managing Heritage in a War Zone. *Archaeologies* 4:495–505.

3
ONLINE PUBLIC OPINION AND ARCHAEOLOGICAL HERITAGE CONSERVATION

A Case Study from Western Canada

David Pokotylo

Introduction

Archaeologists have long acknowledged a responsibility to engage the public and have developed diverse strategies to address this (see McGimsey 1972; Merriman 2004; Okamura and Matsuda 2011;Thomas and Lea 2014; Skeates et al. 2012). The very nature of public archaeology assumes professional–public interaction is vital to society's support of archaeology, ensuring that this aspect of cultural heritage maintains relevance, particularly in today's economic environment, where basic research and heritage conservation values are constantly challenged in public and political arenas. Archaeologists must consider public opinion in their efforts to promote archaeological heritage conservation. If people do not consider the past significant, preservation of the archaeological record will cease to be an important social issue worth supporting, and public funding will diminish, if not disappear. Understanding how 'the public' comprehends and relates to archaeology and heritage conservation policy is thus an essential part of public archaeology and requires serious, sustained research.

More than four decades ago, Lipe (1974) appealed for archaeologists to better understand their public through empirical studies of public attitudes rather than supposition. Systematic surveys in North America (Pokotylo 2002, 2007; Pokotylo and Guppy 1999; Ramos and Duganne 2000), Europe (Bonacchi 2014), and Australia (Balme and Wilson 2004) provide an initial perspective of public opinion on archaeological heritage values and conservation. However, we still have a limited 'baseline' understanding of public appreciation and knowledge of archaeology and attitudes toward (and support for) archaeological heritage values and preservation that remain frontline issues in developing effective public archaeology strategies. Public opinion information is also relevant to those responsible for developing and implementing heritage conservation policy. Governments and politicians are increasingly sensitive to public opinion data to gauge public support for and strength of current policies and practices.

While systematic sample survey remains the most reliable way to assess public opinion, Internet-based commentary has now entered the public opinion research realm in areas such as climate change (see De Kraker et al. 2014; Jaspal et al. 2012; Koteyko et al. 2103) and health science (Henrich and Holmes 2011). Digital technologies have transformed the media and communication landscape and how the public consumes and shares information. The study of this new media has resulted in the 'media ecology' theoretical framework that assumes society is an organism fed by the media environment and modified by it (Naughton 2006; Postman 2000).

Given that Internet usage has been linked to more positive attitudes toward science in general, as well as support for basic research (Brossard and Scheufele 2013), the Internet has a potentially significant role in the formation of public knowledge and perceptions about archaeological research, heritage values, and conservation. Online news media provide increased public access to archaeological information as well as a venue for public opinions on heritage issues. Online news sources can also narrow the knowledge gap produced in traditional media often targeted to highly educated audiences (Dudo et al. 2011). Online newspapers have also transformed traditional one-way forms of communication into participatory ones, with reader comments contributing to diverse and contested social thinking and public discourse. However, the free-ranging nature of the Internet also increases the potential for public misinformation on archaeological matters unless the profession takes an active role in 'virtual' archaeology. Online commentary may also influence perceived public support for heritage conservation policies (see cf. Berkhout 2010) as well as public attitudes and support for these policies (cf. Brossard and Scheufele 2013).

Is the heightened presence of archaeology and heritage issues in online media increasing public understanding and support of (or opposition to) archaeological conservation policies? This question creates a new urgency for public archaeology to include the Internet in order to better understand today's public and the challenges of engaging them in this 'virtual' world (see Bonacchi 2012; Bonacchi and Moshenska 2015). However, analysis of reader comments on online news stories about archaeological conservation issues has not yet been conducted.

Scope and Objectives

This chapter has two objectives: first, to analyze online news reader attitudes/opinions regarding a specific case of an archaeological site threatened with destruction as a proxy for current public opinion on heritage resource conservation policy and practice. This study examines reader comments and ratings to articles concerning the Grace Bay archaeological site, British Columbia, Canada, published on newspaper websites in 2014–2015. This study is unique in focusing on online reader comments as a primary data source for public opinion studies in public archaeology. Second, the online results are compared with past public opinion surveys to see how Internet-based data supplement, complement, or contradict prior (and pre-Web 2.0) understanding of public opinion concerning archaeological heritage conservation. Given these data, the potential of online reader comments as an information source for effectively monitoring public opinions on heritage conservation and policy is also assessed.

Reader Comments to Online News Articles and Public Opinion Research

Many online newspapers now allow readers to post comments to revitalize reader engagement and 'citizen journalism' in which readers actively contribute to news coverage. This allows reaction to article content and issues raised, as well as other reader comments. Commenters (Schuth et al. 2007) may correct perceived misinformation in other reader comments, provide support or argument, and add other 'facts' considered relevant. Readers may also register their agreement or disagreement. Such exchange creates a 'dialogue' in which ideas and perspectives are debated and negotiated in a way not possible in traditional paper-based news media. Online reader commentary may also influence opinions (see Lee 2015) and play a role in shaping general public attitudes. Readers' comments thus become 'civic forums' in which citizens exchange ideas and dialogue occurs (Torres da Silva 2015).

Although online reader comments cannot *a priori* be assumed to represent views of the general population, they can reveal perspectives of 'mini-public' sectors. Virtual environments offer varying degrees of anonymity and reduced social expectations, thus people may divulge more about themselves online, and that disclosure is often more open (Joinson 1999). Reader ratings of an article may be more representative of general public opinion than comments alone, as more people may rate an article than comment (Henrich and Holmes 2013:2; Lee and Yoon 2010).

Online reader commentary and ratings thus provide a venue to monitor current public opinion (albeit a small, self-selected sample) on public archaeology issues: understanding and appreciation of archaeological heritage values, social relevance of archaeological research, support of archaeological heritage preservation policy and practice, and social-political implications (in the case of Canada, issues of economic development and First Nations.[1]

The Grace Islet Heritage Site Case Study

Recently, land development versus archaeological preservation issues involving First Nations precontact archaeological sites in southwestern British Columbia have received considerable local-, regional-, and national-level online news coverage. Land development issues at the Marpole site, Vancouver (Reynolds 2012), the Willows Beach site, Victoria (McCullough 2013), and the Grace Islet site, Gulf Islands (Petrescu 2014a), have raised public awareness of the precontact archaeological record and current protective legislation and generated online public opinion. This online coverage provides an ideal context in which to analyze reader comments as indicators of how the increased online media profile of archaeology and Internet-enhanced public access to information and communication forums may affect current public opinion on heritage values and archaeological site protection/preservation policies.

Grace Islet is a small (0.75-hectare) islet near Salt Spring Island on British Columbia's south coast. Known in local Coast Salish First Nations Hul'qumi'num language as 'shmukw'elu',[2] loosely translated as "a place to have funerals and containers (for bodies)" (Huakari and Peter 1995:71), it was part of the larger First Nations Shiya'hwt waht village at the head of Ganges Harbour. The islet went into private ownership in 1913, then was sold to various owners until 1990. The islet was initially noted as part of the larger Ganges Harbour village recorded in 1966. Subsequent studies identified shell midden deposits and human remains, and in 2006, rock cairn features were recorded. Further investigations confirmed the burial cairns and archaeological deposits dating *ca.* 1000 BP, and the entire islet was placed under the protection of the provincial Heritage Conservation Act (HCA). It remained undeveloped until 2010, when the owner submitted plans under an Archaeological Impact Assessment to build a residence.

In 2011, the B.C. Archaeology Branch issued an Alteration Permit to the site for development. As construction commenced in 2012, rising opposition to the development among First Nations groups, local residents, and other supporters led to protests on and near the islet. Opposition grew, and legal challenges continued through 2014 (Figure 3.1), when a local First Nation—the Cowichan Tribes—filed a claim that granting private ownership of Grace Islet infringed their Aboriginal title. The provincial government intervened in December 2014, halted construction, and started to work on resolving the dispute between the landowner and First

FIGURE 3.1 Gulf Islands Residents and First Nations Protesting House Construction on Grace Islet, August 26, 2014

Source: Photograph by Adrian Lam, Victoria Times Colonist. Used by permission.

Nations. In January 2015, the government partnered with First Nations and a land conservancy to purchase the islet for $5.45 million and develop a joint plan to remove the construction material and restore the ecological and heritage values of the islet. Also in early 2015, the minister responsible for the HCA ordered a review of BC's heritage conservation legislation. To date, the ministry has not provided any details about the review or the expected completion date.

Grace Islet is representative of a larger issue concerning how ancestral burial grounds are protected under law in British Columbia (see Nicholas et al. 2015). In British Columbia, *all* archaeological sites predating 1846, whether on public ('Crown') lands *or* private property, fall under the HCA. Burial sites dating before 1846 also fall under the HCA, whereas designated post-1846 cemetery sites are protected under the Cremation, Interment and Funeral Services Act, which does not cover nondesignated First Nations or settler burial sites. This has resulted in complex political and legal questions surrounding the protection, preservation and ownership of First Nations burial grounds in the face of impending land development (see Paterson 1996).

Study Methods

Although public opinion research using online reader comments is increasing, a methodology for systematic analysis is still evolving (Hine 2005; Henrich and Holmes 2013). This presents challenges for both research design and comparative analysis, including (but not limited to) (1) criteria for screening comments as relevant versus irrelevant with respect to content and issue studied; (2) reliable identification of demographic indicators (e.g., age, gender) in comments; and (3) how to classify and quantify comments. The methodology developed for this study is outlined in what follows.

Content analysis of reader responses to online news articles on the Grace Islet issue is used to identify public perceptions of archaeological heritage values and conservation. The database is derived from reader comments in local and national online newspaper articles representing a start-to-finish chronology of this issue between 2014–2015 (see Table 3.1). Three 'phases' of coverage in

TABLE 3.1 Online Newspaper Reader Comments Database

Phase	Source	Comments	Discussions	Commenters
1	Petrescu Sarah "Attempt to downplay Grace Islet burial ground dismays archaeologist." *Victoria Times Colonist* August 8 2014	65	24	26
2	Hunter, Justine "B.C. may buy Grace Islet home to settle First Nation land dispute." *Globe and Mail* Dec. 2 2014	53	21	28
3	Kines, Lindsay "B.C. buys disputed Grace Islet in Ganges Harbour for $5.45 million." *The Vancouver Sun* February 17 2015	22	12	18

online newspapers are identified: (1) rising public controversy (Petrescu 2014b), (2) resolution negotiations involving the landowner, First Nations, and government (Hunter 2014), and (3) settlement of the dispute (Kines 2015). The newspaper articles sampled were factual/neutral in tone in order to minimize potential effects of reader reaction to explicit criticism or support for heritage preservation issues. The overall sample size is admittedly small (140 comments) due to deletion of reader comments on news sites after an unspecified period, with no archive for future retrieval.

All reader comments were characterized by the relative date of the comment and 'type' of reader reaction-opinion regarding the heritage issue. Given contributors could 'sign' a comment with a made-up name, analysis of gender-based patterning based on the commenter's online 'handle' is problematic and was solely based here on the 'apparent' sex of name in the commenter signature. The distribution of comments across these variables was calculated. A sequence of online responses to an initial comment on an article was analyzed as a 'discussion'. Multiple comments to a given article by the same contributor were aggregated and analyzed as a group to avoid overrepresentation of multiple posts by the same commenter. Content analysis was carried out using NVivo (V. 10) software to (1) identify themes/categories and classify and code comments into nodes, (2) text search queries for words and phrases, viewed in context; and (3) compare material across nodes and identify patterns by coding queries.

To compare the distribution of reader comments with results of previous public opinion surveys, seven commenter 'types' were defined. These types were based on the aggregate of opinions posted by each contributor using keywords and phrase, as well as overall expression in longer comments (see Table 3.2).

TABLE 3.2 Online Reader Comment Types and Characteristics

Commenter type	Characteristic
Positive	supports archaeological site preservation, First Nation heritage rights, land claims
Negative	critical of site preservation, First Nations heritage rights, land claims (particularly on private property); challenges burial ground status of site
Sarcastic-negative	critical of government handling of preservation under the Heritage Conservation Act, addressing First Nations land claims
Critical of landowner character	critical of landowner's character and integrity in developing and selling the property
Critical of media coverage	critical of journalistic bias vs. factual story content
Questioning	reasonable, factual question about the issue (e.g., archaeological values, preservation law)
Ambiguous-irrelevant	vague and/or unrelated off-topic comments

Analysis and Results

Most discussions (55.7%) consisted of a single reader comment but ranged as high as 10, with an average 'length' of 2.4 comments (see Figure 3.2). Most (66.3%) commenters contributed only once to an article, and only 9.3% of contributors posted more than five comments (Figure 3.2). The maximum number of posts a single commenter contributed is 11. More than half (52%) of the commenters used a name that allowed classification of apparent sex—this subsample was predominantly male (80%).

With respect to the general content of reader comments, knowledge of archaeological heritage values and preservation policies generally appeared to be low. Nevertheless, many contributors were outspoken about archaeological heritage preservation and First Nations rights claims. The government-sanctioned protection of an archaeological site on private property was a concern broadly shared. The reader comments also challenge current archaeological assessment and conservation processes and First Nations oral tradition as evidence of past use. This also suggests a lack of support for First Nations' control over archaeological sites and their use of archaeological sites in cultural practice. Many contributors also displayed a sense of distrust directed against not only politicians, First Nations and media but also archaeologists!

Examination of reader ratings of online comments shows that negative comments received more 'agreement' ratings than other types. The comment with the highest number ($n = 29$) of 'agrees' concerned skepticism about the heritage value of precontact burial grounds and rationale for preservation as well as the First Nations land claims process:

> There are bones everywhere. People have lived here for a long time. Dig up any little island and you are bound to find bones. Just because there are some

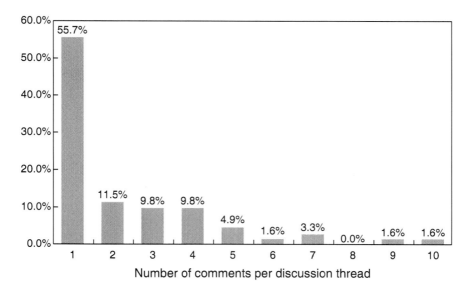

FIGURE 3.2 Distribution of Number of Reader Comments to a Discussion Thread

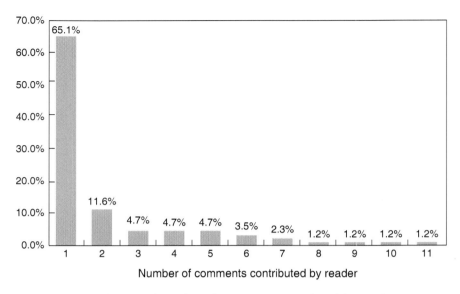

FIGURE 3.3 Distribution of Number of Comments Contributed by Reader

human bones on your land doesn't make it 'sacred'. They are just bones! As humans, we think we are some kind of exalted creature, and our bones are something important. The proper and only true value of our bones is compost. It's time to put away the childish fairy tales that pass for our 'beliefs'. There are no spirits hovering around our bones. We are not talking to the ancestors. Let the guy build his house.

[comment by 'James Richy' in Petrescu 2014b]

The distribution of online commenter types (Figure 3.4) shows a minimal level (4.2%) of contributors made ambiguous-irrelevant comments. Nearly half (44.4%) of the contributors presented negative opinions about First Nations heritage rights, archaeological site preservation, and infringement on private property. The level of negative opinions is nearly double that of positive support (44.4% vs. 23.6%). Equal numbers of contributors (8.3%) either were critical of the landowner's character/integrity or posed questions about the controversy. A relatively small number of contributors (4.2%) were specifically critical of media coverage.

The distribution of online commenter types by controversy phase (Figure 3.5) shows negative contributors predominate throughout, but the level varies between phases. Ambiguous-irrelevant comments were absent in initial phase of rising awareness but subsequently increased to 11.1% of the total in the dispute settlement phase. Questioning comments were also highest in the dispute settlement phase (when more information about the process was known). Looking at the ratio of negative to positive commenters by phase, the highest negative expression (4:1) was

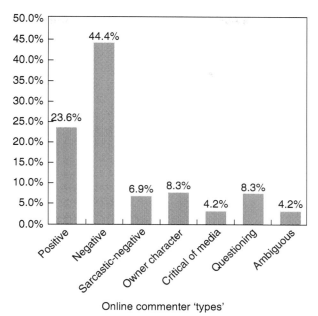

FIGURE 3.4 Distribution of Online Commenter 'Types'

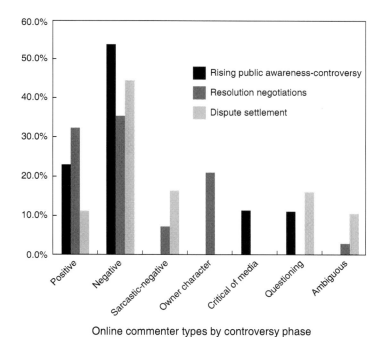

FIGURE 3.5 Distribution of Online Commenter Types by Controversy Phase

in reaction to settlement—government purchase of the property for preservation. Negative expression was also high (2.3:1) during the rise of the controversy, while there was a near-equal split of opinion (1.1:1) during negotiations.

Comparison of online reader comments and contributor types with outcomes of past public opinion surveys on archaeological heritage values and conservation in Canada (Pokotylo 2002, 2007; Pokotylo and Guppy 1999) is difficult. Nevertheless, the following observations can be made by summarizing relevant variables from past surveys to provide a baseline for comparison, as seen in what follows.

At the national level (Pokotylo 2002), most Canadians were quite interested in archaeology but lacked understanding of current practices, nature of the archaeological record, and antiquity of Indigenous settlement. A majority expressed concern about archaeological preservation, supporting laws protecting archaeological sites, but were uncertain or misinformed about heritage conservation laws at the provincial or national level.[3] Most Canadians strongly supported Indigenous Peoples' involvement in archaeological research and rights to use archaeological sites in cultural practices but had a negative attitude towards Indigenous Peoples' control over investigation of archaeological sites. At the regional level, British Columbia residents identified Aboriginal land claims as the predominant issue concerning archaeology (Pokotylo and Guppy 1999). British Columbia is unique in Canada, as colonial and provincial governments signed few treaties with Indigenous groups. The land claims settlement process is ongoing. Archaeology also has a credibility issue—slightly fewer than half of BC respondents did not consider archaeologists the most knowledgeable interpreters of the archaeological record, while a smaller proportion (14.3%) agreed that First Nations are the most knowledgeable.

Relative to the survey results, contributors of online comments show:

1. continued low level of understanding of archaeology and the rationale for heritage conservation,
2. continued misunderstanding of heritage conservation laws, (particularly differential treatment of precontact burial grounds versus 'settler' cemeteries),
3. lessened support for archaeological heritage values and conservation,
4. increased negative attitude towards First Nations' control over archaeological sites, and
5. decreased support of First Nations' rights to use archaeological sites in their cultural practice.

Discussion and Conclusion

In sum, online reader comments to news coverage of the Grace Islet issue show skepticism-concern about the nature and value of archaeological heritage sites and a low perceived relevance of archaeology in society. Concerns expressed online about the economic cost of heritage preservation (e.g., purchase and transfer of ownership into the public trust) suggest resistance to laws protecting precontact archaeological sites, even when threatened by imminent destruction. Comparative analysis of online reader comments shows that, while the relatively low level of contributors' knowledge of archaeological science and heritage conservation is similar to that of public surveys, there is heightened contributor skepticism of archaeological heritage value in society and lessened support for heritage conservation legislation.

How to account for this online negativity about the role, value, and practice of archaeological heritage conservation in current society relative to past surveys? It is not likely attributable to reader reaction to either overly critical or supportive news articles on archaeological preservation, as the articles selected were neutral in tone. One potential factor is the anonymous and immediate nature of online comments, which may offer a more realistic insight into people's opinions than survey questionnaires (see Henrich and Holmes 2013), given a tendency towards socially desirable answers in nonanonymous contexts (see Suler 2004). Taking this latter point into consideration, have previous surveys generated a fundamentally wrong picture of public opinion, or has a shift in public opinion on archaeological heritage conservation occurred since 1999–2000? A more practical (and plausible) explanation may be that contributors of online reader comments are not representative of the Canadian population at large. The distribution of 'apparent' contributor gender showing males comprising a very large majority is a strong indication of bias. Also, research on online reader comments has noted that contributors are often outspoken with dissenting (and provocative) opinions that challenge prevailing social and institutional views in order to gain online notoriety (see Eisinger 2011; McCluskey and Hmielowski 2012; Myers 2010). Thus, 'heritage skeptics' with outspoken opinions on and a desire to express dissent with heritage conservation will likely be overrepresented in online reader comments relative to systematic public surveys.

While this increased negativity is likely not representative of the population at large, it cannot be dismissed. A measure of heritage conservation policy robustness is its degree of societal support and ability to address resistance. The Internet is now the preferred primary information source about scientific issues (in America and likely elsewhere; see Brossard and Scheufele 2013). Internet-based opinions expressed by a small group are read by a large part of the population and thus have the potential to influence opinions of the general public (as well as politicians) on heritage values and conservation (see Berkhout 2010). This may well be the main contribution of online opinion studies to public archaeology—to identify and monitor 'heritage skeptic' viewpoints and their potential effect on public support of heritage conservation policies.

Thus, public archaeology cannot overlook the potential impact of online opinions given ongoing challenges to address the low level of public understanding of heritage values and heritage conservation legislation and the fact that a significant part of social life now occurs online. While the analysis of readers' comments, ratings, and contributor types provides an alternative and potentially useful way to 'take the pulse' of public opinion on heritage values and issues, this research suggests it is best used in combination with other data and methods to provide a stronger, broader-based foundation in deriving a realistic perspective.

Acknowledgements

This chapter benefited from comments provided by Andrew Mason, Andrew Martindale, RG Matson, and Patricia Ormerod. Final figures were prepared by Susan Matson. An initial version of this paper was presented at the Society for American Archaeology 80th Annual Meeting, San Francisco 2015, in the Public Perceptions of Archaeology symposium.

Notes

1 In the case of Aboriginal peoples in Canada, names have changed over time. Although the Indian Act remains in force in Canada, the term 'Indian' is generally disdained by those whom the term is used to describe. While 'Aboriginal' has been used in self-reference, 'First Nations' and 'Indigenous' are more commonly accepted at present. As there is no universally accepted term or definition, these latter terms are used interchangeably here.
2 Shmukw'elu is not so much a specific Hul'qumi'num' place name as a generic reference to any burial place. Activist elders used the term in reference to Grace islet (C. Arnett, personal communication October 25, 2016.)
3 Canada's Constitution Act of 1867 splits legislative powers between federal and provincial governments. The provinces are responsible for managing provincially owned public ('Crown') lands, while the federal government is responsible for federally owned public lands, including those reserved for Canada's Aboriginal people. This is reflected in legislation to protect and manage archaeological heritage. In southern Canada, a minor amount of land is under federal jurisdiction, and provincial statutes dominate.

References

Balme, J., and W. Wilson 2004 Perceptions of Archaeology in Australia Amongst Educated Young Australians. *Australian Archaeology* 58:19–24.

Berkhout, F. 2010 Reconstructing Boundaries and Reason in the Climate Debate. *Global Environmental Change* 20:565–569.

Bonacchi, C. 2014 Understanding the Public Experience of Archaeology in the UK and Italy: A Call for a 'Sociological Movement' in Public Archaeology. *European Journal of Post-Classical Archaeologies* 4:377–400.

———. 2012 Introduction. In *Archaeology and Digital Communication: Towards Strategies of Public Engagement*, edited by C. Bonacchi, pp. xi–xix. Archetype Publications, London.

Bonacchi, C., and G. Moshenska 2015 Critical Reflections on Digital Public Archaeology. *Internet Archaeology* 40. Electronic document, http://dx.doi.org/10.11141/ia.40.7.1, accessed June 16, 2016.

Brossard, D., and D. Scheufele 2013 Science, New Media, and the Public. *Science* 339:40–41.

De Kraker, J., S. Kuijs, R. Corves and A. Offermans 2014 Internet Public Opinion on Climate Change: A World Views Analysis of Online Reader Comments. *International Journal of Climate Change Strategies and Management* 6(1):19–33.

Dudo, A., D. Brossard, J. Shanahan, D. Scheufele, M. Morgan, and N. Signorielli 2011 Science on Television in the 21st Century: Recent Trends in Portrayals and Their Contributions to Public Attitudes Toward Science. *Communication Research* 38:754–777.

Eisinger, R. 2011 Incivility on the Internet: Dilemmas for Democratic Discourse. Paper Presented at the 2011 Annual Meeting of the American Political Science Association, Seattle. Electronic document, https://papers.ssrn.com/sol3/papers.cfm?abstract_id=1901814, accessed November, 1, 2016.

Henrich, N., and B. Holmes 2013 Web News Readers' Comments: Towards Developing a Methodology for Using On-line Comments in Social Inquiry. *Journal of Media and Communication Studies* 5(1):1–4.

———. 2011 What the Public Was Saying about the H1N1 Vaccine: Perceptions and Issues Discussed in On-Line Comments During the 2009 H1N1 Pandemic. *PLoS ONE* 6(4): e18479. doi: 10.1371/journal.pone.0018479.

Hine, C. 2005 Virtual Methods and the Sociology of Cyber-social-Scientific Knowledge. In *Virtual Methods: Issues in Social Research on the Internet*, edited by C. Hine, pp. 1–13. Berg, Oxford.

Huakari, T., and R. Peter 1995 *The Cowichan Dictionary of the Hul'qumi'num' Dialect of the Coast Salish People*. Cowichan Tribes, Duncan, BC.

Hunter, J. 2014 B.C. May Buy Grace Islet Home to Settle First Nation Land Dispute. *Globe and Mail*, December 2. Electronic document, www.theglobeandmail.com/news/british-columbia/bc-may-buy-grace-islet-home-to-settle-first-nation-land-dispute/article21863762/, accessed March 26, 2015.

Jaspal, R., B. Nerlich, and N. Koteyko 2012 Contesting Science By Appealing to Its Norms: Readers Discuss Climate Science in The Daily Mail. *Science Communication* 35(3):383–410.

Joinson, A. 1999 Social Desirability, Anonymity, and Internet-Based Questionnaires. *Behavior Research Methods, Instruments, and Computers* 31:433–438.

Kines, L. 2015 B.C. Buys Disputed Grace Islet in Ganges Harbour for $5.45 million. *The Vancouver Sun*, February 17 [online]. Electronic document, www.vancouversun.com/news/metro/buys+disputed+Grace+Islet+Ganges+Harbour+million/10820096/story.html, accessed March 26, 2015.

Koteyko, N., R. Jaspal, and B. Nerlich 2013 Climate Change and "Climategate" in Online Reader Comments: A Mixed Methods Study. *The Geographical Journal* 179:74–86.

Lee, M. 2015 The Persuasive Effects of Reading Others' Comments on a News Article. *Current Psychology* 34:753–761.

Lee, E., and J. Yoon 2010 What Do Others' Reactions to News on Internet Portal Sites Tell Us? Effects of Presentation Format and Readers' Need for Cognition on Reality Perception. *Communication Research* 37:825–846.

Lipe, W. 1974 A Conservation Model for American Archaeology. *Kiva* 39:213–245.

McCluskey, M., and J. Hmielowski 2012 Opinion Expression During Social Conflict: Comparing Online Reader Comments and Letters to the Editor. *Journalism* 13:303–319.

McCullough, S. 2013 B.C. Had No Authority to Make Oak Bay Homeowner Pay for Archeological Digs, Court Rules. *Victoria Times Colonist*, June 4. Electronic document, www.timescolonist.com/news/local/b-c-had-no-authority-to-make-oak-bay-homeowner-pay-for-archeological-digs-court-rules-1.312652, accessed March 20, 2015.

McGimsey, C. 1972 *Public Archaeology*. Seminar Press, New York.

Merriman, N., editor 2004 *Public Archaeology*. Routledge, New York.

Myers, G. 2010 Stance-Taking and Public Discussion in Blogs. *Critical Discourse Studies* 7:263–275.

Naughton, J. 2006 Our Changing Media Ecosystem. In *Communications—The Next Decade*, Section 1: Trends and Challenges, edited by R. E. Foster and R. Kiedrowski, pp. 41–50. Electronic document, www.ofcom.org.uk/research-and-data/multi-sector-research/general-communications/comms-next-decade, accessed November 1, 2016.

Nicholas, G., B. Egan, K. Bannister, and E. Benson 2015 Intervention as a Strategy in Protecting Indigenous Cultural Heritage. *The SAA Archaeological Record* 15(4):41–47.

Okamura, K., and A. Matsuda, editors 2011 *New Perspectives in Global Public Archaeology*. Springer, New York.

Paterson, R. 1996 Aboriginal Burial Sites and Property Development. *Aboriginal Justice Bulletin* January 1996:6–7, 134.

Petrescu, S. 2014a First Nations Renew Protests Over Building on "Sacred" Grace Islet. *Victoria Times Colonist*, August 26. Electronic document, www.timescolonist.com/news/local/first-nations-renew-protests-over-building-on-sacred-grace-islet-1.1330406, accessed March 20, 2015.

———. 2014b Attempt to Downplay Grace Islet Burial Ground Dismays Archaeologist. *Victoria Times Colonist*, August 8. Electronic document, www.timescolonist.com/news/local/attempt-to-downplay-grace-islet-burial-ground-dismays-archeologists-1.1304718, accessed March 20, 2015.

Pokotylo, D. 2007 Archaeology and the "Educated Public": A Perspective from the University. *The SAA Archaeological Record* 7(3):14–18.

———. 2002 Public Opinion and Canadian Archaeological Heritage: A National Perspective. *Canadian Journal of Archaeology* 26:88–129.

Pokotylo, D., and N. Guppy 1999 Public Opinion and Archaeological Heritage: Views from Outside the Profession. *American Antiquity* 64:400–416.

Postman, N. 2000 The Humanism of Media Ecology. *Proceedings of the Media Ecology Association*, Vol. 1, edited by J. Sternberg and M. Lipton, pp. 10–16. New York. Electronic document, www.media-eology.org/publications/MEA_proceedings/v1/humanism_of_media_ecology.html, accessed November 1, 2016.

Ramos, M., and D. Duganne 2000 *Exploring Public Perceptions and Attitudes About Archaeology*. Report prepared by Harris Interactive Inc. for the Society for American Archaeology. Electronic document, www.saa.org/portals/0/SAA/pubedu/nrptdraft4.pdf, accessed June 14, 2016.

Reynolds, C. 2012 Ancient Musqueam Burial Ground in Marpole to Remain Free of Development. *Vancouver Sun*, September 30. Electronic document, www.vancouversun.com/technology/ancient+musqueam+burial+ground+marpole+remain+free+development/7318280/story.html, accessed August 2, 2016.

Schuth, A., M. Marx, and M. de Rijke 2007 Extracting the Discussion Structure in Comments on News-articles. 9th ACM International Workshop on Web Information and Data Management (WIDM 2007), pp. 97–104.

Skeates, R., C. McDavid, and J. Carman, editors 2012 *The Oxford Handbook of Public Archaeology*. Oxford University Press, New York.

Suler, J. 2004 The Online Disinhibition Effect. *Cyberpsychology and Behavior: The Impact of the Internet, Multimedia and Virtual Reality on Behavior and Society* 7(3):321–326.

Thomas, S., and J. Lea, editors 2014 *Public Participation in Archaeology*. Boydell Press, Woodbridge.

Torres da Silva, M. 2015 What Do Users Have to Say About Online News Comments? Readers' Accounts and Expectations of Public Debate and Online Moderation: A Case Study. *Participations: Journal of Audience and Reception Studies* 12(2):32–44.

4
OBJECTS OF THE PAST
Relevance of Cultural Heritage in 21st-Century Museums

Chen Shen

Introduction

Cultural heritage is defined in this chapter as a legacy of physical artifacts and intangible attributes of a group or society that is inherited from past generations, maintained in the present, and bestowed for the benefit of future generations (see Appendix A: The Toronto Declaration). Heritage influences our lives and our way of thinking concerning the past and the present in contemporary societies. Here, I will focus on objects as tangible heritage that are normally on display in museums or could also have been hidden away for more than a hundred years. It is critical to ask how the past that is represented by these objects can be made relevant in the present and how the stories that are represented by these objects can be told within the context of contemporary society for the education, enjoyment, and betterment of present and future generations.

As we enter the 21st century, museums are transforming their mandates and missions from traditional roles as venues for displaying objects of the past into multiplatform public-facing cultural institutes. The change is inevitable, paralleling changes in lifestyle and expectations of youngsters growing up with social networking and mobile technologies. More and more, a question is being asked, "What should museums look like to build engagement with today's audiences?" While there are many answers that lead to museum strategic planning, a follow-up question should be "Why?"—that is, what are the objectives to engage today's young people who are heavily equipped with social media tools? In addition to welcoming them to enter the museum and view displays of cultural objects, our goal is truly to pave the ways in which a museum can connect a contemporary society to its past—the past that the local community has been built upon. Thus it is the museum that has a unique role in making cultural heritage relevant to today's living societies.

Objects of the Past

Museums are often viewed as treasure hoards, housing enormous collections of objects created in natural and cultural worlds and ranging in age from billions of years old to current cultural historical periods. In the period before formal museums were established, objects were commonly displayed in royal houses as human curiosities and/or trophies of conquest. With the development of museums and the establishment of museum practices, objects of the past are now interpreted in ways that build knowledge and dissolve barriers between one's own perceptions and understandings of the past in different cultural regions. As in U.S. National Park Service Ranger Freeman Tilden's frequently cited quotations: "Through interpretation, understanding; through understanding, appreciation; through appreciation, protection" (1957:38). Therefore, interpretations of objects should allow the public to gain understanding and appreciation of cultural heritage that can then be well protected.

For the purpose of this chapter, objects of the past are defined not only as those recovered from known archaeological sites but also those in which the context is not clear. This can result from unscientific excavation, salvaging, and rooting discoveries, and so forth, as well as family collections passed down from generation to generation. Whether ancient or recent, these objects become part of museum collections in which they are displayed in exhibits or curated. Interpretations of objects, through a variety of historical and archaeological perspectives, seek to reconstruct past societies that may have relevance to contemporary societies. However, the relevance and meanings of objects being displayed to museum visitors often remain unexplored. What do those objects mean to the general public in terms of contemporary focus of the latter on life, education, and entertainment?

What we need to consider in this discussion is how cultural materials of the past can make a relevant connection to the past of societies that value their cultural heritage. Objects of the past in museums should not be simply treated as archaeological materials and stylistic artworks that are merely referenced in university textbooks and/or museum catalogues. What is clear is that these objects serve a multifaceted purpose for the museum visitor: they include not only aspects of exhibition but also education, experience, and identity. Objects are cultural materials from the past that illustrate formations of cultural heritage that are identifiable for specific cultural worlds and regional groups. Tangible artifacts from the past are normally the subjects of preservation. Safekeeping and conservation of these objects at museums are ways of preserving the past—although this is far from enough.

Objects as Path of Connection to the Past

Objects from the past are often interpreted by archaeologists or historians with respect to origin and cultural affiliation. These objects are then displayed with labels that convey a message to museum visitors who may wish to make a connection to their own past. This presents the unique opportunity for objects on display to the public to serve as a gateway not only for understanding one's own past but also bridging the past and the present in one's own cultural heritage. Objects as a path for connecting to the past are viewed and interpreted by visitors, not scholars *per se*. Public interpretations of the objects' connection to their past may or may not be the same as those intended by exhibit designers and subject matter experts/scholars. So a problem arises: how can we—as academics and museum professionals who put cultural objects on exhibit—understand the relevance of cultural heritage to the contemporary societies if the publics' interpretations or desires are not communicated?

Objects as a Tool of Communication with the Past

Objects of the past can and should serve as tools for communication. Objects that were created by people in the past have an active role in shaping people's lives and ways of thinking in contemporary societies, just as powerfully today as in the past (Gosden 2005). These objects do not merely stand as best examples of artworks or historic documents but also trigger dialogues between scholars and laymen, curators and visitors, people understanding the past, and people concerned about the future. Objects of the past connect people from the past with people of the present—and people of the future. The connection includes both sides of the equation: the people to whom cultural heritage matters and those who serve as stewards for heritage. Objects on museum display can and should serve as media or social media that transform the meanings of the objects interpreted by academics into new meanings that have relevance to the museum visitor.

Thus in today's museums, researchers and curators should no longer focus solely on academic research efforts with respect to identification and evaluation of objects but rather on making the story of objects relevant to the people who care about their past and feel that objects can connect them with that past. Museum curators have a responsibility to go beyond the object and bring out the lives of the people behind those objects, because it is people—whose lives might have been either ordinary or heroic—who are relevant to contemporary societies. With this in mind, museum curators can and should help objects to recover sentimental memories of visitors who find themselves connecting to their own past. Exhibits should include various forums and conversations, similar to the functionality of social media today.

People's Heritage: Case Study of an Object

Heritage values in contemporary society are not just identified and applied through displayable tangible artifacts in the museum; rather, heritage values exist in a complicated and multifaceted matrix that links today's life in more meaningful ways when the past is made relevant to the present (Smith et al. 2010). Museums can provide storytelling exhibitions, provocative installations, and interactive programs, but at bottom line is that the museum collections themselves speak for heritage value.

One example is the Royal Ontario Museum (ROM) collection of Chinese ancient jade, the largest such collection outside China. Jade, a naturally hard mineral gemstone, has been carved into various forms and implements for thousands of years in China for the purposes of adornments, decorative arts, and utensils as well as ritual symbolism. Traditionally in Chinese societies, the allure of jade for personal pleasure has proven to be more than a passion—it is an obsession. Jade elicits fascination for its timeless beauty and value and has become a symbol of Chinese heritage that can be viewed in many museums of art and history around the world.

While the jade collection at ROM has been acquired over more than one hundred years, jade acquisition at the museum has become more selective in the past two decades. Western museums are restricted to acquisition of ancient artwork following the UNESCO conventions as well as AAMD (Association of Art Museum Directors) guidelines. To prevent illegally traded artwork from entering museum collections, museums like ROM take precautions for any gifts and purchases of jade. Objects, regardless of their high aesthetic values, will not be considered for acquisition unless they are accompanied by a clear history of provenance, documentation, and/or research support materials that prove they are of genuine origin and legitimate exportation.

In the autumn of 2012, I received an email inquiring if the ROM would be interested in a jade *bi* disc as a gift to the ROM. The current owner is Bernard Rasch, a retired Toronto architecture designer who worked on China's first American-style shopping mall in Shenzhen in 1980s. Rasch inherited this piece from his aunt, Celille Hatskin (1919–2005), who was married to well-known Canadian football player and businessman Ben Hatskin (1917–1990). It was indicated that the archaic Chinese jade disc was obtained from an unnamed Chinese lady by Cecille Hatskin in New York City in the 1940s.

In the beginning, this *bi* disc did not catch the author's curatorial interest to receive it as a gift. The *bi* disc is a classic 4,000-year-old Neolithic Liangzhu culture ritual object, and ROM already has quite a few in its collection. However, the collection history of the family who owned this piece of prehistoric Chinese ritual jade become an interesting subject of inquiry in its own right: why would a Canadian family want to own a piece of Chinese antiquity, and how did a piece of jade that originated from Eastern China turn up in New York before arriving in Canada? And in particular, who was this mysterious Chinese lady?

This situation could have been like that of many objects in museum galleries, in which objects come only with a display label suggesting a brief title, date, material, and credit line at the bottom. However, a surprise came in the form of the wooden display stand for the disc, which allowed me to build a whole story that connects the past to the present. The engraved scripts still visible on both sides of the wooden stand began an investigation on provenance by this author, one that revealed a fascinating story of 150 years of collecting history (Figure 4.1a-b) (Shen 2016).

The scripts on the front side of the wooden stand indicate that the original owner of this bi disc was the author of *Gu Yu Tu Kao* (*Illustrated Study of Ancient Jades*), published in 1889 by the Qing Dynasty statesmen and scholar Wu Dacheng

Objects of the Past 39

FIGURE 4.1a   Chinese Jade *bi* Disc Dated to 4,000 Years Ago, a Ritual Jade Object of Liangzhu Culture in Eastern China, Once in the Collection of China's Famed Wu Dacheng, Is Now the Latest Addition to the ROM

Source: Photo courtesy of the Royal Ontario Museum, used by permission.

(1835–1902) (Wu 1889). Wu is famous in Chinese recent history for his politic life as well as scholarship. Another 15 characters of Chinese shown in the front lower panel are an exact match with script on page 34 of the aforementioned publication. Further study on Wu's preserved diary suggests that he received this jade on March 19, 1889, from his dear friend Mr. Gu. On the back of the wooden stand, the upper panel is inscribed with a passage that says "[the *bi* disc] was originally possessed by Gu Zijia of Nanxun, and exchanged by Xu Hanqin with a bronze square *zun* vessel inscribed with zhu nu. It now belongs to Kezhai". Kezhai is an alternative or scholar name for Wu Dachang.

Further research included trips to Nanxun, Shanghai, Taipei, and Hong Kong. This revealed the fascinating history of five generations of the Gu family, who transformed themselves from silk producers and traders in late 19th-century Shanghai to

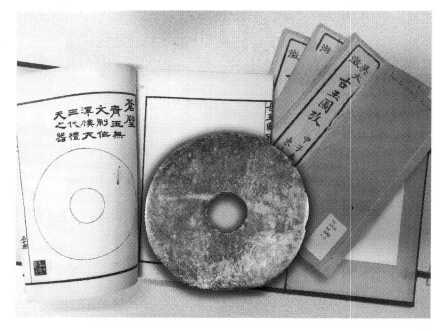

FIGURE 4.1b Chinese Jade *bi* Disc Dated to 4,000 Years Ago, a Ritual Jade Object of Liangzhu Culture in Eastern China, Once in the Collection of China's Famed Wu Dacheng, Is Now the Latest Addition to the ROM

Source: Photo courtesy of the Royal Ontario Museum, used by permission.

a major international entrepreneurial enterprise. Today's Koo (Gu) family focuses on education philanthropy in Hong Kong at present, who have supported thousands of students who are in need to complete high school educations in China. George Koo, whom the author met in Hong Kong in 2014, was not aware that his great-grandfather, Gu Zijia, had once owned this *bi* disc and had a significant relationship with Wu Dacheng. Gu Zijia was a major collector in Nanxun, where the silk production business was booming, making the whole town into one of the richest in China.

Gu's prowess as a collector is evidenced by his possession of an exquisite bronze vessel with an extraordinary inscription that dates to the late Shang dynasty. A similar vessel bearing the same inscription was in Emperor Qianglang's collection in the 18th century. This bronze vessel was exchanged with the jade disc and supposedly remained in the town of Nanxun through the hands of Wu Dacheng. It was probably a tribute to the Qing court at the turn of the 20th century. Today, this bronze vessel is part of the imperial collection at the National Palace Museum in Taipei.

The most intriguing part of the story is how the jade *bi* disc came to Canada via New York City. Through a study of letters in the ROM archives, we understand that after Wu passed away in 1902, part of his jade collection was inherited by his daughter Wu Benxian, who married an elder son of China's first Republic

President, Yuan Shikai. Wu Benxian sold most of these jade pieces to the ROM through Bishop William White, who acted as ROM's agent for collecting Chinese art during 1925–1934. Thus 27 jades that once belonged to Wu Dacheng arrived in Toronto in 1927–1928.

We have reason to believe that this particular *bi* disc was also passed down to Wu Dacheng's favorite daughter Wu Benjing, the young sister of Wu Benxian, given the sentimental value of the *bi* disc with a wooden stand engraved with her father's identity and names of her father's friends. My research also suggests that Wu Benjing's only daughter, Fei Lingyi (a graduate of Columbia University and an English professor in Shanghai) moved with her family to New York city in 1943 at the age of 39. We can only speculate that at this point the young Canadian woman Cecille had an encounter with Ms. Fei in the Big Apple. Therefore, I believe that Fei was the mysterious 'Chinese lady' mentioned in Rasch's email in 2012. In brief, this *bi* disc with its wooden stand is at the center of an extraordinary collecting story that spans more than 150 years. It has passed down through the hands of several legendary figures and is now finally reunited with 27 other ritual jades from the original collection of Wu Dacheng.

As demonstrated with the *bi* disc, a collecting history is a story of human relationships and societal changes. While we feel it is informative to know when and where an object came to the possession of a Canadian museum, in fact the more intriguing story is how this object made its way to Canada and how this can reveal a fascinating tale of the past. While we enjoy the object on display through the glass of the museum showcase, it is more relevant to consider the people and the lives behind the object.

Cultural Heritage: Identity, Sensibility, Controversy

Moving back to the realm of museum displays, artwork of the past may be appreciatively viewed for its beautiful aesthetics and historic narratives. Museum labels and presentations can enhance this understanding and appreciation by clearly identifying the dates and places of origin where the work was created. Such standard information gives a sense of pride for someone coming to visit the museum, where he or she can connect with and explore heritage roots through the exhibits.

One of the greatly successful programs at the Royal Ontario Museum was an annual Heritage Day for a variety of communities including Chinese, Korean, Iranian, and South Asian. For several days, children and parents shared sensations of their roots while being surrounded by works of art that reflect diverse and rich cultural heritages. A museum of art, culture, and nature such as the ROM is a great place where people come to find their own cultural identity within the multicultural society of Canada.

The Of Africa project at the Royal Ontario Museum is a multiplatform initiative to bring to the museum exhibitions and programs that offer diversified perspectives on Africa and the diaspora. With exhibitions and programs, this project challenges monolithic representations of Africa, including museum collections and

42 Chen Shen

colonial histories, through broadening discussions and conversations with members of community partners and by various presentations of what constitutes Africa and African art and cultures (Figure 4.2).

Using collections of family photographs, the family camera project leading to the same-titled exhibition at the ROM explores the relationship between photography (objects) and the idea of family (heritage). As the project describes, our personal photographs document our feelings about family, how we define family, and how we stay connected to loved ones who may be separated as a result of migrations, relocation, and other diasporas.

Museums are also challenged to present cultural sensibility with regard to cultural diversity, religious gestures, and symbolic engagement through gallery development and exhibition presentations (e.g., designing materials, use of colors, and assemblages). Gallery labelling interpretations are key to making heritage relevant to culturally sensitive communities. The family camera project, for example, will preserve a family history for future generations as well as provide a resource for teachers, historians, and scholars to write new histories of family and lifeways through that particular lens.

Museums are responsible for naturalizing concurrent issues rising from historic disputes and cultural conflicts and, as such, are given a golden opportunity to be at the center of important debates. The destruction of heritage sites by the 'ISIS; (also see Burgess this volume) as well as issues of looting of Iraq antiquities during

FIGURE 4.2 The Africa Program at the ROM

Source: Photo by the author.

wartime (see Stone this volume) are good examples of such debates that surround related objects from museum collections. Debates also arise from the lines of political states in history as depicted in exhibitions and gallery, which can trigger discussions of nationalism. Interestingly, debates like these that concern museums' presentations have been commonly centered on lost objects and/or damaged objects.

Museums and Relevance of Cultural Heritage to Contemporary Communities

The relevance of cultural heritage has yet to make its powerful presence fully known to the public through museum programs and exhibitions. To a great degree, cultural identity and sensibility in contemporary society can be better understood through a museum's approach to its cultural materials.

Museums play a pivotal role in engaging with diversified communities and public at large, as cultural heritage value is applied to an understanding of the past that is relevant to everyday life. Museums hold significant collections of natural and cultural worlds that, over the ages, have witnessed climatic and environmental changes (also see Douglas this volume), natural disasters, and human-powered manipulations. The surviving objects that are displayed in galleries and exhibitions today are key to engaging the public in dialogues that foster understanding of cultural heritage. In today's growing multicultural municipalities, museums provide platforms for the public to make meaningful links to the past of their own identity through current technologies and social media, which in turn raise awareness of heritage values and give voice to policy making that affects cultural heritage for local communities as well as the nation they are proud to be a part of.

References

Gosden, C. 2005 What Do Objects Want? *Journal of Archaeological Method and Theory* 12(3):193–211.

Shen, C. 2016 Timeless Destinations: Stories of the People behind Wu Dacheng's Jade Cang Bi. *Orientations*, 47(3):26–33.

Smith, G. S., P. M. Messenger, and H. A. Soderland, editors 2010 *Heritage Values in Contemporary Society*. Left Coast Press, Inc. Walnut Creek, California.

Tilden, F. 1957 *Interpreting our Heritage*. University of North Carolina Press, Chapel Hill.

Wu, D. C. 1889 *Gu Yu Tu Kao*. Tongwen Shuju (publisher), Shanghai.

5

WHAT'S A MUSEUM TO DO? THE GLOBAL TRADE IN ILLEGAL ANTIQUITIES

L. Eden Burgess

> In mid-2015, ISIS beheaded Khaled al-Asaad. Militants interrogated him for a month before he was murdered in the ancient Syrian city of Palmyra. His crime? The renowned antiquities scholar reportedly refused to reveal the locations of the city's ancient treasures. The murder of al-Asaad brought ISIS' practice of selling looted antiquities to fund its activities to the forefront of the challenges facing the antiquities market worldwide, including museums.
>
> (*The Guardian* 2015)[1]

Cultural heritage—various items of cultural, historic, scientific, or religious importance—is being looted from archaeological sites, museums, and many other sources (United Nations 2015).[2] "Hundreds, if not thousands, of priceless historical artifacts have long been stolen, traded, sold and passed through numerous hands only to be spirited away across multiple borders to private collectors" (Mascarenas 2013:9; SAFE 2016).[3] Cultural racketeering is a global crime worth millions that affects not only the country from which goods are stolen but also the nations through which the objects pass on the way to their final destination (Interpol 2016b).

In light of the scale of the problem, the damage caused to the cultural resources and the historical record, and the immense complexity of solving it, what can U.S. museums do to combat the illegal antiquities trade?

Defining the Global Problem

In the last decade, illegal trafficking of cultural heritage has grown—especially in Middle East. For instance, Da'esh (also known as the Islamic State [IS], the Islamic State of Iraq and Syria [ISIS], or the Islamic State of Iraq and the Levant [ISIL]) reportedly has looted upward of 2,000 archaeological sites in Syria alone (Lamb 2014; Sehmer 2015).[4] The United Nations (UN) warns that Da'esh, Al-Qaida, and other groups generate income through the illegal antiquities market to support recruitment efforts, strengthen operational capability, and organize and commit attacks (United Nations 2015).

The U.S. poses some unique problems. First, it is one of the largest markets for looted antiquities in the world (CBS News 2015).[5] In addition, the U.S. suspended diplomatic ties with Syria in March 2014 (Al Jazeera 2014), so it is difficult to obtain accurate information. The U.S. established a bad reputation for itself in Iraq when it allowed the National Museum and the National Library to be looted in 2003 and tolerated widespread pillaging of archeological sites throughout the countryside (ABC News 2013; *Washington Post* 2003).[6] While it later made efforts to rectify those errors (AIA 2004),[7] Iraq continues to suffer the loss of irreplaceable cultural resources (see Peter Stone this volume).

The problem, in short, is vast and devastating, and efforts to combat the challenge have yet to match its scope.

International Efforts to Fight Cultural Racketeering

Many international organizations fight against illegal trafficking of antiquities as part of their mission. One of the tools they rely on is the Convention for the Protection of Cultural Property in the Event of Armed Conflict with Regulations for the Execution of the Convention of 1954, passed in response to the unprecedented looting and destruction of cultural property during World War II (Wegener 2010). The 1954 Convention focuses on the protection of cultural heritage during armed conflict and requires member states to seek to prevent their military forces from engaging in acts of theft and destruction involving cultural items (Ibid.). It also requires that each state implement protective measures for its own cultural heritage (Ibid.; see Arlene K. Fleming this volume).[8]

One highly visible international organization is Interpol, an information-sharing exchange that works to raise awareness among the general public, police, and market participants (Interpol 2016b). Interpol focuses efforts on encouraging an efficient exchange of data between official and private parties; its goal is to centralize information so that nations and global organizations can exchange information in order to return stolen goods to their rightful owners (Ibid.). Interpol created a database of stolen works of art for use by law enforcement officers and other authorized users (Interpol 2016b), as well as another, more limited database accessible by the general public (Ibid.). Europol performs a similar function within the European Union (Europol 2017).

Separately, various arms of the United Nations work to combat the illegal antiquities market. The UN Security Council, chartered on the principle that it will solve international problems by coordinating across nations (UN Security Council 2016), unanimously passed Resolution 2199 in 2015, which condemns the illegal trade in antiquities that may fund terrorist groups in Iraq and Syria (UN Security Council 2015). Resolution 2199 requires all member states to take steps to prevent the trade of cultural heritage taken from Iraq and Syria and enable the return of looted goods (Ibid.).

UNESCO has been engaged in the fight against stolen cultural property for several decades. A landmark step was the 1970 Convention on the Means of Prohibiting and Preventing the Illicit Import, Export and Transfer of Ownership of Cultural Property (UNESCO 1970). This Convention mandates that member states develop a national service dedicated to the protection of cultural heritage, requires certifications for the lawful export of cultural heritage items, and orders nations "to prevent museums and similar institutions within their territories from acquiring cultural property originating in another State Party which has been illegally exported" (Ibid.). It also requires states to refrain from transferring or importing any property that is likely to promote the illegal trade, to restitute the item as quickly as reasonably possible, and to allow rightful owners to pursue actions for recovery (Ibid.).

The International Institute for the Unification of Private Law, or Unidroit, passed the Convention on Stolen or Illegally Exported Cultural Property in 1996 as a follow-up to the 1970 UNESCO Convention (Unidroit 1995). The Unidroit Convention targets the art market and requires that any stolen object be returned (Ibid.). Unidroit also published a set of Model Legislative Provisions to assist legislators in establishing a framework for recognizing ownership of the items and facilitating restitution (Unidroit 2012). Notably, the United States, Iraq, and Syria are not signatories to the Convention and have not adopted the Model Legislative Provisions (Unidroit 1995).

The International Association of Dealers in Ancient Art (IADAA), created in 1993, seeks to improve relations among art dealers, museums, and government agencies to ensure the legal and ethical trade of antiquities (IADAA 2016). The organization encourages its 32 members from eight countries to adhere to a code of ethics (Ibid.) that includes a requirement that dealers conduct due diligence to ensure any item they acquire was not stolen (Ibid.).

Finally, the International Council of Museums (ICOM) represents museums and museum professionals (ICOM 2016). ICOM trains museum personnel to protect heritage through inventory systems and observance of international standards regarding the acceptance of cultural goods (Ibid.). ICOM also created The International Observatory on Illicit Traffic in Cultural Goods, a collaborative website that encourages communication among law enforcement, government entities, and private parties (Ibid.). ICOM publishes the well-known 'Red Lists', transmitted through Interpol, which describe antiquities at risk of being illegally traded (Ibid.).

Until the recent widespread conflicts in Iraq and Syria, the U.S. has generally resisted international efforts both to reduce the incentives for looting and to increase nations' dedication to combatting it. Over the past several decades, again until quite recently, American politicians have infamously opposed the U.S. signing on to international agreements—such as the 1954 Hague Convention and its two protocols—that may interfere with U.S. policy-making independence. However, the U.S. has begun to join global efforts to tamp down the illegal antiquities trade, particularly in recent years.

U.S. Efforts to Combat Antiquities Trafficking

Several U.S. agencies are involved in combatting the trafficking of cultural heritage. The Department of State plays a significant role in America's efforts to slow the illegal antiquities trade. After signing onto the 1970 UNESCO Convention in 1972, it was not until 1983 that Congress passed the Cultural Property Implementation Act, which, among other things, chartered the Cultural Heritage Center at the State Department to implement the principles set forth in the UNESCO Convention (U.S. Congress 1983). Upon execution of a memorandum of understanding (MOU) with a requesting foreign nation, the Act authorizes the Department of Homeland Security to seize archaeological and ethnological objects identified in the MOU (Bureau of Educational and Cultural Affairs 2016).

In addition, the U.S. Department of Homeland Security is empowered to investigate trafficking and smuggling, which can lead to recoveries and restitutions (U.S. Department of Immigrations and Customs Enforcement 2016). Under U.S. customs laws, Homeland Security Investigation can seize property illegally brought into the United States and return it to its rightful owners, as well as investigate art theft crimes (Ibid.). Homeland Security has recovered thousands of priceless items of cultural heritage (Ibid.).

The Federal Bureau of Investigation (FBI) created the Art Crime Team with agents specially trained in art and cultural property investigations (FBI 2016). The Team has recovered $150 million worth of stolen items since 2004 (Ibid.). The Art Crime Team also works with foreign law enforcement officials to assist in worldwide art-related investigations (Ibid.).

The United States has passed various pieces of federal legislation focused on the criminalization of transporting stolen goods. The National Stolen Property Act (18 U.S.C. § 2311, *et seq.*) makes it a federal crime to transport goods worth more than $5,000 known to be stolen (U.S. Congress 1987). Also, a new statute called the Protect and Preserve International Cultural Property Act imposes restrictions on the importation of Syrian Antiquities and directs an Assistant Secretary of State to coordinate the cultural heritage protection efforts of the Departments of State, Defense, Homeland Security, and Justice (U.S. Congress 2015). While the U.S. government has taken measures to participate in the world's efforts to protect and preserve cultural heritage, few states or localities have adopted parallel measures. Los Angeles has the only police department with an Art Theft Detail, a full-time municipal law enforcement agency devoted solely to art crimes (LAPD 2015).

U.S. Museums

The impact of federal legislation is amplified by cooperation from private-sector response in the United States, specifically among museums and museum professionals. The American Alliance of Museums (AAM), among other things, tracks legislation that affects museums (AAM 2016a).[9] It also issues briefs related to certain areas of law that implicate museums, including issues pertaining to cultural heritage (Ibid.). AAM also promulgates National Standards and Best Practices for U.S. Museums that are free to its members (AAM 2016b). These standards describe the process for ensuring ethical acquisition of objects for a museum's collection (Ibid.). Similarly, AAM has issued standards regarding objects illegally obtained during the Nazi Era that cover acquisition, loans, research, and procedure upon learning of an illegally obtained item (AAM 2016c).[10]

The Association of Art Museum Directors (AAMD) encourages ethical practices, advocating on behalf of museums, and serving as a forum for the exchange of ideas. Specifically, AAMD publishes issue summaries relating to topics affecting museums, including the exchange of cultural property (AAMD 2016d). Regarding the Protect and Preserve International Cultural Property Act, AAMD has issued a statement that expresses concern that the legislation would prevent all import of items from Syria (Taylor 2016). AAMD has also issued a series of standards and practices relating to the collection of objects, including items of cultural significance from areas of crisis (2016b, f). AAMD encourages museums to collect items and serve as a safe haven until they can safely be returned to their rightful owner (AAMD 2016g).

What's a Museum to Do?

How can U.S. museums help tamp down antiquities looting, and do they have any responsibility—legal or ethical—to do so?

U.S. Museums' Legal and Ethical Responsibilities

Museums are not law enforcement agents; most U.S. museums are not even government owned, although the majority are nonprofit and enjoy tax-free status granted by the IRS and their respective states (Institute of Museum and Library Service 2015; U.S. Department of State 2015).[11] Do other legal and ethical obligations apply?

Legal Obligations[12]

Museum law is largely a function of state law, which differs across the country. State attorneys general are responsible for ensuring that nonprofits like museums work in furtherance of their stated missions and do not misuse donated funds and property. Museums may also be impacted by state laws governing contracts, employment, insurance, and wills and estates.

Federal law governs other areas relevant to museums, such as copyright and trademark. For purposes of this chapter, the National Stolen Property Act (NSPA) is becoming increasingly pertinent. The NSPA treats antiquities as 'stolen property' under U.S. law if they were improperly taken from a foreign country that makes the government the sole and rightful owner of such artifacts.[13] While the NSPA does not, on its face, prohibit museums from acquiring antiquities, the possibility of a broader enforcement of its provisions—particularly since the exponential growth of the black market in antiquities—should dampen a museum's willingness to make risky acquisitions.

The Cultural Property Implemetation Act (CPIA) (19 U.S.C. § 2601, *et seq.*) also potentially influences museum acquisitions, although museums are generally expected to acquire only antiquities with a clear provenance traceable back to 1970. It does not provide criminal penalties but does provide for seizure and forfeiture of illegally imported objects (see 9 U.S. Code § 2609). The CPIA requires, however, that a country apply for the statute's special protections, such as the control of exports, imports, and international commerce in specific cultural materials (Bureau of Educational and Cultural Affairs 2016).

The law's procedures have proved burdensome. Since looters often take advantage of unrest to pilfer sites and objects, nations are often too busy handling those immediate challenges to address cultural heritage protection. As a result, only 15 countries have successfully negotiated a memorandum of understanding with the State Department since the CPIA's enactment in 1983.[14] For example, the unrest in Egypt during January 2011 has had a "devastating effect" on its sites and artifacts (Ikram 2014). But because of that same internal turmoil, Egypt was not in a position to request special protections until spring 2014 (AIA 2014).

Therefore, unless an object is known to be stolen (NSPA) or on a list of objects protected by an MOU (CPIA), no federal law requires that museums take special precautions when acquiring antiquities. Their acquisition policies are therefore limited not by federal or state regulation but by state property laws, museum association guidelines, and each museum's own acquisition policy.

Ethical Obligations[15]

The AAM's Code of Ethics reminds its members that "legal standards are a minimum. Museums and those responsible for them must do more than avoid legal liability" (AAM 2016c). More specifically, in 2008, the AAM adopted Standards Regarding Archaeological Material and Ancient Art (Ibid.). Those Standards include three basic rules for acquiring antiquities:

- "[M]useums should not acquire any object that, to the knowledge of the museum, has been illegally exported . . ."
- Museums should obtain "documentation that an object was out of its probable country of modern discovery by November 17, 1970" (adoption date of the 1970 UNESCO Convention).
- For objects exported from their country of modern discovery after 1970, museums should "require documentation that the object has been or will be legally exported . . . and legally imported into the United States" (Ibid.).

AAM thus provides a loophole by advising that museums not acquire objects *known* to be illegally exported (Ibid.). Also, AAM stops short of advising its members *never* to acquire poorly documented antiquities, explaining that in some cases, "it may be in the public's interest for a museum to acquire an object, thus bringing it into the public domain, when there is substantial but not full documentation [of the] provenance" (Ibid.). Finally, AAM includes about 799 museums as accredited members—only 2.2% of the estimated 35,000 museums in the U.S.—meaning the impact of these restrictions is limited; nevertheless, since AAM guidelines reflect best practices in the museum field, non-AAM museums ignore these rules at their peril (AAMD 2016e).

The AAMD's Guidelines on the Acquisition of Archaeological Material and Ancient Art take a stronger position since the 2013 revisions, which were intended to "provide more detail about the considerations to be taken into account when deciding whether to acquire a work that is either archeological material or ancient art" (AAMD 2016f). The AAMD advises that member museums "normally should not acquire a Work *unless provenance research substantiates* that the Work was outside its country of probable modern discovery before 1970 or was legally exported … after 1970" (AAMD 2016h). While the AAMD, similar to the AAM, allows museums to "consider acquisitions that do not have a complete provenance if they meet the criteria described in the guidelines" (AAMD 2016f), it does provide detailed criteria—including that the museum make an informed judgment as to the provenance and "carefully balance the possible financial and reputational harm of acquiring the Work against the benefit" (AAMD 2016h)—and requires that the museum promptly publish its reasoning for the acquisition of an object with inadequate provenance and list the object on the AAMD website to give it public exposure (Ibid.).

No More Antiquities?

Some steps, then, have already been taken to encourage U.S. museums to combat looting. In theory, requiring high standards for acquisition reduces incentives to loot and to smuggle looted objects, since museums are *unlikely* to buy or accept donations of such objects under strict standards. But the impact appears to be minimal thus far, as looting is still rampant, and the U.S. remains one of the world's leading markets for stolen objects. As Vlasic (2011) has noted, "Without the markets for stolen cultural property in Europe and North America, there would be little scope for nefarious attempts at taking advantage of the current instability of cultural treasures in North Africa and the Middle East".

The next step would be to *prohibit U.S. museums from acquiring any new antiquities*. U.S. museums have some experience with such a ban already due to the UN Security Council's ban on the trade in Iraqi artifacts in 2003 (UNESCO 1970), followed by the United States' emergency import restrictions on materials from Iraq pursuant to the Emergency Protection for Iraqi Cultural Antiquities Act of 2004 (U.S. Congress 1983). Similarly, UN Security Council Resolution 2199, unanimously adopted in February 2015, "condemns the destruction of cultural heritage and adopts legal measures to counter illicit trafficking of antiquities from Iraq and Syria" (Perlsen 2015). The resolution resulted from concerns that Islamic State and other groups are generating funds from the antiquities trafficking. The U.S. Senate later implemented the measure by voting to "ban the import of virtually all ancient art and artifacts from Syria to discourage the looting and trafficking of illicit objects by the Islamic State and other armed groups" (Myers 2016).

In both instances, the United States adopted bans on trade in artifacts from wartorn Middle Eastern nations, although some would argue this was too late, after international organizations had already taken the lead. Most observers agree that the UN ban and other national efforts helped Iraq recover from the rampant looting in the wake of the U.S. invasion and have urged the same steps to be taken with respect to Syrian objects—but the United States did not enact an appropriate law until 2016 (The Syria Campaign 2014).

Thus far, the FBI has declined to advise U.S. buyers to refuse to buy any antiquities (Martinez 2015). Considering the success of the suspensions of trade in Iraqi and Syrian antiquities, however, perhaps it is time to consider a broader approach: one that would prevent museums from acquiring *any* antiquities, unless the object comes with documentation of legal export from its country of origin before 1970 and a reliable provenance, also dated to at least 1970, independently verified by museum staff or consultants (SAFE 2016).[16] U.S. museums attempted nearly this approach *via* an AAMD 2008 strict ban on acquiring poorly documented antiquities; however, the dearth of well-documented antiquities drove the AAMD, in 2013, to broaden the scope of the exceptions.

Conclusion

Neither enforceable nor unenforceable restrictions on U.S. museums require these institutions, which hold their collections in trust for the public, to refuse to acquire antiquities, even where the export documentation or provenance is inadequate. Adopting and enforcing a stricter ban on antiquities will impact the incentive overseas to loot sites and should impact ISIS's ability to fund its terror campaign by committing terrorist acts against the world's invaluable cultural heritage. Cultural heritage must be protected in order for it to maintain relevance to contemporary society, and we owe it to ourselves and future generations to take every possible step to save our history.

Acknowledgments

Ms. Burgess, a partner with Cultural Heritage Partners, PLLC in Washington, DC, and a Professorial Lecturer in Law at the George Washington University Law School, sincerely thanks Melissa Sprinkle, a student at Georgia State University Law School, without whom this chapter would exist only in the author's imagination. Thanks also go to Tom Kline and Jen Morris for their thoughtful editing.

Notes

1. As widely reported, ISIS destroyed Palmyra later that year.
2. Some famous examples of looted treasures whose proper home has been long debated are the Rosetta Stone (looted first from Egypt by Napoleon, then from Napoleon by the British), and the Parthenon (or Elgin) Marbles.

3 Saving Antiquities For Everyone (SAFE) cautions, however, that it is impossible to quantify the exact size or value of the black market trade in antiquities due to its illicit nature.
4 'Cultural cleansing' refers to the "'systematic destruction' of important historical sites in an attempt to erase cultural identities" and often occurs alongside cultural racketeering.
5 According to U.S. Marine Col. Matthew Bogdanos, who led the investigation into the 2003 looting of the National Museum of Iraq, the four destinations for looted objects are New York, Paris, London, and Tokyo.
6 Charges of neglect by U.S. armed forces to properly protect the Museum prompted Martin E. Sullivan, chairman of the President's Advisory Committee on Cultural Property, to resign.
7 For example, by passing the Emergency Protection for Iraqi Cultural Antiquities Act of 2004.
8 The United States ratified the resolution in 2009.
9 For example, AAM issued a brief in support of the proposed Protect and Preserve International Cultural Property Act.
10 During the Nazi regime, millions of objects of cultural heritage were destroyed, looted, and sold across borders. The extent of the looting in cultural property has become clear in more recent years, which has prompted museum professionals to focus on identifying and assist in the return of such objects.
11 According to the Institute of Museum and Library Services, the U.S. has approximately 35,000 museums. In most of the world, museums are largely supported by the government. American museums raise their own funds from government sources and the private sector.
12 For a more fulsome discussion of legal issues governing museums, see Courtney 2015.
13 *United States v. McClain*, 551 F.2d 52 (5th Cir. 1977).
14 Other federal laws that impact archaeological objects and antiquities—but rarely impact museums directly—include the Antiquities Act of 1906 (16 U.S.C. §§ 431–433), the Archeological and Historic Preservation Act of 1974 (16 U.S.C. § 469–469c), and the Archaeological Resources Protection Act of 1979 (16 U.S.C. § 470aa, *et seq.*). Also, the Native American Graves Protection and Repatriation Act of 1990 (25 U.S.C. § 3001, *et seq.*), requires museums that receive federal funding to repatriate Native American remains and 'cultural items'. 25 U.S.C. § 3001(3), (8). These statutes are beyond the scope of this chapter. For more information, see: Department of Interior. Electronic Document, www.doi.gov/museum/laws-and-regulations, accessed April 22, 2016.
15 Ethics codes not discussed here include the College Art Association (available at www.collegeart.org/guidelines/) and individual museum policies and codes of ethics, such as the J. Paul Getty Museum's (available at www.getty.edu/about/governance/pdfs/acquisitions_policy.pdf). A longer list is available here: www.ifar.org/professional_guidelines.php.
16 Provenance of antiquities should reach back to at least 1970.

References

ABC News 2016 Who's to Blame for Iraq Museum Looting? April 19, 2016. Electronic document, http://abcnews.go.com/Nightline/story?id=128469&page=1, accessed April 17, 2016.

Al Jazeera 2014 US Suspends Diplomatic Relations With Syria, March 19, 2014. Electronic document, www.aljazeera.com/news/middleeast/2014/03/us-suspends-diplomatic-relations-with-syria-2014318153828980578.html, accessed April 27, 2016.

American Alliance of Museums 2016a Public Diplomacy and Protection of Cultural Property. Electronic document, www. aam-us.org/docs/default-source/advocacy/brief-public-diplomacy.pdf?sfvrsn=6, accessed April 27, 2016.

———. 2016b Product: National Standards and Best Practices for U.S. Museums. Electronic document, www.aam-us.org/ProductCatalog/Product?ID=3410, accessed April 27, 2016.

———. 2016c Standards Regarding the Unlawful Appropriation of Objects During the Nazi Era. Electronic document, www.aam-us.org/resources/ethics-standards-and-best-practices/collections-stewardship/objects-during-the-nazi-era, accessed April 27, 2016.

———. 2016d Issue Summaries: Cultural Property Issues. Electronic document, www.aam-us.org/sites/default/files/key-issue/Cultural%20Property%20Issue%20Summaries%2010-2015.pdf, accessed April 27, 2016.

———. 2016e Statistics. Electronic document, www.aam-us.org/resources/assessment-programs/accreditation/statistics, accessed April 27, 2016.

———. 2016f Strengthened Guidelines on the Acquisition of Archaeological Material and Ancient Art Issued By Association of Art Museum Directors. Electronic document, https://aamd.org/for-the-media/press-release/strengthened-guidelines-on-the-acquisition-of-archaeological-material, accessed April 27, 2016.

———. 2016g The AAMD and Nazi-era Claims—A Principled Response. Electronic document, https://aamd.org/sites/default/files/key-issue/FINAL_%20The%20AAMD%20and%20Nazi-Era%20Claims%20-%20A%20Principled%20Response.pdf, accessed April 27, 2016.

———. 2016h The AAMD Guidelines, Sections III.E, F, H. Electronic documents, https://aamd.org/sites/default/files/document/AAMD%20Guidelines%202013.pdf, accessed April 27, 2016.

Archaeological Institute of America 2014 CPAC to Discuss Egypt's Request for Import Restrictions, Review of Nicaragua MoU. Electronic document, www.archaeological.org/CPAC, accessed April 27, 2016.

———. 2004 Emergency Protection for Iraqi Cultural Antiquities Act Passes, November 1. Electronic document, www.archaeological.org/news/sitepreservation/143, accessed April 17, 2016.

Bureau of Educational and Cultural Affairs 2016 Cultural Heritage Center: Background. Electronic document, http://eca.state.gov/cultural-heritage-center/cultural-property-protection/process-and-purpose/background, accessed April 27, 2016.

CBS News 2015 Following the Trail of Syria's Looted History, September 9. Electronic document, www.cbsnews.com/news/isis-looted-syrian-ancient-artifacts-black-market-us-and-europe/, accessed April 17, 2016.

Courtney, J., editor 2015 *The Legal Guide for Museum Professionals*. Rowman & Littlefield, Lanham, MD.

Europol 2017 Illicit Trafficking in Cultural Goods. Electronic document, www.europol.europa.eu/crime-areas-and-trends/crime-areas/illicit-trafficking-in-cultural-goods-including-antiquities-and-works-of-art, accessed February 18, 2017.

The Guardian 2015 Beheaded Syrian Scholar Refused to Lead Isis to Hidden Palmyra Antiquities, August 19, 2015. Electronic document, www.theguardian.com/world/2015/aug/18/isis-beheads-archaeologist-syria, accessed April 27, 2016.

ICOM 2016 The Observatory. Electronic document, http://obs-traffic.museum/observatory, accessed April 27, 2016.

Ikram, S. 2014 The Loss and Looting of Egyptian Antiquities. Electronic document, www.theepochtimes.com/n3/648156-the-loss-and-looting-of-egyptian-antiquities/, accessed April 27, 2016.

Institute of Museum and Library Services 2015 Museum Universe Data File, FY 2015 Q3 Release: Documentation. Electronic document, www.imls.gov/sites/default/files/mudf_docuemenation_2015q3.pdf, accessed April 22, 2016.

International Associate of Dealers in Ancient Art 2016 Chairman's Address. Electronic document, www.iadaa.org/en/chairman-sAddress, accessed April 27, 2016.

Interpol 2016a Works of Art FAQ. Electronic document, www.interpol.int/Crime-areas/Works-of-art/Frequently-asked questions, accessed April 27, 2016.

———. 2016b Works of Art. Electronic document, www.interpol.int/Crime-areas/Works of-art/Works-of-art, accessed April 27, 2016.

Lamb, F. 2014 Looting Is the Greatest Threat to Our Cultural Heritage in Syria. *Foreign Policy Journal*, December 29. Electronic document, www.foreignpolicyjournal.com/2014/12/29/looting-is-the-greatest-threat-to-our-cultural-heritage-in-syria/, accessed April 27, 2016.

Los Angeles Police Department 2015 About the Art Theft Detail. Electronic document, www.lapdonline.org/about_the_art_theft_detail, accessed April 27, 2016.

Martinez, A. 2015 FBI Warns US Art Dealers: ISIL-Looted Antiquities Are Hitting the Market. *The Observer*, August 27, 2015. Electronic document, http://observer.com/2015/08/fbi-warns-us-art-dealers-isil-looted-antiquities-are-hitting-the-art-market/, accessed April 27, 2016.

Mascarenhas, H. 2013 Priceless Artifacts Museums Should Return to Their Home Countries, *Mic*, December 11, 2013. Electronic document, http://mic.com/articles/76321/9-priceless-artifacts-museums-should-return-to-their-home-countries#.kpc35AbrF, accessed April 27, 2016.

Myers, S. L. 2016 Senate Votes to Ban Imports of Syrian Art and Antiquities. *The New York Times*, April 14, 2016. Electronic document, www.nytimes.com/2016/04/14/world/middleeast/senate-votes-to-ban-imports-of-syrian-art-and-antiquities.html, accessed April 27, 2016.

Perlsen, M. 2015 UN Bans Export of Antiquities To Target Islamic State Revenue. Electronic document, https://news.artnet.com/art-world/un-bans-export-of-antiquities-to-target-islamic-state-revenue-255058, accessed April 27, 2016.

SAFE 2016 Facts and Figures. Electronic document, http://savingantiquities.org/safe-resources/facts-figures/, accessed April 27, 2016.

Sehmer, A. 2015 Isis Guilty of "cultural cleansing" across Syria and Iraq, Unesco Chief Irina Bokova Says. *The Independent*, October 5, 2015. Electronic document, www.independent.co.uk/news/world/middle-east/unesco-chief-irina-bokova-accuses-islamist-groups-of-cultural-cleansing-isis-a6679761.html, accessed April 27, 2016.

The Syria Campaign 2014 Open Letter Calling on UN to Ban Trade in Syrian Artifacts. Electronic document, https://diary.thesyriacampaign.org/un-ban-the-trade-in-syrian-antiquities/, accessed April 27, 2016.

Taylor, S. M. 2016 Letter from American Alliance of Museums President to Congressmen Royce and Engel Concerning H.R. 1493. Electronic document, www.aamd.org/sites/default/files/key-issue/FINAL%20STATEMENT7471527_4.pdf, accessed April 27, 2016.UN Security Council 2016 What Is the Security Council? Electronic document, www.un.org/en/sc/about/, accessed April 27, 2016.

UNESCO 1970 Illicit Trafficking of Cultural Property: 1970 Convention. Electronic document, www.unesco.org/new/en/culture/themes/illicit-trafficking-of cultural-property/1970-convention/text-of-the-convention/, accessed April 27, 2016.

UNIDROIT UNESCO 2012 UNIDROIT Model Provisions on State Ownership of Undiscovered Cultural Objects. Electronic document, www.unidroit.org/instruments/cultural-property/model-provisions, accessed April 27, 2016.

———. 1995 The 1995 UNIDROIT Convention on Stolen or Illegally Exported Cultural Objects. Electronic document, www.unidroit.org/overviecp/english, accessed April 27, 2016.

United Nations 2015 UN Security Council Unanimously Adopting Resolution 2199 (2015), Security Council Condemns Trade with Al-Qaida Associated Groups, Threatens Further Targeted Sanctions. Electronic document, www.un.org/press/en/2015/sc11775.doc.htm, accessed April 27, 2016.

Congress 2015 Protect and Preserve International Cultural Property Act, H.R. 1493. Electronic document, www.congress.gov/bill/114th-congress/house-bill/1493, accessed April 27, 2016.

———. 1987 National Stolen Property Act, 18 U.S.C. §§ 2314–2315. Electronic document, www.unesco.org/culture/natlaws/media/pdf/usa/usa_natstolenpropertyact_1983amended1987_enorof.pdf, accessed April 27, 2016.

———. 1983 Convention on Cultural Property Implementation Act 2016 19 U.S.C. § 2601 et seq. Electronic document, http://eca.state.gov/files/bureau/97-446.pdf, accessed April 17, 2016.

U.S. Department of Immigrations and Customs Enforcement 2016 Cultural Property, Art and Antiquities Investigation. Electronic document, www.ice.gov/cultural-art-investigations, accessed April 27, 2016.

U.S. Department of State 2015 How Are Museums Supported Financially in the U.S.? You Asked Series. Electronic document, http://iipdigital.usembassy.gov/st/english/pamphlet/2012/05/201205155699.html#ixzz46ezJyD5q, accessed April 22, 2016.

U.S. Federal Bureau of Investigations 2016 Art Theft: Art Crime Team. Electronic document, www.fbi.gov/about-us/investigate/vc_majorthefts/arttheft/art-crime-team, accessed April 27, 2016.

Vlasic, M. 2011 Stamping Out the Illicit Trade in Cultural Artifacts. *The Guardian*, August 7, 2011, Electronic document, www.theguardian.com/commentisfree/cifamerica/2011/aug/07/egypt-antiquities-trade, accessed April 27, 2016.

The Washington Post 2003 Charges of Neglect by U.S. Armed Forces to Properly Protect the Museum Prompted Martin E. Sullivan, Chairman of the President's Advisory Committee on Cultural Property, to Resign. Paul Richard, Bush Panel Members Quit Over Looting; Cultural Advisors Say U.S. Military Could Have Prevented Museum Losses. April 17, 2003, Section C1.

Wegener, C. 2010 The 1954 Hague Convention and Preserving Cultural Heritage. *Archaeological Institute of America*, October 19, 2010, Electronic document, www.archaeological.org/news/hca/3137, accessed April 27, 2016.

6

PUBLIC PERCEPTION AND POLICY CHANGES OF CULTURAL HERITAGE MANAGEMENT IN CHINA

Jigen Tang

Introduction and Background

In modern China, the principles for protecting the cultural heritage were established by the Law of the Peoples Republic of China on Protection of Cultural Relics, which was first adopted in November 19, 1982, and revised in 1991, 2002, 2013, and 2015. Before the law was issued, policies for protecting the ancient artifacts and archaeological remains were based on cultural traditions and political needs. The law and policies have shaped cultural heritage management in China and changed the attitudes of the public—however, the people's attitudes toward cultural heritage can also challenge the policies, and sometimes even the principles, of the law.

China has a very ancient and continuous cultural heritage and therefore a long tradition of collecting ancient artifacts. Scholars in the Northern Song dynasty (960–1127 A.D.) viewed the inscriptions on the ancient bronzes and stones as very important resources for learning historic knowledge from their ancestors. They developed a discipline known as *Jinshixue*, or studies of ancient bronzes and stones. During the Qing dynasty (1644–1912 AD), Jinshixue became one of the main streams in Chinese scholarship. Even during the period of chaos and war in China in the first decades of the last century, Chinese scholars never gave up collecting and studying the ancient artifacts.

The People's Republic of China was established in 1949. Following Marxist doctrine, the new government led by the Communist Party treated cultural heritage as an important tool of interpreting the Marxist historical theory. Therefore, policies were made to encourage people to protect archaeological sites and present historical knowledge behind the ancient remains and artifacts. The best examples are the establishment of two archaeological museums, the Zhoukoudian Museum in Beijing that presents the famous Paleolithic site and its findings of human remains 50,000 years ago, and the Banpo Museum in Xi'an for presenting the Neolithic site of 6,000 years ago. The two museums were built to demonstrate that China experienced both the primitive society and matriarchal society, just as Marxist Stalin predicted in his work (Q. E. Wang 2000). This was summarized by Mao Zedong, the founder of the People's Republic of China, as "let the past serve for the present".

Unfortunately, the attitude of the Chinese government toward cultural heritage and the past turned negative because of new political needs after 1966. During the Cultural Revolutionary period (1966–1976), a movement of 'sweeping the four olds' developed in China. To break up old thoughts, old culture, old customs, and old habits, Chinese people started to give up or even damage cultural relics. Many great works of architecture, books, and monumental buildings were destroyed. Fortunately, most archaeological sites avoided being destroyed because they are buried underground.

After 1978, Chinese government terminated the Cultural Revolutionary movement and turned to developing the national economy. Cultural heritage was viewed as an important source for the recovery of strength of the country. By 1979, the government established the Terracotta Army Museum. The public was attracted by the terracotta warriors surrounding the mausoleum of the great emperor Qinshihuangdi, and many became proud of China's history after visiting the site. By then, both the government and the public realized the importance of protecting China's cultural heritage. This became the background of the 1982 enactment of the protection law on cultural heritage.

The adoption of the Law of the Peoples Republic of China on Protection of Cultural Relics in 1982 was a milestone for protecting cultural heritage in China, and Chinese people began to change their attitude. The best example of this change is the strides made to develop the discipline of archaeology in universities. In 1983, Peking University branched out its archaeology studies from the Department of History and established an independent Department of Archaeology. Jilin University followed suit by branching out archaeology studies from the history department. In the early 1990s, the discipline of Archaeology started to emphasize the reinforcement of the functions of archaeology, the expansion of services the discipline can provide, and the practical usage of working models.

According to the Protection Law of 1982, all developers are required to invite qualified archaeologists (mainly from archaeological institutes at central and provincial levels) to investigate the land if development is planned. Yet more museums were established to meet the need to house and exhibit items recovered during archaeological excavations. Although the protection law played a decisive role in the protection and use of the cultural heritage, public attitudes about cultural relics vary depending on their educational background, their social position, and even where they live.

My own observation is that the urbanization process played the most important role in affecting public attitudes toward cultural heritage. Urbanization is a process during which human population and industrial activities begin to congregate in certain spaces, and rural areas quickly or gradually become urbanized. Starting in

1978, the migration of population from rural areas to cities increased sharply. In 1978, China's urban population accounted for only 17.92% of total population of China. In 2010, the percentage reached around 47%, and at the time of this writing, it has reached almost 60%.

When it comes to preferences concerning geography, climate, and especially resources, modern people have many similarities with their ancestors. Therefore, the places where modern cities are established usually overlap with ancient sites. A typical modern city is densely populated yet rich with cultural heritage. Urbanization highlights the struggle between modern urbanization and preservation of ancient sites, particularly buried ones. On one hand, as the population grows, more land is required to build more housing and production facilities; on the other hand, the State Administration of Cultural Heritage must take up the responsibility of preserving and protecting ancient sites.

The Problem of Urbanization

Prior to 1990, the State Administration of Cultural Heritage was able to maintain control, and archaeologists could conduct their research without much interruption. If a site was vandalized, the administration would send out a notice, and usually the malicious actions would stop. Archaeologists and cultural heritage management departments at that time generally practiced very simple protection and preservation methods. For example, officials would map out the area of the ancient site, fence it up, and put up a sign saying 'Protection Unit'. Infrastructure construction was forbidden in this area, and no change was to be made to the geological surface of the site. This practice was to some degree a type of 'unmodified preservation'.

Unmodified preservation did achieve certain effects during that period. Anyang City in Henan province gives an example. Yinxu is the capital site of the Shang dynasty (c.1600–1046 BCE). The site's importance is also linked with the earliest Chinese writing system, because it is the place where the famous oracle bone inscriptions were found. In the mid-1980s, the original development plan of the city was to 'move west', and the planning division decided to build the Anyang City Hall in the Yinxu Site. The archaeology division stepped in and discouraged the plan. Finally, in the mid-1990s, the city government changed the original 'move west' plan to 'expand into the east and move into the south', thus avoiding the ancient site.

In the 1990s and especially after 1995, urbanization developed more rapidly in China (Shan 2006). Expanding infrastructures in the cities not only threatened the already-known ancient sites within the city area but also began to affect more and more previously buried sites. However, archaeology scholars and officials who were used to dealing with ancient site protection with the traditional unmodified preservation method did not modify their policies accordingly. The protection and preservation of ancient sites triggered great conflict between experts and officials in cultural heritage and those from other government branches. Archaeologists and cultural heritage officials accused the other government departments and infrastructure divisions of deliberately neglecting the protection law, while the latter group

FIGURE 6.1 A Shang Dynasty Chariot under Excavation at Yinxu
Source: Photo by Dr. Yue Hongbing. Used by permission.

claimed that the former were hindering economic growth and thus were responsible for the unsightly 'ruins' (ancient sites covered with weeds and debris) littered all over the city. As the fierce arguments carried on, cases of vandalism of ancient sites increased. According to a comprehensive report, 544 cases of violation to the cultural heritage in the country were reported to the State Administration of Cultural heritage between 2006 and 2008. The Annual Report on the development of China's Cultural Heritage Management System, published in 2009, also points out:

> Some of the city officials who make decisions are short-sighted. Their main concern are economic profits, therefore they allow large-scale constructions on old towns and cities, over-commercialized operations, and development plans that alter the premises greatly. They have leveled historical areas which are saturated with culture and history, destroyed numerous traditional buildings that signify the uniqueness of the regional culture, and torn down many cultural heritage protections.
>
> *(Liu 2008, translated from Chinese)*

The report was written to support cultural heritage preservation, intending to emphasize the damage urbanization in China causes on cultural resources. Yet should the cultural heritage and archaeology departments not shoulder some blame for letting the situation become so desperate?

For dealing with the multiple, sometimes controversial attitudes toward cultural heritage, the government took the measurement by issuing specific policies and regulations in the 21st century. This begins with the premise that ancient sites are historical memories of cities. If modern city development ignores the existence of ancient sites, the city rejects its own historical memory, and this leads to grave consequences: thousands of dull cities with no distinctive character or style. Yet there are ways to combine city park designs with ancient cultural site preservation. Parks can be planned around ancient sites, which then can become the cultural 'soul' of parks. By doing so, ancient sites are preserved, and citizens have a place to enjoy green trees, fresh air, and ancient cultural beauty. Ancient sites are the embodiment of local history, a physical existence, and display of local traditions and characteristics.

Understanding this, archaeologists started to cooperate actively with government officials. As a result, a number of ancient sites have been successfully preserved in cities. The attitude of the local officials and the local residents has become very positive to the cultural heritage, particularly to archaeological sites nearby the cities. The success of unifying archaeological sites with public planning has set a good example for larger society. In order to meet the emerging challenge of urbanization, the State Administration of Cultural Heritage of China began to consider revising the Law of the Peoples Republic of China on Protection of Cultural Relics.

Updating the Law

In 2000, after observing various international practices and experiences, the State Administration of Cultural Heritage of China, with the assistance of the Getty Conservation Institute (U.S.) and the Australian Heritage Council, announced the Principles for Conservation of Heritage Sites in China. The principles, which were drafted based on the actual situation of cultural heritage preservation in China, introduced policies for Chinese heritage preservation that comply to international archaeology concepts, adding new ideas to those already existing.

Following the adoption of the Principles for Conservation of Heritage Sites in China, the Law of the Peoples Republic of China on Protection of Cultural Relics was amended in 2002. This finalized the system for the establishment of historical culture blocks and historical culture villages/towns. Starting in 2005, Shan Jixiang, the director of the State Administration of Cultural Heritage of China, regularly visited different areas to study and observe local cultural heritage preservation progress around the nation. In 2007, more than a thousand participants from more than 23 countries and areas, including mayors, planners, architects, culture scholars, and historians, gathered in Beijing and released the Beijing Declaration of Urban Culture. The event was organized by the State Administration of Cultural Heritage of China. The declaration states that:

> When developing city culture, history should be taken into consideration. Traditional culture should be honored, preserved, and promoted. Any negative

impact caused by commercialized development and abuse of cultural heritage and environment should be reduced. We need not only commercial cities and industrial cities, but also, more importantly, cultural cities.

(Shan 2009, translated from Chinese)

During the National Working Conference on Cultural Heritage held in December 2009, the policy for the protection and utilization of cultural heritage was summarized by Shang Jixiang:

> During the event of learning and practicing scientific development theory, we underwent a vast range of studies, learning and in-depth investigation and research. We now understand better why and how we should develop a new model of cultural heritage preservation, and also for whom we are doing it, and who can be of assistance. By protecting our cultural heritage and preserving the dignity that our culture deserves, we can transform our cultural heritage into the most tasteful cultural aspects of our development, and the pride of our country and people. Cultural heritage preservation should be integrated with the development of local economy and society, the enhancement of the quality of life of local residents, the infrastructure of cities, and improvement of local environment. The public should be able to enjoy the fruits of cultural heritage preservation. They should have a more active role, which will strengthen the emotional bond and connection between the mass public and cultural heritage, and emphasize the people-oriented aspect of the projects. We will continue to preserve our cultural heritage, carry on our traditional skills, and let the public enjoy the results of our labor. And we will thrive to let the preservation of cultural heritage benefit the heart, mind and body of our people.
>
> *(Shan 2009, translated from Chinese)*

At the same time, the State Administration of Cultural Heritage of China proposed the establishment of National Archaeological Parks. This action was a formal confirmation from the state supporting the integration of parks and archaeological sites. The conventional unmodified preservation method was no longer mainstream. In 2010, the State Administration of Cultural Heritage officially announced 12 National Archaeological Parks, including Yinxu in Anyang (Figure 6.2), the Jinsha site in Chengdu, and Liangzhu in Hangzhou. By 2013, 12 more National Archaeological Parks were announced, including Niuheliang in Liaoning and the Luoyang city site of the Han-Wei periods in Henan.

The new policies align with the Law of the Peoples Republic of China on Protection of Cultural Relics while they bring benefits to the public. The new policies shed light on bringing archaeological sites and relics back to life. By benefiting from the protection and utilization of cultural heritage, more people take positive attitudes toward cultural heritage relics and values.

FIGURE 6.2 The National Archaeological Park of Yinxu, Created in 2010

Source: Photo by Zixing Li, Anyang Field Station, Institute of Archaeology, Chinese Academy of Social Sciences. Used by permission.

The Influence of History on Today's Laws

The evolution of cultural management practices in China has clearly been influenced by China's unique history of mutual interaction between the policy making and the public response. From 1949 to 1966, both the tradition of respecting history and the Marxist political atmosphere created good conditions for protecting cultural heritage in China. With the beginning of the Cultural Revolution, the past was utilized to serve new political needs. This led to a split of public attitudes. Mao and followers like as the Red Guards (mainly students) favored the utilitarian policy because of political fanaticism. However, educated people like professors continued to respect the ancient artifacts. Although some cultural relics were damaged during the destruction of the 'four olds', archaeology was able to continue as a discipline because it could be recruited to prove Marxist historic theory.

The divergence of public attitudes toward cultural heritage put pressure on policy makers after the end of the Cultural Revolution in the 1970s. This became the important background of the Law of the Peoples Republic of China on Protection of Cultural Relics. This law was mainly made to prevent damage to cultural heritage relics. However, in practice, the law quickly exposed a weakness in balancing protection versus utilization. From my point of view, the law overwhelmingly emphasizes protection but leaves very little room for utilization of cultural heritage for the public. Under this law, all policies were designed to protect archaeological sites by separating them from the public. As a result, neither the government nor the public could derive any benefit from cultural heritage.

This situation lasted for more than 20 years. Without knowing their value, people didn't respect archaeological sites and ancient artifacts. Vandalism to sites increased day by day. In the 1990s, a cultural landscape approach called the 'Qujiang model' was adopted for Xi'an. The basic concept is to improve the commercial value of peripheral lands by creating the site as a cultural landscape. The Qujiang model was welcomed by both the local government and the residents. However, this model conflicts with the traditional ideology of static cultural heritage protection, so the situation called for the policy change and revision of the law. After the issuance of new policies in 2000, the law was revised in 2002. Thus, the response of policy makers to pressure from the public can be summarized in three points:

1. to preserve the dignity of our cultural remains,
2. to let the public benefit from cultural heritage, and
3. to integrate cultural heritage preservation with the development of economy and society

Following the new policies, creating a cultural landscape or site park or simply building a museum (or a combination of these) were all recognized as good ways to respect the dignity of archaeological sites while serving the local economy and benefiting the public. In following decades, many more site parks and cultural landscapes were built.

After years of practice, how do members of the public evaluate the new policies of creating cultural landscapes and museums in archaeological sites? To understand this, I conducted a survey at the Yinxu National Archaeological Park (Figure 6.3). Survey results show that different 'stakeholders' have very different attitudes to this cultural landscape. Archaeologists view the site park positively. They benefit from carrying out excavations and research activities in a better landscape condition than before.

However, some senior scholars are not satisfied with the modification to the site, viewing visitors as a potential threat to the site's integrity. Also, to local governments, the current situation of Yinxu is not favorable. These officials hope to tell more stories of the Shang dynasty in the site and exhibit more artifacts in the Yinxu museum. They feel that the Yinxu landscape should attract more visitors, and therefore more modification based on archaeological work is needed. Tourists say the site can be difficult to understand even if they spend a whole day in Yinxu. They complain that the archaeologists don't tell stories clearly, presenting the Shang dynasty in obscure academic terminology. Members of the local community, mostly farmers, hold little interest in Yinxu and the stories behind the archaeological site and Shang artifacts. What they really care about is if the Yinxu site can finally improve their household incomes. So far, local people are not happy because Yinxu hasn't brought any direct benefits. Several local residents made it clear that the quality of life never improved after Yinxu was inscribed into the World Heritage List. A survey of annual incomes also suggests that the villages inside the Yinxu site are actually poorer than those outside the site. These controversies reveal that policies behind management practices never meet the requirements of all the 'stakeholders'.

64 Jigen Tang

花园庄的居民

1. 基本资料

姓名	王	男/女	男(圈)	出生年	1974
教育程度	高中			老家	许昌

有哪些家庭成员（有几口人）： 四口，两小孩，媳妇花园庄人，姐妹三人。

地址： 一期十五号

2. 村民生计与工作的转变

- 目前主要收入来源为何？ 单位（字钢）
- 2006 申遗之前主要收入来源？ 单位（字钢）
- 2006-2010期间的主要收入来源？
- 2011-2015 期间的主要收入来源？

3. 花园庄 – 拆迁状况

- 原来的房子多大？ 14米
- 全家在新区拿到几套房子？贴了多少钱？ 五套（分三套，买两套），贴几十万。(三套也贴) 1500/平，买1700平
- 家庭成员如何分配搬家后拿到几套房子？
- 还会想回到旧家吗？

4. 花园庄 – 现况与改变

- 搬离花园庄的时间？ 2009年底 2015年底搬入新村
- 过渡期间住过哪些地方呢？ 王裕口、大司空
- 对于拆迁工程的态度转变？ 不愿意拆，后来没法只能拆。
- 满意现在的生活吗？ 与以前差不多。
- 搬家时哪些东西是非得一起带到新家呢？还会回到花庄庄旧址吗？ 没有。

4. 对于安阳殷墟的文化遗产的认识与态度

- 去过殷墟博物馆吗？（何时？或多久去一次？） 好几次，开放日会去。
- 喜欢（或看不懂？）殷墟博物馆的哪个部分？（喜欢看博物馆的器物呢？还是遗迹？还是建筑复原？还是妇好墓？） 妇好墓
- 殷墟申遗后生活的具体影响？ 往好的地方发展，大公园不错，有休闲
- 是否有察觉到殷墟申遗后安阳的改变、殷墟周遗的改变、博物馆的改变？

其他：建议、不满、或期待？

FIGURE 6.3 A Questionnaire Used to Survey the Attitude of Local Residents at Yinxu

Source: Created by Shuli Wang, used by permission.

To develop a cultural landscape or build a museum at an archaeological site has obvious advantages to protect cultural heritage resources and present their values to the public. These activities also benefit the local government by obviously improving the land price of adjoining areas. However, there is still a lot of work to be done before this strategy can meet the diverse demands of stakeholders. This requires policy makers to make more efforts to analyze the relevance between the cultural heritage and all stakeholders, thus ideally allowing for relevance to be calculated.

The public attitudes we learned about from the survey at Yinxu strongly indicate that policy makers must consider the needs of different groups of people. In the case of China, archaeologists have a much stronger voice in archaeological site management than other stakeholders. Policy makers therefore should consider issuing policies with more flexible options so that in practice, the utilization of cultural property becomes workable.

Traditionally, archaeologists have influenced policy makers to view archaeological sites as merely academic resources. To emphasize that utilization, Du Jinpen proposed to use the term 'archaeological cultural property' as a substitute for 'cultural heritage' (Du 2015). This new concept shows the attitude changes of some scholars toward traditional cultural heritage management. At the same time, policy makers should pay more attention to the views of visitors, local residents, and local governments. Cultural landscapes should be accessible and readable. To make an attractive landscape, archaeologists should decide how to balance the importance of landscapes and museums. If a museum has been proposed, the location and exhibited artifacts should be consistent with the landscape. Archaeologists have an obligation to present the knowledge of the cultural heritage in words that can be easily understood. One of the reasons that local residents might have no interest in a site is because they think they have nothing to do with that site. This suggests archaeologists should find spiritual links between modern residents and the past in order to assure that it stays relevant to people today.

In the case of Yinxu and many other archaeological sites, the local residents paid a price for the protection of the cultural heritage. Often, they have sacrificed their land and their lifestyle for the public good. Thus policy makers should discuss how to compensate these people. To let the public share the benefits of cultural heritage management, the concept of activating cultural heritage has been widely accepted by various groups of Chinese people. China is now in a good position to improve the management of its rich cultural heritage. However, listening to multiple voices and meeting the demands of different people is a long-term challenge: continuing rapid urbanization in China will require flexibility and continual communication of cultural heritage managers with diverse stakeholders.

References

Du, J. P. 2015 A Discussion to the Protection of Archaeological Property. *Kaogu*, 2015(1):58–68.

Liu, S. J., editor 2008 *Blue Book of Cultural Heritage: Annual Report on the Development of China's Cultural Heritage Management System 2008*. Social Sciences Academic Press, Beijing.

Shan, J. X. 2009 Speech on the National Working Conference on Cultural Heritage. *Proceedings of the 2009 Annual Conference of the Directors of Provincial Bureau of Cultural Heritage*. National Bureau of Cultural Heritage, Beijing.

———. 2006 *Urbanization Development and Cultural Heritage Preservation*. Tianjin University Press, Tianjin.

Wang, Q. E. 2000 Between Marxism and Nationalism, Chinese Historiography and the Soviet Influence: 1949–1963. *Journal of Contemporary China* 9(23):95–111.

7
VALUE AND VALUES IN HERITAGE TOURISM FROM THE GRAND TOUR TO THE EXPERIENCE ECONOMY

Uzi Baram

The Promise of Heritage Tourism

The promise of tourism includes economic development bringing tourists and hard currency to areas without other economic possibilities in today's global economy—but also follows the Mark Twain quip from *The Innocents Abroad* (1869:650): "Travel is fatal to prejudice, bigotry, and narrow-mindedness, and many of our people need it sorely on these accounts. Broad, wholesome, charitable views of men and things cannot be acquired by vegetating in one little corner of the earth all one's lifetime". Cultural relativism, coexistence, cosmopolitanism, and even peace are the goals put forward for travel and its commercial offspring—tourism. However, the reality is more complicated.

Anthropologists have investigated the implications of tourism for local communities for decades. Castaneda (2015) offers a sequence for the anthropology of tourism from the 1960s through 1980s with a wave of initial studies, then a crest in the 1980s through the middle of the 2000s, and another swelling of studies in the last decade. While some easy generalizations can be made regarding tourism, most have condescending implications regarding the masses. This chapter will avoid such moves. As Castaneda (2015) has advocated, one can study tourism beyond the tourist to break the slippage between the belief in possessive individualism and the social structures. Importantly, one should avoid synchronic snapshots and rather use histories for tourism.

Since the 1990s, archaeologists have expressed increasing concern for the use of the past in the present (see Rowan and Baram 2004). Some have diagnosed the issues involved (see Meskell 2005), and others have brought archaeologists and tourist scholars together, recognizing the complexity of the encounter (Walker and Carr 2013). This chapter, focused on the historical development of heritage tourism, offers a differentiation between the value of heritage for tourism and the values of heritage tourism by recounting the adventures and comments of an American traveler whose clever writing delineates the transition to tourism across Europe and the eastern Mediterranean. The various facets of tourism, tourists, and tourist infrastructure are changing the past in ways that should concern those committed to heritage as an avenue for meeting the challenges of contemporary gross global economic and social inequalities.

From the Grand Tour to Tourism

Critiques and criticisms of tourism are not unique to anthropological literature. Mark Twain offered the now-famous positive line about travel as fatal to prejudice, but alternatively in his classic *The Innocents Abroad*, Twain provides a humorous critique of travel across Europe to the eastern Mediterranean, with insights into its inhabitants and his fellow travelers. Just as during Mark Twain's time, heritage tourism today encourages awareness of the disruptions and challenges of the present (see Fleming this volume) and repercussions of tourism for communities, knowledge, and ecology. There are important lessons from the earlier age of travel for today's heritage tourism.

From the 16th through 19th centuries, European travel was best known through the Grand Tour, the expectation for young western European elites to see the sights of the imagined origins for what they considered their civilization: Rome, Athens, the Great Pyramids of Giza, and Jerusalem. The 1867 voyage of the vessel *Quaker City* came at an important hinge in history. For the United States, the adventure, two years after the Civil War ends, is part of the process of establishing the new American identity, and for travel, the enterprise is one of the first organized endeavors. During the same era in Britain, Thomas Cook creates what became known as Cook's Tours, facilitating vacations for the working classes to see famous places. *The Innocents Abroad* documents the transition from travel to tourism, as becomes clear in reading Twain's comments on people, travel, and places. For example, his remarks on Leghorn (now Livorno) remind us that the *Quaker City* voyaged before tourism. As he wrote (1869:253): "The stupid magnates of this Leghorn government cannot understand that so large a steamer as ours could cross the broad Atlantic with no other purpose than to indulge a party of ladies and gentlemen in a pleasure excursion. It looks too improbable". But no longer. Tourism for that Italian city now encourages the large-scale visits by cruise ships.

Twain's humor offers a critique of national identity, the goal of visitations, and the welcome in places from the Azores to Jerusalem. *Innocents Abroad* was written as a travel account; its keen observations offer important insights into the peoples encountered (Baram 2002) and places visited. In Venice, Twain wrote (1869:217): "One ought, indeed, to turn away from her rags, her poverty and her humiliation, and think of her only as she was . . ." He was not impressed with the "funny old city" (1869:220), comparing it to a flooded Arkansas town (page 158). Yet Venice continued to attract attention, with implications as discussed later in this chapter. Twain observes something that anthropologists rediscovered only in the second half of the 20th century: people see what they want to see (1869:511):

> I am sure, from the tenor of books I have read, that many who have visited this land in years gone by, were Presbyterians, and came seeking evidences in support of their particular creed; they found a Presbyterian Palestine, and they had already made up their minds to find no other, though possibly they did not know it, being blinded by their zeal. Others were Baptists, seeking Baptist evidences and a Baptist Palestine. Others were Catholics, Methodists, Episcopalians, seeking evidences indorsing [sic] their several creeds, and a Catholic, a Methodist, an Episcopalian Palestine. Honest as these men's intentions may have been, they were full of partialities and prejudices, they entered the country with their verdicts already prepared, and they could no more write dispassionately and impartially about it than they could about their own wives and children.

Mark Twain's observations foreshadow tourism scholarship of the late 20th century. The social and political economic forces supporting tourist infrastructure continue to grow, with far-reaching implications. And in some places, the results of the tourist interest transform landscapes in such a way that terms such as 'imagineering' are

FIGURE 7.1 Tourists Disembarking from Cruise Ship at Cozumel

Source: Photograph by author.

FIGURE 7.2 Theming for Disney World Begins on the Highway

required. Whether cruise ships that bring thousands to the shops and performances at Cozumel in Mexico (Preble 2014) and the airports and interstate highways that lead to the Magic Kingdom at Disney World in Orlando, Florida, or the congestion around the Great Pyramids at Giza, Egypt, the attraction becomes a focal point for massive commodity consumption and entertainment and for new identities for the locations beyond the connections with nearby communities.

Heritage has a remarkable recursive dynamic. Kirshenblatt-Gimblett (1995) refers to heritage as a mode of cultural production, encouraging interest in presentations and representations. The curiosity for displays is often tied to tourism. Understanding the exhibitory aspects of heritage through tourism requires recognizing and defining heritage tourism.

Defining Heritage Tourism

'Heritage' is an ever-expanding term in both popular and academic discourse. To provide a foundation for further academic research, Samuels and Rico (2015) offer 15 keywords for heritage studies (though it is not meant to be all-encompassing, and one term not included is 'heritage tourism'). Following their approach, heritage tourism deserves redescription, paying attention to its complex intersections with heritage and tourism. There are parallel discourses on heritage tourism as driving economic inequalities and as a potential productive resource for heritage preservation and sustainability.

Depending on the component words used, approaches to heritage tourism shift dramatically. From the tourism industry perspective, Timothy and Boyd (2003) in *Heritage Tourism* recognize the significance of heritage tourism in travel, recognizing the diversity of heritage for tourism. Like many who comment on tourism, they (2003:7) note the key is experience: people want to take away good memories from their travels. For successful heritage tourism, Misiura (2005:2) offers a marketing textbook to help organizations with their sites, noting

> The essence of heritage marketing process ... is to find out what the customer wants and to deliver it, subject to any constraints that might prevail, such as the need to protect parts of a heritage site or historic property because of the increased wear and tear resulting from the extra footfall stimulated through marketing initiatives.

From a business perspective, customers want to visit historic sites and also have their needs met.

Others provide suggestions and caveats for tourism. Godfrey and Clarke (2003:57), recognizing that cultural resources "have become a tourism resource out of consequence rather than a result of their original function or primary intent", note, "Tourism is no economic panacea, and is best suited as a supplement to a local economy" (2003:5). The scholarship of tourism has nuanced insights into the dynamics of heritage tourism for tourists and the tourism industry as well as for the sites, surrounding communities, and countries.

The other component term is 'heritage'. Ever since Lowenthal (1997) compiled the examples from around the globe demonstrating explosive growth in heritage as a social phenomenon in the late 20th century, scholars have offered a wide range of definitions and descriptions for heritage. In this chapter, a distillation for heritage is as a pathway to the past that opens up possibilities for understanding history as well as our circumstances today. From a heritage perspective, tourism offers visitations focused on the past and history, potentially contributing to productive and sustainable management of sites.

'Heritage tourism' is more than the sum of its component terms, with its own meaning. In the United States, the National Trust for Historic Preservation (2016) defines cultural heritage tourism as traveling to experience the places, artifacts, and activities that authentically represent the stories and people of the past and present. It includes cultural, historic, and natural resources. This approach is increasingly significant. The popularity of heritage tourism can be seen in the growth of locations listed by UNESCO as World Heritage sites (also see Tang this volume). The development of heritage tourism with local nuances and contingencies makes the trajectory seem inevitable: heritage becoming heritage tourism. Archaeologists have noticed the influence of heritage tourism on their research (see Rowan and Baram 2004), with the tourist industry continuing to grow. For those who envision heritage as more than a tourist experience, the implications should become a pressing concern.

Heritage Tourism in the Early 21st Century

Historic preservation in the U.S. started with grassroots efforts that, by the 20th century, led to the national government's encouraging, facilitating, and ensuring preservation. After mid-century the dynamic became international. Today heritage sites are expected to be economically self-sufficient institutions and mechanisms that encourage visitation provide financial opportunities to sustain heritage locales. But this is not a simple formula. As a new dynamic, organized and sustained by today's neoliberal political economy, implications include the role of the state and explosive growth in heritage tourism. Harvey (2007:2) offers,

> Neoliberalism is in the first instance a theory of political economic practices that proposes that human well-being can best be advanced by liberating individual entrepreneurial freedoms and skills within an institutional framework characterized by strong private property rights, free markets, and free trade. The role of the state is to create and preserve an institutional framework appropriate for such practices.

One aspect of the explosive growth in heritage is presentation to the public. Lowenthal (1997) explored the negative aspects of heritage: destructive chauvinism, elitism, incoherence and inanition, commercial debasement, and 'bad history'. Yet the productive aspects of heritage are accelerating in the neoliberal age, and as Lowenthal (2015:2) recently noted, the study of heritage needs "a plausible synthesis out of extremely heterogeneous materials". It is not "wantonly eclectic or absurdly disparate" (Lowenthal 2015:3) but does need to notice expanding dynamics. Heritage is a broad but useful category in the experience economy that describes the current political economy of our world (Pine and Gilmore 2011). In the experience economy, where themes and customization are stressed and goods and services require a stage to encourage consumption (Ibid.), archaeological/historical sites offer representations of social identities, the past as foreign (as Lowenthal 2015 explains), and materiality as an experience. For Meskell (2005:130), the "tourist industry combines services, culture, and ethnicity and results in a product that unifies and packages society, culture, and identity". Pine and Gilmore (2011) note that products are no longer sufficient, thus experience becomes the framework for consumption. Whereas travelers on the Grand Tour gained experiences by encountering places and people, with goals of social polish and cultural capital, the new dynamics in tourism focus on experiences, packaged with concise information, places to stand for the self-taken photograph, gift shops, restaurants, and memories of the visit to be shared via stories or images in person or online. This reshaping of heritage sites has implications for the presentations of the past that are remembered by the visitor and for local community members whose history is commodified for the pleasure of others.

The implications of this trajectory and influences of the neoliberal global economy can be seen with a very famous tourist city that captured Mark Twain's attention during his tour of the Mediterranean: Venezia.

The conventions of the Grand Tour for northwest Europeans included seeing the sights of the classical world on the Italian peninsula. Venice offered a place where the young gained experiences for their trajectory to join the elite of their nations. The experiences in Venice added to the storehouse of cultural capital for these elites.

Travelers and tourists returned to their home countries, and through their writings, paintings, and conversations, interest in Venice increased, and the development of tourism, as *Innocents Abroad* illustrated, encouraged even more visitations. Venice became famous as a famous place to visit. In North America, the imagery for Venice led to place names: Venice, Florida, founded in 1888; another in California in 1905; and other 'Venices' in states like Illinois, Louisiana, and New York; Canada has a Venice in Alberta. A simple Internet search can locate almost countless hotels been named for the city of Venice.

Concern for the heritage of Italian Venice triggered the United Nations movement toward historic preservation. After the 1965 White House Conference in Washington, DC, called for a World Heritage Trust, the flooding in Venice that destroyed artwork and left thousands homeless led the United Nations Educational, Scientific and Cultural Organization (UNESCO) along with other organizations offer help for the city to preserve its art for all of humanity. In 1972, UNESCO adopted the Convention concerning the Protection of the World Cultural and Natural Heritage. In 1987, Venice and its Lagoon joined the World Heritage Listing.

FIGURE 7.3 Venice at Disney World

Source: Photograph by author.

Thus Venice, through these global efforts and attention, has become a theme. And the experience economy goals encourages Venice the theme to be projected anywhere; for instance, Epcot in Disney World Orlando features idealized canals, San Marcos Plaza, and even gondolas.

Venice is an example and warning regarding heritage tourism. Davis and Marvin (2004:1) start their discussion of the city by noting:

> Tourism is ... the life and life's blood of Venice, Italy ... while sitting in Piazza San Marco on an August afternoon, we have felt like the better part of those 664 million [figure from 1999] were passing right before our eyes. Venice may well be, for its size and population, the most touristed city on the planet ... the epitome of the tourist experience.

The city belongs to tourists. As Davis and Marvin (2004:3) explain, this was a 19th-century choice made by the Venetians. In early 2015, Italian courts overturned a ban on cruise ships sailing through the city's central canal. The image of a 96,000-gross-ton cruise ship next to the Rialto Bridge, dwarfing the houses on the canals, is the type of startling, massive materiality that transforms cultural landscapes. While airports and roads bring huge numbers of tourists to Venice, the cruise ships bring even more to gaze at the city.

FIGURE 7.4 Tables and Tourists at Piazza San Marco

Source: Photograph by author.

Whether professionals choose to critique the growth of tourism or jump on the tourist train (Slick 2002), the continuing expansion (e.g., Mak 2004) requires critical consideration. Neoliberalism encourages governments to treat material heritage as a commodity that provides an economic value. And the processes that encourage visitation seemingly continue to grow. Terrorist attacks against tourist sights are a danger for places, but in the absence of violence or even after a few years of the absence of increasing tourism, the trajectory seems to move ever upward. And in the politics of neoliberalism, there seems to be no alternative to commodifying heritage (whether archaeological or otherwise representing the past) even as archaeologists grapple with funding and presentation of research. But there are alternatives.

Value is a key conclusion from the lessons of Venice in considering the intersection of archaeology in the experience economy. To encapsulate the critiques of tourism along with the positive possibilities of travel, recognizing that either assessment is within a neoliberal context, there needs to be a redescription of heritage tourism (Samuels and Rico 2015). Many efforts by heritage scholars consider the value and values of heritage for contemporary society, economics, and political engagements, through academia or national and international organizations. Some approach the issues in terms of values (see Smith this volume) and others by defining cultural heritage for countries (see Altschul this volume), museums (see Burgess this volume), and communities (see Hassan this volume). Many heritage scholars recognize the significance of tourism to contemporary heritage (see Werkheiser et al. this volume). Yet the term 'values' is not simply the plural of 'value'; Miller (2008) explains the difference. For Miller (2008:1123), value "can mean the work involved in giving a monetary worth to an object. . . . almost synonymous with price", while values "refers to the inalienable as opposed to the alienable value". Going further, Graeber (2013) asserts value is ". . . a key issue if we see social worlds not just as a collection of persons and things but rather as a project of mutual creation, as something collectively made and remade". The differences between values and value shift within the larger context of decisions and actions, uneven and with multiple interests involved in the creation and recreation of places and representations. These differences have social implications, as indicated by the discussion of the anthropological literature on tourism and the consideration of Venice.

A community's concern for its heritage and the educational potential of heritage versus the possibilities for financial resources and expansion of infrastructure—that seems the range between values and value for tourism to a place. For Miller (2008:1130), "the creative potential of value, lies not in what it is, nor how it is conceived, but rather in what it actually does". As Gmelch (2003:9) states from ethnographic research on Barbados, "Tourism has contributed less to long-term economic development than expected", Still, central governments invest in infrastructure for tourism because of the perceived potential of its financial value. And since tourists expect their purchases and services to be an experience, and some will seek out new and different experiences from what their families, neighbors, and friends have had, heritage tourism offers to meet expectations: travel to a locale provides experiences in difference, whether temporal or cultural.

Heritage as a pathway to the past is an experience. Engaging heritage objects or places, even the intangible heritage of performances, is meant to be moving, emotionally or socially. The choices for the professional can be stark, representing the excavated past as a commodity for consumption in the experience economy versus education and understanding or financial capital versus social capital. But rarely is the choice a glaring one. The dynamics are more likely trajectories for decisions and opportunities. Recognition that the analysis and interpretation of the material past occurs in the present, in the gross inequalities of today's globalized world, is the necessary first step for navigating the intellectual terrain of archaeological research and representations. Since archaeological excavations offer potential for new experiences, through the craft of archaeology or its finds, these values must be considered.

Overconsumption of the Past

The dilemma is not only between goals and ownership. The 'golden horde', to use the title of Turner and Ash (1977), can overcome the meaning of a heritage site. The question gets asked: can increased visitation be too much of a good thing? When tourists visit archaeological sites, for example, do they destroy the aura they wish to experience? When the parking lot is paved, entry has a fee, the ruins are roped off, and the gift shop is the busiest location at the place, something is missing for the values of archaeology even if the value of the place fits neoliberal concerns. There are studies that address the clash between the values of preservation and presentation and the financial value of mass tourism and oversuccessful marketing of a place. As the number of tourists increases, the weight is felt by the ruins themselves. Peru requires guides to control crowds at Machu Picchu; Great Britain controls admission to Stonehenge; Venice is overwhelmed by water and tourists. The visitor faces restriction to accessing the materiality.

Not all heritage places become overwhelmed by the neoliberal experience approach for tourism. People travel for new experiences because they seek out education to better themselves in the tradition of the Grand Tour. This is still an elite endeavor, but it can sustain heritage as a pathway to the past for communities with all their dynamics and contradictions, struggles and successes. The global does not determine the local experience, as Tsing (2005) illuminated through the concept of friction, but the uneven power relations were clear even to Mark Twain in the mid-19th century.

Relevance in Contemporary Society

Having heritage to visit allows the positive aspects of travel to flourish, the chance to learn about a different time, way of life, and place. How people encounter heritage is the challenge for contemporary tourists, travelers, and visitors. The dynamics of heritage tourism matter because tourism shapes perceptions of places, creating assumptions regarding the past and history (Baram 2011). Returning to Disney

World in Orlando, Florida, where Venice is one of hundreds of heritage locales recreated for tourists, offers the key lesson. Disney is a goal for many tourist endeavors: a place popular for being popular, successful beyond imagination in terms of visitations and reputation, well known globally. One of the sources of the success, as Knight (2014:73) notes, comes from Disney situating the visitor at the center of the experience, at the 'Happiest Place on Earth', a vacation 'Where Dreams Come True'. Disney World is so successful that the complex of theme parks has reshaped the central Florida landscape. Competing for experiences, the all-encompassing and best-advertised themed parks drove out what are commonly known as Old Florida attractions. These dynamics shaped Florida into a low-wage, low-tax, and governmental services state.

Heritage tourism, with the past as its theme, offers the paradox of increased visibility for archaeological and historic sites but one that requires the neoliberal individualism that alienates nearby and descendant communities, sometimes scholars, and even the tourist from their object of consumption. The critical assessment of value versus values opens up recognition for the social relevance of the past beyond the materiality upon which tourists will gaze for entertainment purposes. We might find sites competing not to be the happiest place on earth but against each other, with a similar emotive draw and vacuous result.

A powerful discourse has been sustained with heritage tourism for neoliberal purposes, but we might find optimism in an engaged public archaeology that avoids battles over proprietary walls by expanding the definition of development to include community building, the creation of social capital, and active citizen engagements: values that fit the ideals for archaeology even if development is usually situated in terms of financial value in the contemporary globalized world. While the trajectory from the Grand Tour to today's experience economy implies archaeology as simply a source for a new type of commodity, there are alternatives in the form of heritage tourism that stress other values over the value of travel to a location for consuming experiences. Education can be the tourist experience, by engaging a range of experiences from seeing excavations and laboratory research, from delineating the research process with local community members and studying the history and heritage recovered and presented. Recognition of the larger-scale processes and historical legacies of tourism will be an asset in encouraging learning rather than just experiencing the past for new tourist endeavors, going beyond intersections with merely corporations (see Werkheiser et al. this volume), recognizing that there will be regression and progress (see Soderland and Lilley this volume) for positive dynamics for local and descendant communities and for the sites themselves. The critical assessment of value versus values opens up recognition for the social relevance of the past beyond the materiality upon which tourists will gaze. The critique of tourism is not a criticism of heritage, since travel is part of human heritage. Heritage sites should be places to learn the past, to study what happened in particular times, and to meet the idealism of travel, as expressed by Mark Twain, to encourage coexistence and peace.

Acknowledgments

Since coediting *Marketing Heritage: Archaeology and the Consumption of the Past*, the paradoxes of heritage tourism have continued to intrigue me. My thanks to archaeology colleagues, New College of Florida undergraduates, and tourism professionals for engaging my concerns—apologies for not listing the specific individuals who helped me over the last decade. Gratitude to Pei-Lin Yu, George S. Smith, and Chen Shen for inviting me to the Toronto workshop and for facilitating a robust consideration of the dynamics of the relevance and application of heritage.

References

Baram, U. 2011 Archaeology in the Public Interest: Tourist Effects and Other Paradoxes That Come With Heritage Tourism. In *Ideologies in Archaeology*, edited by R. Bernbeck and R. H. McGuire, pp. 107–129. University of Arizona Press, Tucson.

———. 2002 Seeing Differences: Travelers to Ottoman Palestine and Accounts of Diversity. *Journeys: The International Journal of Travel and Travel Writing* 3(2):29–49.

Castaneda, Q. 2015 Anthropology of Tourism. Online webinar presentation, October 1, 2015.

Davis, R., and G. Marvin 2004 *Venice, the Tourist Maze: A Cultural Critique of the World's Most Touristed City*. University of California Press, Berkeley.

Gmelch, G. 2003 *Behind the Smile: The Working Lives of Caribbean Tourism*. Indiana University Press, Bloomington.

Godfrey, K., and J. Clarke 2003 *The Tourism Development Handbook: A Practical Approach to Planning and Marketing*. Thompson, London.

Graeber, D. 2013 It Is Value That Brings Universes Into Being. *HAU: Journal of Ethnographic Theory* 3(2):219–243.

Harvey, D. 2007 *A Brief History of Neoliberalism*. Oxford University Press, Oxford.

Kirshenblatt-Gimblett, B. 1995 Theorizing Heritage. *Ethnomusicology* 39(3):367–380.

Knight, C. 2014 *Power and Paradise in Walt Disney's World*. University Press of Florida, Gainesville.

Lowenthal, D. 2015 *The Past Is a Foreign County: Revisited*. Cambridge University Press, Cambridge.

———. 1997 *Possessed By the Past: The Heritage Crusade and the Spoils of History*. The Free Press, New York.

Mak, J. 2004 *Tourism and the Economy: Understanding the Economics of Tourism*. University of Hawai'i Press, Honolulu.

Meskell, L. 2005 Sites of Violence: Terrorism, Tourism, and Heritage in the Archaeological Present. In *Embedding Ethics*, edited by L. Meskell and P. Pels, pp. 123–146. Berg, Oxford.

Miller, D. 2008 The Uses of Value. *Geoforum* 39:1122–1132.

Misiura, S. 2005 *Heritage Marketing*. Elsevier Butterworth-Heinemann, Oxford.

National Trust for Historic Preservation 2016 Heritage Tourism. Electronic document, www.preservationnation.org/information-center/economics-of-revitalization/heritage-tourism/#.Vr5J3_krLcs, electronic document, accessed April 26, 2016.

Pine II, B., and J. Gilmore 2011 *The Experience Economy: Work Is Theater & Every Business a Stage*. Harvard Business Review Press, Cambridge.

Preble, C. 2014 Imperial Consumption: Cruise Ship Tourism and Cozumel, Mexico. Unpublished PhD dissertation, State University of New York at Albany, Albany NY.

Rowan, Y., and U. Baram, editors 2004 *Marketing Heritage: Archaeology and the. Consumption of the Past*. Altamira Press, Walnut Creek.

Samuels, K., and T. Rico, editors 2015 *Heritage Keywords: Rhetoric and Redescription in Cultural Heritage*. University of Colorado Press, Boulder.

Slick, K. 2002 Archaeology and the Tourism Train. In *Public Benefits of Archaeology*, edited by B. Little, pp. 219–227. University Press of Florida, Gainesville.

Timothy, D., and S. Boyd 2003 *Heritage Tourism*. Prentice-Hall, Harlow.

Tsing, A. L. 2005 *Friction: An Ethnography of Global Connection*. Princeton University Press, Princeton.

Turner, L., and J. Ash 1977 *The Golden Hordes: International Tourism and the Pleasure Periphery*. St. Martin's Press, New York.

Twain, M. 1869 *The Innocents Abroad, or the New Pilgrims Progress Being Some Account of the Steamship Quaker City's Pleasure Excursion to Europe and the Holy Land; With Descriptions of Countries, Nations, Incidents and Adventures, As They Appeared to the Author*. American Publishing Company, Hartford.

Walker, C., and N. Carr, editors 2013 *Tourism and Archaeology: Sustainable Meeting Grounds*. Left Coast Press, Walnut Creek.

8

HERITAGE IN A CHANGING WORLD AND HIGHER EDUCATION FOR HERITAGE MANAGERS

A Pilot Program from Egypt

Fekri Hassan

Introduction

Higher education programs in cultural heritage management are emerging in a few institutions worldwide as a response to a paradigmatic shift in the role of archaeology in a world that has changed drastically from the mid-20th century, a time when archaeology departments were proliferating rapidly. Then, archaeologists were more concerned with debates on the theoretical and philosophical foundations of archaeological inquiry, with little attention to the social ends and relevance of their discipline. This contribution documents the emergence of a pilot program in cultural heritage management in Egypt and reviews the changing role of archaeology in society.

While archaeologists were debating the merits of what they posited as contrastive approaches to archaeological inquiry (Thomas 2015), ever-greater numbers of sites were being destroyed as world population spiraled, industrialization intensified, urban construction expanded, and demands for hydropower led to mega-dams with mega-reservoirs. Public concern increased for protecting and conserving threatened sites. The Aswan High Dam (1960–1971), built to meet Egypt's growing demands for water and electricity, caused the emergence of the notion of 'world heritage' sites and monuments and was one of the first international projects to safeguard sites of special importance to the history of humankind (Hassan 2007a).

In the United States, the protection of sites during construction of dams and pipelines began with the Historic Sites Act of 1935, one of several economic relief laws of the Great Depression. Thereafter, the Reservoir Salvage Act of 1960 originated from the need to rescue archaeological sites from the development of a national water resource program. The National Environmental Policy Act (1969) and the National Historic Preservation Act (1966) covered all federal undertakings, not just reservoir developments. The major boost to protecting sites, however, was due to the Moss-Bennett Bill of 1974. This bill encouraged archaeologists to engage in public and community archaeology as a key component of what became known as cultural resource management (CRM). The skills and competence involved in CRM, including project management, business planning, conservation, outreach programs, dissemination of public information, and mounting exhibitions were new elements in the tool kit of professional CRM archaeologists. However, 'academic' archaeology curricula were not quick to integrate these components.

The 1960s was a period of tremendous social change, witnessing the liberation of many countries previously occupied by European states for decades. Notions of freedom, resistance, and protest became embedded in the minds of a new generation of students and young scholars across the world. The civil rights and feminist movements gained momentum, and chauvinistic fervor of WWII as a sign of ultra-nationalism and the stronghold of Nazi and fascist ideologies yielded to a critical attitude toward hegemonic power of the state and increasing awareness of the rights of ordinary people, the disenfranchised, the poor, and those exhausted by colonial rule. In that context, the generation of archaeologists who were in their 20s in the 1960s, then their 40s and 50s in the 1980s and 1990s, were in a position through their academic and professional posts to engage with the political role of archeology in society (Smith 2004). One influential scholar of this generation was Peter Ucko, who was deeply concerned with the political and social dimensions of archaeology in contemporary cultures, raising fundamental questions about ownership, identity, authenticity, and the role of the past in the present (Jones 2014). Individual efforts by archaeologists at that time ran parallel to institutional changes on a global scale as UNESCO established its World Heritage Centre and convention in 1972. One can hardly underestimate the efforts by the Centre to safeguard sites as much as can be done with limited funds and bureaucratic obstacles, but one cannot also ignore the differential political weight of different countries (Meskell 2015).

I am concerned with the continuation of a 'preservationist' rather than a 'developmental' paradigm and the lack of a clear vision of the functions of cultural heritage in contemporary societies (Hassan 2017). In addition, the selection of sites and monuments on the basis of 'universal' and 'outstanding' value requires critical examination of the social significance of archaeological relics, sites, landscapes, and their relationships and relevance to living communities and contemporary society. My position is that cultural heritage studies and management must be guided by humanistic ethics in order to make the world a fitting home for the fulfillment of human potential in a socially supportive and enabling environment while guarding against intolerance, strife, discrimination, marginalization, exploitation, and destitution (Hassan 2017).

Professional Education in Heritage Management—Changing Times

The concept and the strategy of managing heritage as a social construct thus clearly moved from a means to claim world dominance to a weapon in the call for liberation, independence, national sovereignty, and emancipation (including feminist movements). Heritage is now an element in the gambit to establish a new global order and the transformation of the global economic and political scene to accommodate multinational corporations, the inherited modern nation-state, regional coalitions and unions, and rising economic powers in developing nations.

Archaeology and Its Discontent

Since the 19th century, archaeology has contributed to the making of a then-novel world order, dominated by European colonial nation-states. 'Heritage' was based in Western discourse founded upon intellectual and economic inequities. Bahrani (1998), for example, describes how Europeans constructed 'Mesopotamia' as a distant, historical place of 'ancient' civilizations, unrelated to modern Iraq or Iran—the cradle of civilization. From there, civilization 'emigrated' to grow up into the fully fledged civilization of Europe while the ancient land (often also viewed in Biblical terms) was overrun by Muslims (Arabs and Turks). This grand narrative still informs tourism, in which the past is hardly connected with the cultures of living communities. In Egypt, the situation is not much different. Ancient Egypt was dissociated from contemporary Egypt, and that 'exotic', remote Egypt is a land for adventure, treasures, and horror-movie mummies (Hassan 2010).

Archaeological remains are also primarily treated as 'national antiquities'—a source of pride sometimes bordering on chauvinism—rather than a source of understanding of the complexity of how the past is constructed and the social meanings and context of archaeological narratives. In transforming archaeological research into socially meaningful narratives, we must emphasize that archaeology is concerned with the past in a context of 'heritage' consisting of material proxies, oral histories, and texts that may be interpreted to learn more about where we came from, how our sense of self, identity, and life-projects has been shaped and processes and dynamics by which societies function. Only then can we critically examine our current situation, creatively engage with our collective past, and, with better understanding of the causes for current affairs, contribute to the making of a better future. In a global society, going beyond national identities to the notion of a common human cultural heritage has the potential to unify humankind through recognizing cultural diversity as a result of geographic distances, localized trajectories, and communalities as a result of common human biology and frequent cultural exchanges and intercultural transmissions.

Although several higher education institutions now teach cultural heritage management and some offer masters' degrees, this is rather recent. Archaeology even today remains detached from cultural heritage issues, and the education of archaeologists rarely addresses situations raised by the historical tide that highlight the need to link archaeology with social issues. We are missing an explicit concern for the social objectives of archaeology and its potential role in contemporary society. Is archaeology a means for knowing who we are and where we came from? Or a source of pride in the achievement of one's ancestors? Is it a medium for nation building? A foundation for a sense of common humanity? Or simply for the elevation of taste, the cultivation of refinement, and the enjoyment of beautiful exquisite antiques? Is archaeology concerned with existential issues of death, anxiety, and becoming human? And importantly: for whom do archaeologists address their work? One may argue that archaeology provides materials for dealing with any or all of those queries, but how can archaeology produce the kind of knowledge needed to deal with these issues if they are not regarded at the start of archaeological inquiry?

In the public mind, archaeology is regarded as a romantic pursuit for treasures, full of adventure and thrills (McGeough 2006). This may be attributed to the entertainment and tourist industries, but what are archaeologists doing to present archaeology under a different light? Admittedly, archaeology has a charm and public appeal that can hardly be enjoyed by other fields of inquiry like physics, chemistry, or economics. More related to psychology and history, archaeology arouses interest in issues of interest to the human psyche and for understanding oneself—who am I? where did I come from? What are my capabilities? How can I change my situation? More than psychology and history that deal with the 'past' on a personal and social dimension, respectively, archaeology deals with the social past through tangible objects that have a potent sensorial impact compared to textual or oral narratives (Hassan 2007b).

Unlike economics or sociology, archaeology is almost 'primordial' in its appeal, seemingly less complicated and sophisticated in its methods. This may explain why archaeology is attractive to the entertainment industry and can easily be manipulated for persuasion for political, religious, or ethnic or national goals. However, archaeology, like other disciplines, is not independent of the ethos of the times and concerns of societies or international affairs. As such, archaeology cannot remain isolated from contemporary issues engendered by decolonization, postcolonial discourses, globalization, the weakening of the hegemonic rule of nation-states, the flow of information through the social media, and growing dissatisfaction with how the world is run and fears of where we are going. Archaeology also must engage with concerns for terrorism, fanaticism, inequity, poverty, and climate change.

None of these issues can be addressed through an academic platform concerned only with its own narrow methodologies or the soundness of explanatory schemes. Archaeological ethics as a framework for learning have to include the principles of stewardship, accountability, and avoidance of commercialization (Bender 1997) but also must include the 'social relevance' principle that allows us to use the past to help think productively about the present and the future (Ibid.). My own position is that archaeological and other heritage-related fields should also ground their inquiries and actions on the principle of the social good by engaging in making the world a better and safer place, enabling people to realize their creative potential by elucidating how human creativity has guided the course of cultural evolution, helping ordinary people understand the cultural roots of their predicament, and vistas for change illuminated by the social dynamics of ancient societies (cf. Hassan 2006a). The way archaeologists look at the past in terms of 'artefacts' also requires a fundamental change to shake the strong bond between archaeological inquiry and technology. This requires a view of the past from a different starting point, in which society and cultural dynamics become the core and guiding light of archaeological inquiry (Hassan 2006b).

Archaeologists' concern for 'heritage' (see Meskell 2015:1–2) is strongly colored by their emphasis on 'materiality', making it difficult to surrender their own appropriation of the past and authority as the legitimate guardians of the past as defined and represented in books, professional journals, and museums. Even when archaeologists express a desire to engage in the current discourse on heritage, they do not seem to recognize that intangible beliefs are not confined to indigenous peoples and that heritage is not a 'supplement' to history. Rather, heritage is a celebration and valorisation of those elements of the past curated in proverbs, tales, performances, practices, and material relics. I take issue with the statement that "it is not simply historical accounts or narratives that have salience for living populations, but rather tangible places and objects are necessary to mobilize identifications, significations and memorialisation" (Ibid. p. 1). To the contrary, tangible places and objects become salient for living populations only inasmuch as they are material proxies of intangible oral and narratives and historical accounts, as well as performances and practices. The pyramids and other Egyptian monuments and remains were pillaged, destroyed, and ignored until a historical narrative of their significance to world history was created. This narrative was transformed into poetry, novels, and movies, making it a salient element in the Egyptian sense of identity and a key ingredient in Egypt's construction of its national identity in 1919 and of citizenship and revolutionary ideals during the 2011 revolution (Hassan 1998).

Tangible places and objects have a sensorial quality that make them 'potent' means of substantiating intangible 'heritage' (Hassan 2007b), but the role of Quran recitals has a profound impact on the living populations in the Moslem world. Another example is the musical performances of the Al-Sira Al-Hilalyia (a saga about the invasion of Tunisia by a tribe from the Arabian peninsula, with Abu Zeid al-Hilali as a hero), which had a much greater impact on the living population in rural Egypt before the prevalence of radio and television shows and dramas. Thus the admission that tangible places and objects become socially meaningful and significant only through (intangible) narratives and practices is the first step to reenvision archaeology and to acknowledge the need for a profound transformation in the way archaeology is taught and practiced.

Reorienting Archaeology—from Protection to Proactive Engagement in Contemporary Society

The lack of integration between archaeology and conservation was captured by Angel Cabeza in Agnew (2003:17):

> Where I see a problem is in the universities, what you call academic archaeology. They want to keep their way of doing things. If we want a more rapid

integration between archaeologists and conservators in fieldwork, we have to have more impact in the universities and in the education of the new generation of professionals.

However, why we should protect or conserve sites and artefacts and for whom has not been adequately addressed. In addition, what are the criteria that should be invoked to select certain sites or collections for conservation? And perhaps more importantly for setting up the criteria, what is the schema for valuing sites and artefacts? Were such questions raised in the United States after 1966, when archaeologists became engaged in CRM, recognizing that without this endeavor, numerous sites that would have been lost in the expansion of cities and the construction of dams and highways were saved?

Perhaps a key development in archaeological paradigms is the introduction of the UNESCO 1972 Convention's recognized world heritage sites, with its use of the term 'heritage'. This has opened the door later to speak of 'intangible heritage' as a counterpart to 'tangible heritage' (which refers to archaeological sites and objects, architectural structures, and historic cities). The introduction of the category of 'cultural landscapes' by UNESCO has also led to an integration of geography, ecology, social ideas and practices (intangible), and their material modifications as well as the built environment. However, the integration of tangible and intangible heritage as complementary and transconstitutive elements of cultural heritage (Hassan 2004, 2014b) has yet to be fully realized as vital for any cultural heritage management activity.

Not only did such conceptual developments open the door for reconsideration of the subject matter of archaeology and its connection with other disciplines like architecture, history, sociology, and folklore, but it also led to consideration of the intellectual, religious, social, scientific, and aesthetic in the process of nominating values for sites, landscapes, and artefacts on the World Heritage List. Within the context of these conceptual developments, the notion of 'management' first introduced in 'cultural resource management' became necessary in the para-academic process of selecting sites, landscapes, and artefacts for protection and conservation, in implementing legal measures, and more recently in engaging local communities in protecting sites. By 2003, Fagan predicted that archaeology may become almost entirely a profession focused on managing the past if current trends continue. However, what are the 'domains' and 'objectives of management'? The first generation of CRM archaeologists was mostly involved in archaeological surveys connected with major construction projects to ensure that valuable archaeological sites are not destroyed and archaeological materials are retrieved and curated. By contrast, a new generation of CRM archaeologists is needed to oversee a transition in the practice and scope of archaeology into a field guided by the social significance of archaeology and its active role in contemporary social affairs (Hassan 2007b) for social welfare that includes but is not limited to mobilizing heritage, especially in impoverished societies, and for generating jobs and income to local communities and toward national economic development. This will require acquisition of new skills that range from conservation to project management and from community participation to mounting exhibitions.

On a theoretical level, it is essential to engage professionals and archaeology students to discuss and debate the very notion of 'heritage'. In this regard, it would be useful to differentiate between the different 'heritages': (1) as a construct by professionals working with, independently or even in opposition to governments and policy makers and heritage regardless of what it means to local communities, indigenous peoples, and communities, populations and (2) the 'heritage' celebrated and valorized by such communities (Ndoro and Wijesuriya 2015). There is also 'world heritage', national heritage, and community heritage. It is futile not to realize the chasm between the two or overlook the different constructs of heritage created on the basis of religion, ethnicity, politics, geography, gender, generation, education, and occupation.

The political scene and the structure of social power often determine how different heritage constructs are presented and valued. Therefore, it is especially important to study the dynamics of heritage making and the role of civic society, social movements, economics, transnational entities, postcolonial strategies, international heritage organizations, and tourism, as revealed in the reader compiled by Meskell (2015).

The First Cultural Heritage Management Program in Egypt

In 2010/11, the first cultural heritage management program in Egypt was launched at the French University in Egypt (UFE). The program was designed to qualify applicants from different disciplines to become acquainted with the scope of cultural heritage management; realize the social and economic dimensions of heritage; gain skills in project management, information technologies, and academic research; and manage heritage resources for social well-being and development. The broad spectrum of courses covers heritage and society, intangible heritage, site management, education, museums, architectural heritage, historic sites, and international and national laws and conventions. The educational program was designed for rehabilitating those already working at the ministries of 'antiquity' and tourism and to encourage graduates to start their own businesses.

The program at UFE was the culmination of ideas that were consolidated when I was privileged to serve in 1988/89 as advisor on archaeological affairs to the Egyptian Minister of Culture, gaining the opportunity to see firsthand the shortcomings in the management of Egypt's archaeological heritage and the inadequacy of the existing educational programs that produced 'antiquities inspectors' to staff the office entrusted with the management of Egypt's archaeological resources. By 2001, the author, in collaboration with Prof. Fathy Saleh, then-director of the National Center for the Documentation of Cultural and Natural Heritage (the first organization in Egypt to use 'heritage' in its contemporary sense) produced and edited the UNESCO-UNDP document, *Strategic Approach to Egypt's Cultural Heritage* (Hassan 2001:166–184). In this document, I presented a preliminary proposal for a professional cultural heritage management education program in Egypt. The educational program was guided by the premise that archaeological sites, monuments, and collections are part of an inheritance for mobilizing the past for a better future. The label 'cultural heritage management' (CHM) was adopted with clear objectives for interpreting and presenting the past as an active force in contemporary cultural life and development.

In 2006, the first International Conference on Cultural Heritage and Development in the Arab world convened in Alexandria (January 20–22, 2006) and recommended the establishment of a Heritage Academy (Hassan 2008). In the same year, in a paper presented on British–Egyptian relations from Suez from 1956 to 2006, I made the case for an Institute for Egyptian Heritage and made a plea for funding support from the Egyptian–British Association, British scholars, and Egyptian and British philanthropists, recalling the support given a century earlier to Emilia Edwards to launch the Egypt Exploration Society (Hassan 2007c). The institute would have marked a new turn in Egyptian–British relations tuned to the present, but this came to naught, even after a generous offer from an Egyptian philanthropist who for unknown reasons did not honor his promises.

Around the same time, reviewing UNESCO efforts in salvaging sites and monuments in the course of building the Aswan High Dam, I recommended that UNESCO and the Egyptian government hold an international workshop to review the results of the UNESCO–Egyptian collaboration. The focus would be on capacity building, which has lagged behind, creating a crisis in Egyptian heritage management (Hassan 2007a:92).

Heritage for a Better Future—Designing the Curriculum

Cognizant of the great need for training archaeologists and others in cultural heritage management and encouraged by the support of the president of UFE (then Prof. Osman Lotfy), a curriculum was designed and presented to a forum of prominent opinion leaders in Egypt for discussion and recommendations. Subsequently, a partnership was forged with the University of Paris 1, Sorbonne-Panthéon, with Prof. Maria Gravari-Barbas to serve as codirector of the program. This partnership was vital to provide the program with international expertise and link students with the international community and research network. The joint program also ensured international standards for admission, coursework, and grading.

The program of teaching was designed to develop and valorize the role of cultural heritage management in society, and the course of study adheres to contemporary concepts of heritage in accordance with the UNESCO and international conventions and emphasizing the role of heritage in human and economic development, heritage and cultural continuity, solidarity, and the social good. Specifically, the program addresses the following principles.

1. **New concepts of heritage.** Heritage is a social construct of past events, personalities, and practices that are often but not necessarily tethered to material

remains. It includes all cultural manifestations that survive from the past, ranging from temples, mosques, and monasteries to historical houses and from proverbs, artworks, and tales to musical performances, festivals, and celebrations. It is the living memory of the nation and a resource for social and economic development. The construction of heritage is a transgenerational dynamic process feeding and nurtured as a living memory of the past. Heritage, as such, is a major force in socialization and is often manipulated to legitimize ethnic, national, political, religious, or economic claims. It has a powerful role in shaping world views, social development, and the making of self as well as 'identity'. Heritage has been exploited in the context of the 'heritage industry', which can have a negative impact on local communities and ecosystems. However, heritage's role, if properly guided, in helping to alleviate poverty, provide jobs, and enhance social development must be acknowledged, especially in developing countries.

2. **Heritage and Society.** The program is designed to explore the links between heritage and living societies and the role of heritage in nation making, social cohesion, and how people view themselves and their future. Heritage is socially constructed for social goals by previous generations and is curated, valorized, deployed, and modified by living communities in response to changing social conditions. Heritage has a role to play in ensuring well-being, a sense of belonging, consolidation of social values necessary for a 'good' society (such as solidarity, common vision, recognition of cultural diversity, understanding cultural continuities and culture change), stimulating creativity, and economic development.

3. **Safeguarding Heritage.** Given the current threats to the survival and perpetuation of cultural heritage resources, the educational program shall provide the basis for managing conservation efforts to safeguard heritage resources.

4. **Heritage and Human Sustainable Development.** In general, and especially in countries that are struggling to meet economic exigencies and yet are rich in heritage resources, the cost of protecting, maintaining, restoring, and preserving cultural heritage resources is often beyond available funds. This makes it necessary to ensure that heritage resources are mobilized for economic development in a manner that prevents the facile exploitation of such resources for irresponsible tourism that can endanger the integrity and social fabric of local communities, interfere with the health of ecosystems, and alienate host communities from their own heritage. The educational program must therefore consider issues related to how heritage is linked to tourism and other economic pursuits and how it can be a means, as in creative industries, for economic development without compromising the social good.

These principles required an educational program that emphasizes (1) general theoretical and conceptual knowledge of heritage fields, inclusive of archaeology, history, anthropology, social sciences, economics, architecture, and ethics, (2) an interdisciplinary knowledge of interrelated fields of specialties so that graduates are aware at a professional levels of the theories, history, scope, and methods of allied heritage disciplines, (3) professional heritage management skills, and (4) academic research skills.

Future Prospects

Graduates from the program, now exceeding 50, are already changing the landscape of cultural heritage in Egypt. Some are already placed in the Ministry of Antiquities and the Ministry of Tourism. Others have already or are in the process of developing their own professional careers in the private sector and civic society organizations. The program succeeded in securing scholarships from UFE, UNESCO, and the Ministry of Tourism and has attracted students from the United States, Spain, Japan, and Pakistan. In addition to the MA, the program has been actively engaged in conducting research and participating in international projects. In 2012, UFE, leading a consortium of international institutions, won a bid to train the staff of the New Museum of Civilization (NMEC). UFE was also contracted by UNESCO and United Nations World Tourism Organization (UNWTO) to train local community heritage guardians and local tour guides (Hassan 2014a). In 2016, UFE and the University of Kent received a grant from the Newton-Mishrafa fund to undertake a project entitled 'The Living Heritage of Egypt' and another grant for 'Earliest Egypt-Conservation, Valorization, Development and Capacity Building'" with the University of Edinburgh. The program is also part of an Erasmus+ consortium of Egyptian and European universities to develop a curriculum for museum studies (EduMUST).

Of special importance was the program's role in establishing 'cultural heritage' as a matter of national importance and drawing attention to the value of cultural heritage as a means of social and economic development. In this regard, UFE has recently established a Heritage Research and Development Center as the first research facility for heritage studies and management for development in Egypt. The UFE Cultural Heritage Management Program continues to be active in protecting and safeguarding Egyptian heritage and has adopted a Policy Regarding the Illicit Looting and Trade in Cultural Properties (Antiquities), mounted a campaign to put the UNESCO project for the safeguarding of Hassan Fathy New Gourna back on track, and made a public call for saving Egyptian heritage.

Conclusion

To make sure archaeology maintains its relevance in a changing world, the teaching of archaeology can no longer be isolated from the global transformations that have shifted attention from nationalist agendas to local and international social issues with special concern for 'people', inequities, poverty, gender, health, and civic liberties, as well as the threats of hegemonic global economic 'cartels', deteriorating environmental conditions, climatic upheavals, transnational terrorism, and the specter of chauvinistic extremism and xenophobia.

Archeology played a role in nation-building and it now has a role to play in the context of the broader and more socially meaningful 'cultural heritage' concept. As such, educational programs in archaeology need to revise their curricula to include cultural heritage management as a principal component and to embed socially significant issues in the courses taught. There is also a need to develop master's-level programs in cultural heritage management to qualify a new generation of heritage managers who will be guided by the changing notions of heritage (including archaeological relics), of the role of society in constructing heritage, the social consequences of 'exploiting' heritage, of the problematic issues of conservation, and the potential to mobilize heritage for social and economic development in the context of honoring human rights, celebrating creativity, and buttressing the capacity for social transformations toward a better future.

Acknowledgement

The undertaking reported here would not have been possible without the support of Prof. Fathi Saleh and Prof. Osman Lotfy, ex-president of UFE, and Prof. Maria Gravari Barbas and her team from Paris 1, Sorbonne Pantheon, for embracing and supporting the program since its inception. I also owe a special debt to Peter Ucko, with whom I had numerous discussions concerning the establishment of a cultural heritage management program in Egypt. I am, in particular, deeply thankful to the students attending the cultural heritage management program at UFE who have renewed my faith in Egyptian youth. They have become a force for marshalling heritage toward a better future for Egypt and reinterpreting heritage for Egypt and humanity. It is to them and others who will follow in their tracks that I dedicate this contribution.

References

Agnew, N. 2003 Closing the Divide: A Discussion About Archaeology and Conservation. *Conservation, the Getty Conservation Institute Newsletter* 18(1):11–17.

Bahrani, J. 1998 Conjuring Mesopotamia: Imaginative Geography and World Past. In *Archaeology Under Fire: Nationalism, Politics and Heritage in the Eastern Mediterranean and Middle East*, edited by L. Meskell, pp. 159–174. Routledge, London.

Bender, S. J. 1997 A Proposal to Guide Curricular Reform for the Twenty-first Century. In *Teaching Archaeology in the Twenty-First Century*, edited by S. J. Bender and G. S. Smith, pp. 31–48. Society for American Archaeology, Washington, DC.

Fagan, B. 2003 A Responsibility for the Past. *Conservation, the Getty Conservation Institute Newsletter* 18(1):4–10.

Hassan, F. A. 2017 The Future of Cultural Heritage Management: Ethics and Development. In *Collision or Collaboration-Archaeology Encounters Economic Development*, edited by Peter Gould and K. Anne Pyburn, pp. 15–27. Springer, New York.

———. 2014a Training of Local Community Youth in Dahshur, Egypt, as Local Tour Guides and Heritage Guardians. *Almatourism: Journal of Tourism, Culture and Territorial Development* 5(2) Special Issue pp. 39–49 (*presented in* Tourism Management and Sustainability of

Heritage Sites: The Role of Education and Training, Assisi, Italy, November 23, 2013, F. Dallari, and M. S. Minuti, editors).

———. 2014b Tangible Heritage in Archaeology. In *Encyclopedia of Global Archaeology*, edited by C. Smith, pp. 7213–7215. Springer, New York.

———. 2010 Egypt in the Memory of the World. In *Egyptian Archaeology*, edited by W. Wendrich, pp. 259–273. Blackwell, United Kingdom.

———. 2008 Heritage for Development: Concepts and Strategic Approaches. In *Cultural Heritage and Development in the Arab World*, edited by F. Hassan, A. de Trafford, and M. Youssef, pp. 12–54. Bibliotheca, Alexandrina.

———. 2007a The Aswan High Dam and the International Rescue Nubia Campaign. *African Archaeological Review* 24:73–94.

———. 2007b Liberating Power of Archaeology: Changing Aims and Directions in Archaeology. In *A Future for the Past: Petrie's Palestinian Collection*, edited by B. Butler, F. Hassan, R. T. Sparks, and P. Ucko, pp. 37–46. UCL Press, London.

———. 2007c Conserving Egyptian Heritage: Seizing the Moment. In *British Egyptian Relations from Suez to the Present Day*, edited by N. Brehony and A. El-Desouky, pp. 209–233. Saqi, London.

———. 2006a The Lie of History: Nation-states and the Contradictions of Complex Societies. In *Integrated History and Future of People on Earth (IHOPE)*, edited by R. Costanza, L. J. Graumlich, and W. Steffen, pp. 169–196. MIT Press, Cambridge, MA.

———. 2006b Objects of the Past: Refocusing Archaeology. In *A Future for Archaeology: The Past in the Present*, edited by R. Layton, S. J. Shennan, and P. Stone, pp. 217–227. UCL Press, London.

———. 2004 Proceedings of the *International Conference on the Safeguarding of Tangible and Intangible Cultural Heritage: Towards an Integrated Approach*, October 20–23, Nara, Japan. Conceptual Framework for Interdisciplinary Management: Debate Summary, 212–215 and General Summary and Discussion, 218–221. Agency for Cultural Affairs, UNESCO, Japan.

———. editor 2001 *Strategic Approach to Egypt's Cultural Heritage*. UNDP/UNESCO, National Center for Documentation of Cultural and Natural Heritage, Cairo, Egypt.

———. 1998 Memorabilia: Archaeological Materiality and National Identity in Egypt. In *Archaeology Under Fire: Nationalism, Politics and Heritage in the Eastern Mediterranean and Middle East*, edited by L. Meskell, pp. 200–216. Routledge, London.

Jones, S. 2014 Cultural Heritage Management. In *Encyclopedia of Global Archaeology*, edited by Ucko, Peter, pp. 7398–7402. Springer, New York.

McGeough, K. 2006 Heroes, Mummies and Treasure: Near Eastern Archaeology in the Movies. *Near Eastern Archaeology* 69:174–185.

Meskell, L. 2015 Introduction: Globalizing Heritage. In *Global Heritage—A Reader*, edited by L. Meskell, pp. 1–21. Wiley Blackwell, Hoboken, NJ.

Ndoro, W., and G. Wijesuriya 2015 Heritage Management and Conservation: From Colonization to Globalization. In *Global Heritage a Reader*, edited by L. Meskell, pp. 131–149. Wiley Blackwell, Hoboken, NJ.

Smith, L. 2004 *Archaeological Theory and the Politics of Cultural Heritage*. Routledge, London.

Thomas, J. 2015 Why the Death of Archaeological Theory. In *Debating Archaeological Empiricism*, edited by C. Hillerdal and J. Siapakas, pp. 11–37. Taylor and Francis, London.

9

HIGHER EDUCATION AND CULTURAL HERITAGE MANAGEMENT PROGRAMS

A Personal Perspective

George S. Smith

Introduction

Over the past 30 years working in cultural heritage management (CHM), I have watched higher education programs in CHM emerge in academic institutions worldwide due to ever-increasing population and environmental pressures and the need to protect and manage cultural heritage in the public interest. In order to effectively do this, CHM programs under various titles have been developed and implemented to provide students with the skills, knowledge, and abilities beyond philosophical discipline foundations. This includes education and training (see Hassan this volume) that reflect global concerns (see Fleming this volume, and demonstrates the relevance and application of cultural heritage in contemporary society and its ability to contribute to the quality of life and improve the environment (see Douglas this volume) for current and future generations. This is critical with respect to the tremendous impact on cultural heritage resulting from development (see Werkheiser et al. this volume), tourism (see Baram this volume), insufficient management (see Altschul this volume), the illegal antiquities market and looting (see Burgess this volume), war and conflict (see Stone this volume), public perceptions of cultural heritage (see Pokotylo; Tang; Chilton this volume), and indigenous leadership relating to cultural heritage (see Watkins; Yu this volume). The challenge has been and continues to be to develop CHM programs and courses that produce heritage professionals who can effectively balance cultural heritage with the needs and concerns of contemporary society to maintain relevance and compete effectively with other worldwide agendas.

Cultural Heritage Management Programs

Based on what I have observed with respect to CHM and CHM-related programs worldwide and my own experience in helping organize workshops on diverse but related cultural heritage topics (Teaching Archaeology in the 21st Century; Cultural Heritage Management in Global Perspective; Heritage Values in China: Identifying, Evaluating, and Treating Impacts to Cultural Relics; and Heritage Values in Contemporary Society), in addition to managing, protecting, teaching, and writing about CHM (Smith and Ehrenhard 1991; Bender and Smith 2000; Smith, Messenger, and Soderland 2010; Messenger and Smith 2010), I have found a number of topics that are important components of CHM programs and resulting courses that help train and educate cultural heritage specialists. These topics and short discussions are presented in what follows.

1. *Balance cultural heritage with the needs and concerns of contemporary society by applying legal, ethical, managerial, economic, and scientific perspectives in a manner that is accountable and sustainable and includes the ethical responsibility to interact, consult, and work with stakeholders while not compromising the quality of life for future generations.*

The inclusion of stakeholders is an increasingly important theme of CHM in defining, applying, and valuing cultural heritage. Ethical responsibility in CHM absolutely requires meaningful and inclusive engagement with the spectrum of cultural heritage stakeholders. Engagement calls for establishing and maintaining respectful and substantive dialogues between the stakeholders and those who seek to use, investigate, and preserve cultural heritage. In CHM education, student education and training should offer opportunities to participate in such dialogues.

2. *Provide information regarding the numerous conventions, laws, regulations, policies, and guidelines that impact cultural heritage.*

Most, if not all, conventions, laws, regulations, policies, and guidelines dealing with cultural heritage note that the dignity and value of culture must be respected as a fundamental human right because cultural heritage is a basic element of civilization and understanding between peoples, the well-being of humanity, and the progress of civilization. An integral part of these documents is that cultural heritage is an important element in the history of peoples, nations, and their relationships with each other. CHM programs enhance student education and training by examining and discussing the variety of laws dealing with the protection of cultural heritage worldwide and how they are applied and enforced within the context of various governmental structures.

3. *Demonstrate how cultural heritage is valued.*

Any discussion of what gets valued, including cultural heritage, begins in the realm of ethics and morals. Values, in no small part, are also based on memory. In exploring the concept of values, some common themes emerge that have direct application to what is valued and why. These include the belief that value is assigned and influences the quality of life for individuals, communities, and nations. CHM programs enhance student education and training by addressing whose values to include, how that choice impacts who speaks and who listens, and how this can affect complex issues such as those dealing with land tenure, social conflict, indigenous rights, public involvement, economic development, decision-making processes, and above all, accountability.

4. *Include discussion of the terminology used in the establishment of laws, regulations, policies, and guidelines that can influence how cultural heritage is studied, managed, and used.*

Clear and inclusive terminology is key to including stakeholders in the development of management philosophies. CHM programs enhance student education and training by discussing how terminology can influence cultural heritage. Concepts that diverge from views of time as a linear progression or authenticity as something existing in its pristine state need to coexist with practices that might alter the original character of a cultural heritage resource to maintain its contemporary relevance. Successful use of inclusive terminology can influence communication about important issues and the decision-making processes regarding cultural heritage at all levels.

Course Topics

In order to effectively address the relevance of cultural heritage and its application in contemporary society, CHM programs benefit from courses that help students understand core principles. This includes best practices to do the following:

a. Grasp the full extent of our collective cultural heritage and methods for quantifying these values so that they can be considered with respect to local, national, and international policies, strategies, and financing to ensure that cultural heritage is defined broadly and applied fairly.
b. Enlist the fiscal and human resources of developers, national and local governments, local communities, nongovernmental agencies, professional and international organizations, funding agencies, regulators, researchers, educators, and the public.
c. Effectively deal with development, tourism, international partnerships, and networks in order to build reciprocal cooperative bridges.
d. Develop and promote the cultural heritage sector as an advocate for our cultural patrimony to help integrate institutional and financial support.
e. Foster stewardship and understanding for cultural heritage resources that are nonrenewable and finite and must be managed in a sustainable manner.
f. Explore how and why various publics have a stake in cultural heritage.
g. Articulate the ways in which cultural heritage can be used to think productively about the present and the future.

h. Communicate goals, results, and recommendations to diverse audiences and to think critically, write effectively, and speak clearly.
i. Learn how connecting to cultural heritage gives insight to who we are, how we live our lives, how we view and treat others, and how we treat cultural heritage itself.
j. Learn how cultural heritage is examined and explained within the context of contemporary society and how it is influenced by social, political, religious, and/or scientific factors.
k. Address the many ways of viewing cultural heritage in terms of who talks and who listens and taking into consideration various perspectives relating to cultural heritage, some of which may be conflicting.
l. See how knowing about cultural heritage and guarding against a concept of cultural heritage that is dominated by only a few voices is critical to telling our collective story and empowering the public to make informed decisions about multiple and often conflicting explanations and agendas regarding cultural heritage.

It is important that such topics be considered for CHM programs and associated courses and that these courses are taught by faculty and staff with appropriate knowledge and experience. Also, CHM programs must address how cultural heritage is understood within the context of various agendas and how that influences the way it is valued, protected, studied, and used. It would be beneficial for courses and topics to be broad enough to demonstrate that the cultural heritage sector includes not only those who study, manage, and protect cultural heritage, but also those whose heritage is under consideration (stakeholders).

Managing cultural heritage is contingent upon valuing and protecting it. It is difficult to manage what is not well documented and even more difficult to manage cultural heritage that is being lost to man-made or natural threats. Thus studying, managing, and protecting cultural heritage can be considered a public good not only locally but at the national and global levels. Capturing the public value of cultural heritage is vital to understanding that a sense of identity and place is also an important part of our cultural heritage. Therefore, it is important when assessing the public interest in cultural heritage to have reliable data about what stakeholders think is important to long-term studies. Students thus need to be aware of the relevance of cultural heritage to 21st-century communities.

Conclusion

It is clear that our collective cultural heritage and national and international policies on a worldwide scale provide fertile ground for developing CHM programs to help educate and train students to articulate the need for effective, sustainable, and responsive policies and practices regarding cultural heritage. Such programs provide students with education and training to deal effectively with cultural heritage in contemporary society in a way that is clear, accountable, and based on a decision-making process that includes stakeholders and helps to advance local conditions while not compromising the quality of life for future generations. Demonstrating how cultural heritage can be incorporated into mainstream planning and demonstrating the relevance and application of cultural heritage in contemporary society are important skills for cultural heritage professionals.

Acknowledgments

I have participated in several workshops and resulting publications as well as other opportunities to discuss topics and issues regarding the relevance and application of cultural heritage in contemporary society and the skills, knowledge, and abilities that best prepare students to work in the cultural heritage field. I would like to acknowledge these colleagues for their contributions, in alphabetical order: Jeffrey H. Altschul, David Anderson, Uzi Baram, Brenda Barrett, Ian Baxter, Susan Bender, Susan Benton, Judith Bense, Dennis Blanton, Neil Brodie, Eden Burgess, Heather Burke, Kathleen Byrd, Ian Campbell, Hong Chen, Elizabeth S. Chilton, Joelle Clark, Kate Clark, Suzanne Copping, Kirk Cordell, Pam Cressey, Karina Croucher, Hester Davis, Paulo DeBlasis, Janette Deacon, Diane L. Douglas, Ricardo Elia, Maria-Luz Endere, Brian Fagan, Arlene K. Fleming, Nelly Robles Garcia, Patty Gerstenblith, Peter Gould, Roy Graham, Fekri Hassan, Margaret Heath, Valerie Higgins, Cornelius Holtorf, William Jansen II, Zibgniew Kobylinski, Dorothy Krass, Ian A. Lilley, William Lipe, Lilia Lizama-Aranda, Thanik Lertcharnrit, Mark Lynott, Andrew Mason, Randall Mason, Akira Matsuda, Charles McGimsey III, Francis McManamon, Phyllis Messenger, Skip Messenger, Barbara Miller, James Miller, David Morgan, Nancy Morgan, S.B. Ota, Katsuyuki Okamura, Patrick O'Keefe, Nick Petrov, David Pokotylo, Anne Pyburn, Bruce Ream, Ian Russell, Joseph Schuldenrein, Chen Shen, Neil Silberman, Jorge Silva, Claire Smith, Hilary Soderland, Vincas Steponaitis, Peter Stone, Jigen Tang, Brijesh Thapa, Joe Watkins, Marion Werkheiser, Nancy White, Willem Willems, and Pei-Lin Yu. The opinions expressed in this chapter are mine, and I am solely responsible for the content.

References

Bender, S. J., and G. S. Smith, editors 2000 *Teaching Archaeology in the 21st Century*. Special Report, Society for American Archaeology, Washington, DC.

Messenger, P. M., and G. S. Smith, editors 2010 *Cultural Heritage Management: A Global Perspective*. University Press of Florida, Gainesville.

Smith, G. S., P. M. Messenger, and H. A. Soderland, editors 2010 *Heritage Values in Contemporary Society*. Left Coast Press, Walnut Creek.

Smith, G. S., and J. E. Ehrenhard, editors 1991 *Protecting the Past*. CRC Press, Boca Raton.

10

ENGAGING "THE PUBLIC" IN HERITAGE

Which Public and Whose Heritage?

Elizabeth S. Chilton

Having been trained as an archaeologist in the tradition and era of burgeoning 'cultural resource management', for many years I considered the overarching goal of archaeology to be 'saving the past for the future'. I understood my mission to be the protection of archaeological sites and data, and the curation of collections from archaeological sites for perpetuity. The title "Saving the Past for the Future" was used for two conferences sponsored by the Society for American Archaeology in the 1990s. This title and several variations thereof were what Spenneman (2011:9) describes as "almost a battle cry" and were used by numerous other professional organizations. In some of my early professional positions I was asked to serve as a 'public education' coordinator, imparting both the content and importance of archaeology and spreading the message of 'saving the past for the future' to audiences to 'the public', that is, non–heritage professionals. These nonprofessional groups included tourists, school groups, local community members, avocational archaeologists, administrators, politicians, potential donors, and the like. The goal of this 'public education', while often implicit, was centered on garnering support for archaeology and preservation. But a lot of the rhetoric placed the archaeological record itself as the "ethical client" (Blakey 2008:21), as if the cultural resource management specialists were giving voice to and guaranteeing a future for the archaeological record itself.

In my early career, I never really questioned why 'saving the past for the future' was important. Part of the reason I went about it in a fairly unquestioning manner was that I was focused on precontact Native American history through archaeology—a history that was seemingly lost, erased, purposefully buried. I felt it a kind of moral obligation to uncover that history and share it as widely as possible.

But what—beyond data and objects—were we preserving, and for whom? Beyond serving as a series of cautionary tales and as lessons to not repeat the mistakes of human history, I did not question the other reasons future peoples would care about historical narratives or objects being preserved today. As Avrami et al. (2000) put it, "the benefits of cultural heritage have been taken as a matter of faith". Sharing that faith through public education was seen as a logical step in passing on knowledge to future generations. After just a few years as a cultural resource management specialist, I began to think more seriously about which sites were selected for preservation and study and why. And even if my own personal goal was to contribute to uncovering a hidden history, I felt I lacked the critical skills to know how to do that well. Experiencing my first professional and personal existential crisis, I did the only logical thing: I applied to graduate programs. I had come to realize that the stories that people tell about the past—and their ability to tell such stories publicly—are related to their access to power in the present. This is what led me to anthropology. For me personally, the most critical question in heritage studies today is not what should be saved and why but "who gets to decide?"

In this chapter, I argue that the relevance of the past in the present is context specific. I also argue that finding that relevance stems from engaging a variety of stakeholders is intrinsic to heritage work and working toward a deep understanding of the historical and contemporary cultural contexts. The broader impacts of heritage work require a comprehensive analysis of why the past matters to particular groups and individuals and who has power in the present to make decisions about what gets 'saved', commemorated, erased, or forgotten.

Heritage as a Profession

For the purpose of this chapter, I define heritage as "the relevance of the past in contemporary society—the full range of inherited traditions, monuments, objects, and living environments, and, most importantly, the range of contemporary activities, meanings, and behaviors that are drawn from them" (Chilton and Mason 2010). This is very much in line with Smith's (2006:1–2) more succinct definition of heritage: "the act of making meaning in and for the present . . . a cultural and social process, which engages with acts of remembering that work to create ways to understand and engage with the present". As such, I view the goal of heritage studies to be the creation of a scholarly field that is dedicated to building a "social science of the past" (Chilton and Mason 2010). In the context of this definition, heritage includes both the tangible and intangible remains of the past (e.g., artifacts, buildings, remains of structures, crafts, and languages) and the full range of associated activities (preservation, purposeful destruction, commemoration, interpretation, repatriation, policy making, and tourism). Therefore, the historiographical experts—archaeologists, historians, classicists, architectural historians, and so forth—are but one (albeit diverse) group that holds a stake in how such materials, remains, and historical narratives are preserved, interpreted, displayed, and valued. Pannekoek (1998) refers to the historiographical experts as the "heritage priesthood" and attributes the alienation of nonexperts from their heritage to the growing authority of heritage professionals. Smith (2006:4) defines such experts as the actors behind the authorized heritage discourse (AHD), which "privileges expert values and knowledge about the past and its material manifestation, and dominates and regulates professional heritage practices".

  This is not to deny the need for historiographical experts or the necessary dedication and training. It takes many years of training to become a heritage professional and, as many readers know well, this includes gaining knowledge about methods, theory, deep historical knowledge, and, very often, an advanced degree. Most heritage professionals do this because of great passion for their work and a high level of dedication. Nevertheless, the professional and personal self-interests of heritage professionals have to be acknowledged inasmuch as the self-interest of any other stakeholder group is acknowledged. One of the great contributions of postmodernism to academic scholarship is a trend toward greater self-reflexivity and careful attention to the cultural contexts of knowledge production and knowledge consumption. In many ways, postmodernism—and, in archaeology, postprocessualism—was a critique of the AHD (and other claims to greater access to 'truth' or authenticity). By emphasizing multivocality, postprocessual archaeology paved the way for archaeologists to "consider the wider publics and stakeholders" of the past (Chilton 2009:147). But as Smith (1994) points out, postprocessual archaeology—and arguably postmodernism—were largely introspective and not particularly productive in reaching beyond the walls of the academy. So, if the influence of postmodernism has led at least some heritage professionals to reach out to nonspecialists in the formulation of heritage values, who are all these various 'publics' we want to reach, how do we reach them, and why?

Moving Beyond 'the Public'

The term 'public' is often used by those in the AHD to make a distinction between (1) those who generate and preserve knowledge about the past, and (2) those who consume that knowledge. Within this dichotomous view—knowledge production versus consumption—public education is often a one-way sharing of information. In museum settings, for example, this is an obvious distinction: objects and records are kept secure and 'private' (to be viewed by a select minority, with the AHD as gatekeeper). Then there are exhibits and narratives specifically designed for 'the public' to consume, to touch, to react to. In archaeology in particular, there is a mostly implicit but qualitative distinction between knowledge created by experts and knowledge disseminated to the public. This is embodied in the distinction between reports written by cultural resource management professionals for clients and state archives versus 'popular reports' created for public consumption. Likewise, in the academy, there is a value-laden distinction made between the production of knowledge for other experts versus 'popular' writing, and the reward system in the academy reflects this distinction.

  By drawing this distinction between 'private' records (the knowledge and powerbase of the AHD) and the various kinds of information made available to the 'public', my intention is not to criticize the need for some distinction. It is a necessary facet of collecting fairly technical data, the need for documentation, legal considerations, and, in some cases, privacy. However, the danger of carrying the us/them, professional/nonprofessional, AHD/public dichotomy too far is that non–heritage professionals become excluded as legitimate producers of knowledge and values concerning official heritage. If one accepts the definition of heritage as laid out earlier—the relevance of the past in contemporary society—then oral histories and traditions are as critical as archaeological sites, buildings, and artifacts in considerations about heritage conservation. More importantly, if heritage is about relevance in the present, then stakeholders beyond the AHD must participate in the discussion of significance, values, and priorities. It is neither possible nor desired to keep everything in the world exactly as it is today and to save it *in toto* for the future. Thus, broadening our definition of heritage resources requires a commensurate broadening of heritage stakeholders and audiences. But how exactly does one 'engage stakeholders', and exactly what does that mean?

From Engagement to Collaboration

Terms like 'engagement' and 'collaboration' have become increasingly popular over the past decade in archaeological research, heritage management, social sciences, and humanities. Collaboration and engagement can run the gamut from simply keeping stakeholders informed, consulting them and getting feedback to codesigning research projects and outcomes (see Cowell-Chanthaphonh and Ferguson 2007; and Mullins 2011). Pannekoek (1998:8) notes that many projects with education or public involvement goals often have "no intention to involve the community fully in setting priorities". Of course, not all stakeholders have the desire or ability to be involved in heritage projects. In fact, some stakeholders—especially descendent communities—harbor real skepticism from bad experiences with heritage professionals. But given that heritage is part of the cultural and political process of defining criteria of social inclusion and—by extension, exclusion—it is intimately related to the exercise of power (Graham et al. 2000:34). Therefore, the spectrum of collaboration correlates with the amount of power and control afforded to the respective collaborators or stakeholders and also with the potential for the project to work against or reinforce social exclusion.

To this last point, Cook (2009:109) notes that the goal of collaboration should be "leveling the epistemological and ideological space between ethnographer and research community or consultants". But this is the biggest challenge in collaborative or engaged heritage research. One of the more radical and distinctive aspects of critical heritage studies—itself a child of postmodernism—is the movement away from the heritage professional as the sole authority on heritage values and significance (Chilton and Mason 2010). However, by letting go of some power as exerted by 'experts', heritage professionals can become the focal point of power struggles and are sometimes ill-equipped to navigate complex political situations. Cook (2009:113) notes that when anthropologists undertake collaborative research, "they implicitly assume an activist stance" by aligning with particular groups of stakeholders. This can be politically dangerous, and pretenure academic scholars often steer away from collaborative projects out of professional or personal self-interest or the strong advice of senior colleagues. The power dynamics and key actors in each case are distinct, and the ethical dimensions of heritage projects are complex, making decisions about engaging in such projects all the more salient. By opening the door to engaging stakeholders, allowing for multivocality, foregrounding competing narratives and values, the "democratization of knowledge merges epistemological concerns with ethical ones" (Blakey 2008:20). When the ethical considerations of promoting and preserving certain historical narratives are foregrounded, the goal of saving one past for one future becomes obsolete. Even referring to 'the past' as a singular, definite article marks it as concrete and "subject to the judgment of experts such as archaeologists and historians" (Smith **2006**:29).

Thus, I argue that heritage professionals should undertake deep collaboration, which is much more than communicating well with nonprofessionals. Collaboration "depends on negotiating research questions that are mutually agreeable and beneficial to all stakeholders" (Ray 2009:3). The process of collaboration often leads to knowledge discovery (e.g., Heckenberger 2009), the generation of new research interests (e.g., Murray et al. 2009), and even changing methods in field contexts (e.g., Chilton and Hart 2009). The goal of collaborative archaeology and heritage practice should not be simply sharing research results, maintaining or building friendly social relationships with stakeholders, or educating the 'public'. Instead, true engagement and collaboration changes what we do in profound ways. It opens doors to new epistemologies, helps heritage scholars to question their underlying assumptions and taken-for-granted methods, expands the data sources available, and ensures that we are conscious of the contemporary applications of our work in a way that is ethically grounded (Blakey 2008).

Many have written about the importance of deep collaboration in anthropology and archaeology (e.g., Blakey 2008; Fluehr-Lobban 2008; Kerber 2006; Little and Shackel 2007; Smith and Wobst 2005; Watkins 2001). But I would like to offer a few key attributes of a baseline for effective collaboration in heritage projects and, therefore, how we might think about engaging with various 'publics'. Elsewhere I have outlined the complexities and challenges of collaboration through a critique of my own archaeological projects involving contemporary heritage management and associated conflicts (Chilton 2012; Chilton 2006; Chilton and Hart 2009). Here I summarize key takeaways from my own experiences/viewpoint and the literature on engagement—assuming that the goal is to engage in ethical and sustainable heritage projects.

Start with the Intangibles

I know that starting with the intangibles sounds strange coming from an archaeologist. A few years ago, I argued in "The Archaeology of Immateriality" (Chilton 2012) that "tangible and intangible heritage are inextricable, and meanings and values are continuously created and recreated in the present by a variety of stakeholders" (Chilton 2012:221). As stated earlier, the alienation of nonexperts from cultural heritage is a product of the rise of the 'heritage priesthood', which has resulted in a focus on physical remains from the past (Pannekoek 1998). When projects start from the purely tangible forms of heritage—buildings, artifacts, material culture—we privilege the 'experts' who claim specialized knowledge of these heritage 'resources' (Chilton 2012). If the project is centered on 'things', then we lose the opportunity to change the power relationships and positioning of the various 'publics'. This is especially true in collaborative projects with indigenous peoples and other groups that have been disenfranchised from influencing public narratives about their heritage. As someone who absolutely loves the field of archaeology including the field and lab work itself and has spent the majority of her life in academic and professional contexts in archaeology, I acknowledge that it can be difficult for heritage professionals to move beyond comfortable areas of expertise. I am reminded, though, of one of my favorite quotes of all time: "Give a small boy a hammer and he will find that everything he encounters needs pounding" (Kaplan [1964] in Moore and Keene [1983:3]).

Smith and Wobst (2005:5) point out that archaeologists often presume that archaeology is useful, but sometimes the situation does not really call for archaeology at all, or at least not at first. Likewise, starting with the tangible objects associated with contemporary heritage immediately creates a power imbalance that is difficult to move away from. One outstanding and inspirational example of an alternative approach that focused on the intangibles comes from the New York African Burial Ground project; Michael Blakey (2008) advocates an approach that includes (1) a solid grounding in critical theory (and acknowledgement of the political and ideological implications of a heritage project), (2) public engagement with the communities most affected by the research program, (3) the use of multiple data sets (interdisciplinary approaches), and (4) a broader historical and social justice context, in this case an African diaspora frame of reference. Of course, every heritage project is different, but it seems to me that these four principles are widely applicable and hold great promise for working toward a more relevant and ethically grounded approach to heritage.

Acknowledge Your Stake in and Impact on 'the Past'

Heritage professionals are but one group of stakeholders. If heritage is not about what happened in the past, but what people in contemporary society do with the remains and narratives of the past, then archaeologists and historians should be seen as the subjects of heritage studies just as much as indigenous peoples or other descendant groups. Many of us make our livelihood and gain a degree of cultural capital by being experts about the past. It took me a while to acknowledge this personal stake, especially when I was making $5/hour as an archaeologist in my first full=time job. As Spenneman (2011:13) argues, "We have to face up to the reality that we are shaping the past in our image, that we are doing this for the present. Essentially, we are preserving the past for our own benefit, we are preserving the past for ourselves". So even when we have noble reasons for being involved in heritage projects, we need to be able to turn the critical lens on ourselves and acknowledge both our own stake and the legacy and political contexts of past heritage practice.

One example of this is the archaeological record itself. In the United States, the known archaeological record (e.g., sites that are on file at the various state offices) are representative of either where sites have been found accidentally or where professional or avocational archaeologists have decided to look. Each state has its own history and policy concerning cultural resource management, such that the number of sites and their location is influenced as much by the practice of archaeology as by ancient Native American settlement patterns. This becomes especially clear when GIS and other computer mapping programs help us to see that the distribution of sites most often follows modern highways or where Professor X held her field school every year (see Keegan and Keegan 1999).

Thus, there is a great need for an archaeology of heritage. In 2011, Cornelius Holtorf and I organized a session for the Society for American Archaeology entitled "An Archaeology of Heritage: What Does the Preservation of Remains from the Past Reveal about the Present?" In the session abstract, we asked: what do heritage activities and artifacts (signposts, guidebooks, preserved buildings, reconstructions, museums, traditional performances, etc.) reveal about our own time? And to what extent is the discipline of archaeology a manifestation of the modern heritage discourse? The papers from that session were published in a special issue of *Heritage & Society* (2012:5[2]). Holtorf's (2012) paper in that volume argued for a value-centered and inclusive approach to cultural heritage and a movement away from a commemorative focus on heritage objects and sites. Many heritage professionals are not comfortable being the objects of study and are loath to relinquish claims of expertise about the past. However, self-reflexivity and acknowledging our own professional stake in 'the past' is perhaps the most important first step toward a more ethical and sustainable heritage.

Focus on Why Heritage Matters

The key importance of cultural heritage is in maintaining the health of individuals and communities by fostering a sense of identity in the present (Chilton and Mason 2010; Spenneman 2011). Heritage contributes to "how lives are lived, and to the ways in which identities and relationships are formed" (Auclair and Fairclough 2015:3). This is why, in the end, heritage is about social justice—in the past, present, and future—whether we are explicit about the connection or even conscious of it. Heritage impacts a wide range of activities and decisions that we make in the face of climate change, natural disasters, and new technologies (Brabec and Chilton 2015:267). Therefore, it is the key to understanding sustainability, adaptation, and resilience in the face of change (Auclair and Fairclough 2015:3). Auclair and Fairclough (2015:9) note that heritage and sustainability share the most common ground "when both are perceived as being ongoing processes rather than . . . end products . . . and as being people-centred . . . rather than object-oriented". Thus, developing new approaches that encompass all aspects of heritage—not only the built environment and material remains—and engage stakeholders on a profound level from early on will contribute to more inclusive models of sustainable development and social justice in cultural heritage (Brabec and Chilton 2015:283).

The world and the heritage profession have changed over the past few decades. Thus "Saving the Past for the Future" seems like a rather outdated tag line. We now understand more fully the impacts of climate change on the sustainability of societies and the planet, and we are also experiencing intense and violent social conflicts in the face of globalization and displacement. Heritage as a social process and product is vital to mitigating the effects of trauma and maintaining a sense of ontological security and overall wellness (Fullilove 2005; Grenville 2007). The challenge for heritage professionals is to develop better research and public policy engagements on the ways that heritage can mitigate the impacts of trauma brought about by climate change and displacement and embrace and collaborate with a wide range of stakeholders on understanding all of the many intangible aspects of heritage.

Acknowledgments

I wish to thank Pei-Lin Yu, Chen Shen, and George S. Smith for editing this volume and organizing the conference that precipitated it. A special thanks to George for dragging me into the world of heritage values and introducing me to many of the people I have collaborated with in the past decade, many of whom are cited in this paper. The intellectual influence of many of my UMass colleagues is evident here, including Martin Wobst, Art Keene, and Bob Paynter. Of course, any flaws in this work are exclusively my own.

References

Auclair, E., and G. Fairclough, editors 2015 *Theory and Practice in Heritage and Sustainability: Between Past and Future*. Routledge, New York.

Avrami, E., R. Mason, and M. de la Torre 2000 *Values and Heritage Conservation: Research Report*. Getty Conservation Institute, Los Angeles.

Blakey, Michael L. 2008 An Ethical Epistemology of Ethically Engaged Biocultural Research. In *Evaluating Multiple Narratives: Beyond Nationalist, Colonialist, Imperialist Archaeologies*, edited by J. Habu, C. Fawcett, and J. M. Matsunaga, pp. 17–28. Springer, New York.

Brabec, E. and E. S. Chilton 2015 Towards an Ecology of Cultural Heritage. *Change Over Time* 5(2):266–285.

Chilton, E. S. 2012 The Archaeology of Immateriality. *Archaeologies (Journal of the World Archaeological Congress)* 8(3):225–235.

———. 2009 Teaching Heritage Values Through Field Schools: Cases Studies from New England. In *Heritage Values: The Past in Contemporary Society*, edited by Hillary Soderland, George Smith, and Phyllis Messenger, pp. 147–158. Left Coast Press, Walnut Creek.

———. 2006 From the Ground Up: The Effects of Consultation on Archaeological Methods. In *Cross-Cultural Collaboration: Native Peoples and Archaeology in the Northeastern United States*, edited by Jordan Kerber, pp. 281–294. University of Nebraska Press, Lincoln.

Chilton, E. S. and S. M. Hart 2009 Building Collaborative Archaeologies from the Ground Up: Two Case Studies from New England. *Collaborative Anthropologies* 2:87–107.

Chilton, E. S., and R. Mason 2010 "NSF White Paper: A Call for a Social Science of the Past". Submitted to SBE 2020. Electronic document, Future Research in the Social, Behavioral & Economic Sciences. Electronic document, www.nsf.gov/sbe/sbe_2020/submission_detail.cfm?upld_id=297, accessed April 27, 2016.

Cook, S. 2009 The Collaborative Power Struggle. *Collaborative Anthropologies* 2:109–114.

Cowell-Chanthaphonh, C., and T. J. Ferguson 2007 *Collaboration in Archaeological Practice: Engaging Descendant Communities*. Rowman & Littlefield, Lanham MD.

Fluehr-Lobban, C. 2008 Collaborative Anthropology as Twenty-first Century Ethical Anthropology. *Collaborative Anthropologies* 1:175–182.

Fullilove, M. T. 2005 *Root Shock: How Tearing Up City Neighborhoods Hurts America, and What We Can Do About It*. One World/Ballantine, Toronto.

Graham, B., G. Ashworth, G., and J. E. Tunbridge 2000 *A Geography of Heritage: Power, Culture and Economy*. Arnold, London.

Grenville, J. 2007 Conservation as Psychology: Ontological Security and the Built Environment. *International Journal of Heritage Studies* 13(6):447–461.

Heckenberger, M. J. 2009 Mapping Indigenous Histories: Collaboration, Cultural Heritage, and Conservation in the Amazon. *Collaborative Anthropologies* 2:9–32.

Holtorf, C. 2012 The Heritage of Heritage. *Heritage & Society* 5(2):153–174.

Kaplan, A. 1964 *The Conduct of Inquiry*. Chandler, San Francisco.

Keegan, W. F., and K. N. Keegan, editors 1999 *The Archaeology of Connecticut: The Human Era—11,000 Years Ago to the Present*. University Press of New England, Lebanon, NH.

Kerber, J. E., editor 2006 *Cross-Cultural Collaboration: Native Peoples and Archaeology in the Northeastern United States*. University of Nebraska Press, London.

Little, B. J., and P. A. Shackel 2007 *Archaeology as a Tool of Civic Engagement*. Rowman & Littlefield, Lanham, MD.

Moore, J. A., and A. S. Keene, editors 1983 *Archaeological Hammers and Theories*. Academic Press, New York.

Mullins, P. R. 2011 Practicing Anthropology and the Politics of Engagement: 2010 Year in Review. *American Anthropologist* 113(2):235–245.

Murray, W. F., N. C. Laluk, B. J. Mills, and T. J. Ferguson 2009 Archaeological Collaboration with American Indians: Case Studies from the Western United States. *Collaborative Anthropologies* 2:65–86.

Pannekoek, F. 1998 The Rise of the Heritage Priesthood or the Decline of Community Based Heritage. *Historic Preservation Forum*, Spring 1998:4–10.

Ray, C. 2009 Emerging Consensus and Concerns in Collaborative Archaeological Research. *Collaborative Anthropologies* 2:1–8.

Smith, C., and H. M. Wobst, editors 2005 *Indigenous Archaeologies: Decolonizing Archaeological Theory and Practice*. Routledge, New York.

Smith, L. J. 2006 *Uses of Heritage*. Routledge, New York/London.

———. 1994 Heritage Management as Postprocessual Archaeology? *Antiquity* 68(259):300–309.

Spenneman, D. H. R. 2011 Beyond "Preserving the Past for the Future": Contemporary Relevance and Historic Preservation. *CRM: The Journal of Heritage Stewardship* 8(1–2):7–22.

Watkins, J. 2001 *Indigenous Archaeology: American Indian Values and Scientific Practice*. Altamira Press, New York.

11

REGULATING INDIGENOUS HERITAGE

Impacts of Governmental Policies and Procedures on Indigenous Heritage

Joe Watkins

In the United States, the more common terminology related to the protection of cultural materials by governmental agencies is 'cultural resource management' (CRM), a term that sprang up during the establishment of governmental programs following the passage of the National Historic Preservation Act in 1966. Tom King (2008:15–31) offers a brief history of the development of CRM in the United States, but basically it can be said that CRM was seen primarily as a means of 'managing' the impacts of federal actions on the physical manifestations that represented the 'culture' of past or contemporary populations. While it is not my intent to jump quickly through the minefield of semiotics, it is important to note that in my perspective, 'culture' in CRM more often is seen as the material items produced by groups; to me, 'heritage' relates more to the underlying meanings that populations bring or ascribe to those items—more of the intangible aspects of meaning, belief, and relationships. Chilton (this volume) defines heritage as "the relevance of the past in contemporary society—the full range of inherited traditions, monuments, objects, and living environments, and, most importantly, the range of contemporary activities, meanings, and behaviors that are drawn from them" (Chilton and Mason 2010).

In 2008 I specifically stated that I don't believe that 'cultural resources' and 'heritage resources' are interchangeable terms (Watkins and Beaver 2008:11). I used 'heritage management' because of the more global use of the term, something I now regret. I agree with Erve Chambers that heritage management in the United States is more often "associated with a 'heritage industry' that is sometimes more concerned with the desire for favorable and commercially successful representations of the past" (Shackel and Chambers 2004:206), a concept discussed by Baram (this volume) concerning heritage tourism, where "[T]he stories, legends, and insights of elders can be shared as a value added component of the experience".

There exists a conflict between the use of the terms 'cultural resource management' and 'heritage management'; the latter is less often associated with the management of impacts to heritage by government-led or -sponsored projects. George Smith (this volume) notes, "the use of... cultural resource management suggests to some, use and exploitation, while the term cultural heritage management suggests conservation and acknowledgment of other ways of knowing and dealing with the past". Altschul (this volume) talks about cultural heritage management "to describe a community's assertion of rights to define who they are and what's important to them". Regardless of what 'heritage management' may mean on the global stage, the use of that term is developing very slowly (if at all) within any formal, governmental policy in the United States.

National Historic Preservation Programs

In the United States, the relationship with America's Indigenous groups[1] (American Indians or Native Americans) and federal agencies is defined by a series of laws and regulations outlining the special relationship that has arisen from the federal government's trust responsibilities to the Tribes derived from treaties made with the early Tribal nations. This trust responsibility has been likened to that between a trustee and a ward, with the federal government maintaining a fiduciary responsibility over the Tribes (see D'Errico [2000] for a more detailed discussion of the history of the concept of sovereignty in Indian law). Most of the distinct federal guidance dealing with interactions with Tribes relates to federally recognized Tribes, even though non–federally recognized groups may have standing in some states (California, for example) that is nearly equivalent to that of federally recognized Tribes.

Perhaps the strongest guidance concerning interactions with Tribal nations occurs in the National Historic Preservation Act of 1966, in which federal agencies are required to consult with Tribes at various points in the process. Consultation, in this circumstance, involves gathering opinion and perspective from the Tribes about specific actions being undertaken, licensed, or permitted by a federal agency. The Executive Department of the federal government also has provided guidance in the form of Executive Order 13084 Consultation and Coordination with Indian Tribal Governments (issued May 14, 1998); Executive Order 13175 Consultation and Coordination with Indian Tribal Governments (issued November 6, 2000); Presidential Memorandum on Tribal Consultation: Memorandum for the Heads of Executive Departments and Agencies (issued November 5, 2009). Federal agencies also provide their own guidance such as the Advisory Council on Historic Preservation's Consulting with Indian Tribes in the Section 106 Process (updated August 22, 2005), the Forest Service's Departmental Regulation 1350–002 Tribal Consultation, Coordination, and Collaboration (issued on January 18, 2013), and the Department of the Interior's Secretarial Order 3317 Department of the Interior Policy on Consultation with Indian Tribes (issued December 1, 2011).

These memoranda and policy statements provide guidance concerning federal agency interaction with Tribes, but those interactions are more often conducted at individual agency program levels with individuals who may or may not be familiar with Tribal culture. As such, interactions between Tribes and the agency can vary considerably, as can the level and quality of interaction between Tribes and agencies with different (but similar) programmatic needs.

Preservation Property Types

Within the historic preservation arena, perhaps the most common means of protecting aspects of heritage are within traditional cultural properties, or TCPs. First described in the National Park Service's Bulletin 38, a traditional cultural property can be defined generally as one that is "eligible for inclusion in the National Register [of Historic Places] because of its association with cultural practices or beliefs of a living community that (a) are rooted in that community's history, and (b) are important in maintaining the continuing cultural identity of the community" (Parker and King 1998:1). In this manner, communities are able to nominate places of importance to the group that can fall outside of other property types listed for protection under the National Register of Historic Places. While these locations require a physical space that can be physically defined, they need not be associated with 'real' people or 'real' events. I place 'real' in quotation marks purposefully, because such properties may relate to locations associated with Tribal cultural heroes, Tribal origin locations, or other such events that might not be deemed real to non-Tribal members. For Western culture, the Garden of Eden might be one such property to which value would be ascribed based on association or values to which not all people would ascribe or believe. King (2003) offers a much more detailed discussion of the place of traditional cultural properties in American cultural resource management.

Recently, the National Park Service has undertaken revision of Bulletin 38. One of its Frequently Asked Questions now notes that the 1990 version of Bulletin 38 used the term 'traditional cultural properties' to be consistent with references throughout the NHPA to historic properties. Many Indian Tribal members, Native Hawai'ians, and other indigenous peoples object to the words' properties, however, because they view them as implying commodification of their heritage. While such an implication was never the original Bulletin's intent, the proposed update[2] reflects the conclusion on the part of the NPS that 'traditional cultural places' is a more appropriate term, and that such usage is fully consistent within the context of the National Register of Historic Places.

Within the national historic preservation system, there are also other aspects that might be viewed as heritage preservation in the broad sense. A cultural landscape is a geographic area that includes both cultural and natural resources and the wildlife or domestic animals therein, associated with a historic event, activity, or person, or exhibiting other cultural or aesthetic values. Central Park in New York City might be an example most Americans would recognize; Mount Rushmore is another, even though American values might be different than those of Tribal members who ascribe significance to the Black Hills within which Mount Rushmore sits.

Little Bighorn Battlefield National Monument in southeast Montana is a cultural landscape that memorializes and commemorates the victory of the Sioux, Cheyenne, and Arapaho warriors over the U.S. 7th Cavalry on June 25–26, 1876. Park staff, Tribal representatives, and other stakeholders have long supported equal recognition of both cavalry and warrior combatants. In addition, the park's 2011 Long Range Interpretive Plan adds the need for recognition of Indian noncombatants, especially women and children, and their role in the conflict.

Throughout the Little Bighorn National Monument landscape, in addition to memorials that commemorate the battle, there are a variety of markers and memorials that indicate where combatants fell: white marble markers for 7th Cavalry soldiers and warrior memorial stone cairns that were added to the landscape shortly after the battle. While the large 7th Cavalry monument was erected in 1881, a program to add red granite markers for Tribal warriors started in 1999, and the Indian Memorial was dedicated in 2003. All these markers and memorials are critical to telling the full story and keeping memories and associations alive.

Another type of cultural landscape is the Bighorn Medicine Wheel of Wyoming. The Medicine Wheel was added to the National Register of Historic Places in 1969 and was designated a National Historic Landmark in 1970. The site has been used as a vision quest area for Tribal members for centuries. The 75-foot diameter Medicine Wheel is a roughly circular alignment of rocks and associated cairns enclosing 28 radial rows of rock extending out from a central cairn. This feature is part of a much larger complex of interrelated archaeological sites and traditional-use areas that express 7,000 years of Native American adaptation to and use of the alpine landscape that surrounds Medicine Mountain.

Numerous contemporary American Indian traditional use areas and features, including ceremonial staging areas, medicinal and ceremonial plant gathering areas, sweat lodge sites, altars, offering locales, and fasting (vision quest) enclosures, can be found nearby. Ethnohistoric, ethnographic, and archaeological evidence demonstrates that the Medicine Wheel and the surrounding landscape constitute one of the most important and well-preserved ancient Native American sacred site complexes in North America. The Bighorn Medicine Wheel is considered the type site for medicine wheels in North America.

Another federal agency—the Bureau of Ocean Energy Management (BOEM)—has prepared a document identifying procedures relating to 'tribal cultural landscapes' (Ball et al. 2015). While the document does not represent an official policy for any federal agency, it is "designed to outline a proactive approach for resource management agencies and indigenous communities" (2015:1). It defines a tribal cultural landscape as

> [a]ny place in which a relationship, past or present, exists between a spatial area, resources, and an associated group of indigenous people whose cultural practices, beliefs, or identity connects them to that place. A tribal landscape is determined by and known to a culturally related group of indigenous people with relationships to that place.
>
> *(Ball et al. 2015:5)*

Tribal cultural landscapes are not tied to the National Register of Historic Places or Section 106 and actually may be seen as a vehicle to move beyond site specific locations to include both landscapes shaped by human action and ethnographic landscapes. Drawing upon guidance developed by the Advisory Council on Historic Preservation (2011), federal agencies can use this concept to raise awareness about the existence and importance of traditional cultural landscapes and develop tools to assist all participants in the recognition and consideration of these places in the Section 106 and NEPA review processes.

And so you see there are aspects of the historic preservation system that are moving more broadly toward heritage management ideas. Federal agencies are not just managing locations where cultural material is evident (archaeological or cultural sites) but are also including heritage aspects of such places.

Tribal Historic Preservation

In the late 1970s, federal agencies began looking at the impact of their policies on American Indian culture. The American Indian Religious Freedom Act of 1978 forced federal agencies to 'examine' the impact of their policies on the free exercise of American Indian religion. The passage of the Archeological Resources Protection Act in 1979 necessitated consultation with Indian Tribes when archaeological excavations occurred on Tribal lands. The 1992 amendments to the National Historic Preservation Act created a process whereby American Indian Tribes could take over functions of the state historic preservation officer on Tribal trust lands. In 1996, 12 Tribes formally took over some of the authorities and responsibilities of the historic preservation duties in their states previously held by state authorities. At the beginning of 2017, more than 14 times as many Tribes (171 Tribes) were participating formally in the national historic preservation program with their own tribal historic preservation offices. Yu (this volume) writes about the increasing number of Indigenous programs that are using "innovative techniques for tracking, protecting, and managing cultural heritage data" of importance to specific Tribal communities.

While these offices are within the historic preservation program as it currently exists in the United States, they should not be considered 'little state historic preservation officers SHPOs'. Perhaps, taken at their base level, these offices work somewhat counter to the goals of the broader United States, whereby "[A]rchaeological remains are . . . treated and presented as 'national antiquities', a source of pride, sometimes bordering on chauvinism, but not as a source of understanding of the complexity of how the past is constructed and the social meanings and context of archaeological narratives" (Hassan this volume).

Tribal historic preservation offices (THPOs) more often serve functions beyond archaeology, and beyond those taken on by the states. For example, with the passage of the Native American Graves Protection and Repatriation Act of 1990, more impetus was placed on American Indian authority to manage materials that belong or related to their cultures (see Soderland and Lilley this volume, for a brief description of this law and its reach). As a result, many tribal historic preservation offices are assigned to deal with issues related to the Native American Graves Protection and Repatriation Act (graves protection issues) as well as archaeological site protection. Often, too, the tribal historic preservation offices deal with language and culture preservation issues as much as land issues. These offices function more fully within the heritage preservation realm (broadly interpreted in the Tribal perspective) than any other such formal historic preservation offices.

Such overlap of duties creates issues for federal agencies. National Park Service funding for the THPOs is limited to funding actions that relate to the National Historic Preservation Act—archeological site survey, National Register nominations, Section 106 consultation, preparation and participation in Programmatic Agreements, Memoranda of Agreement or Memoranda of Understanding—but not to other federal laws or regulations. As such, Tribes may be handcuffed by overlapping duties and responsibilities of those who occupy this position.

An alternate source of National Park Service funding does offer the opportunity for Tribes to fund some of their initiatives to preserve aspects of their heritage. Each year, NPS offers funding to federally recognized Indian Tribes, Alaskan Natives, and Native Hawaiian Organizations authorized by the National Historic Preservation Act of 1966. Tribal Heritage Grants for cultural and historic preservation projects assist Indian Tribes, Alaskan Natives, and Native Hawaiian Organizations in protecting and promoting their unique cultural heritage and traditions. These grants focus on what these groups are most concerned with protecting—Native language, oral history, and plant and animal species important in tradition—as well as sacred and historic places. While this source does not fund existing THPOs, it can be used to assist in developing the background materials necessary for the establishment of tribal historic preservation offices.

Traditional Ecological Knowledge (TEK)—Plants as 'Heritage'

In the National Park Service, Director's Orders are policy statements that serve as written guidance to help managers make day-to-day decisions. The primary source of guidance is the 2006 edition of Management Policies, which is also the foremost element of the Service's directives system. Other elements include Director's Orders, handbooks and reference manuals. It also shows related memoranda, directives and guidelines that remain in effect until superseded. Currently, the National Park Service is developing Director's Order 100: Resource Stewardship for the 21st century. What is interesting about this new policy statement is that it includes traditional ecological knowledge (TEK) as a viable point of reference for managing units within the National Park system.

TEK, as Usher (2000:185) defines it, "refers specifically to all types of *knowledge about the environment* derived from the experience and traditions of a particular group of people" (emphasis in original). Like Western science, TEK is based on the accumulation of observations. It entails a cumulative body of knowledge transmitted through generations, as well as beliefs about how people fit into ecosystems.

TEK is holistic in outlook and adaptive by nature and has been gathered by generations of astute observers whose lives depend on it.

Initially, TEK discussions occurred within anthropological studies, as travelers to various indigenous cultures around the world brought back descriptions of the ways local populations approached plant science, animal husbandry, agriculture, and so forth. However, over time, other researchers began mining that data for information. Now, each branch of science from A to Z—from anthropology to zoology—is involved in trying to understand the myriad ways that cultural groups take advantage of their specific knowledges of their specific situations. Much of the general knowledge can be found in ethnobotany, ethnopharmacology, cultural geography, ecological anthropology, or texts related to subgroups of regularly funded academic research.

However, it is important to recognize that TEK should not be considered to be in opposition to Western science. TEK and Western science each provide different ways of recognizing humans' relationships with nature, and benefits can be derived from integrating both perspectives. TEK, by the very nature of the knowledge encompassed in the Tribal communities, carries with it intangible aspects that can be tied to tribal heritage. This goes beyond basic identification of plants, locations, or relationships that are somewhat inherent in plant ecology, to include the relationships of humans to place and plant and animal kingdoms. And, as Douglas (this volume) notes, impending climate change can have impact on Tribal heritage: "[C]hanges in the distribution of species, especially the spread of invasive species, can do irreparable damage to natural and cultural heritage sites" and to the general biological heritage of Tribal groups as well.

Contemporary Indian Products as Aspects of 'Heritage'

The Indian Arts and Crafts Act of 1990 (P.L. 101–644) is a truth-in-advertising law that prohibits misrepresentation in marketing of Indian arts and crafts products within the United States. It is illegal to offer or display for sale or sell any art or craft product in a manner that falsely suggests it is Indian produced, an Indian product, or the product of a particular Indian or Indian Tribe or Indian arts and crafts organization resident within the United States. Under the Act, an Indian is defined as a member of any federally or officially state-recognized Indian Tribe, or an individual certified as an Indian artisan by an Indian Tribe.

The law covers all Indian and Indian-style traditional and contemporary arts and crafts produced after 1935. The Act broadly applies to the marketing of arts and crafts by any person in the United States. Some traditional items frequently copied by non-Indians include Indian-style jewelry, pottery, baskets, carved stone fetishes, woven rugs, kachina dolls, and clothing.

All products must be marketed truthfully regarding the Indian heritage and Tribal affiliation of the producers so as not to mislead the consumer. It is illegal to market an art or craft item using the name of a Tribe if a member or certified Indian artisan of that Tribe did not actually create the art or craft item. For example, products sold using a sign claiming 'Indian jewelry' would be a violation of the Indian Arts and Crafts Act if the jewelry was produced by someone other than a member or certified Indian artisan of an Indian Tribe. Products advertised as 'Hopi jewelry' would be in violation of the Act if they were produced by someone who is not a member or certified Indian artisan of the Hopi Tribe.

The inappropriate or unauthorized use of another culture's intellectual property is sometimes referred to as misappropriation. When misappropriation violates intellectual property law, it is referred to as infringement. A recent court case involved the use of a trademarked name. In *Navajo Nation v. Urban Outfitters*, Greer (2013:28–29) notes that proactive work by the Navajo Nation allowed them to halt the sale of the 'Navajo hipster panty' product by Urban Outfitters. In conjunction with misappropriation, 'commodification' refers to transforming an item of cultural importance into a product for commercial purposes, an item to be bought and sold in the market.

In 2008 the Intellectual Properties Initiative Heritage Research (IPinCH) project brought an international collaboration of more than 50 researchers and 25 partnering organizations from Canada, Australia, the United States, New Zealand, South Africa, Germany, England, and Switzerland to explore and facilitate fair and equitable exchanges of knowledge relating to heritage (IPinCH 2016). It was concerned with the theoretical, ethical, and practical implications of commodification, appropriation, and other knowledge about the past, and their effects on communities, researchers, and other stakeholders. The seven-year project was codeveloped by George Nicholas (Simon Fraser University), Julie Hollowell (Indiana University), and Kelly Bannister (University of Victoria). Team members represented Canadian and international universities, Canadian and international organizations, and partnering groups including the World Intellectual Property Organization (Geneva), Parks Canada, the Canadian Archaeological Association, and Aboriginal Nations.

The team identified a range of intangible cultural heritage, intellectual property (IP), and ethical concerns faced by researchers, communities, and others, and used the information to generate ideas for norms of good practice and theoretical insights on the nature of knowledge, IP, and culture-based rights. Areas of concern included research on and access to cultural material and cultural heritage sites, cultural tourism, commercial use of rock art and other images, open versus restricted access to information, applications in new products, bioarchaeology and the uses of ancient genetic data, legal protections, and research permissions and protocols. The project funded 15 community-based initiatives employing a community-based participatory research methodology.

The IPinCH research project finished in 2016, but its contributions to information on appropriation and commodification of Indigenous cultural heritage will have far-reaching impacts. As such, the project continues to produce worksheets, web-based publications, and traditional publications in academic articles and books. With the involvement of the Indigenous partners, the products developed will enable those groups to maintain better control over their heritage in the face of Western demands.

Conclusions

Federal actions define and often limit interactions between groups and communities when it comes to lessening harm to places of importance to heritage. Federal agencies are required by historic preservation laws to communicate and consult with any federally recognized Tribes that are impacted by the federal agency's programs or by programs funded or licensed/permitted by the agency. As such, Tribes continue to be placed in the position of having to choose methods to lessen the impact of federal actions on their heritage. Such laws and regulations, while they acknowledge the existence of locations of Tribal heritage, generally work from the assumption that the federal agency will carry out the project regardless of the impacts to the location; these laws are primarily procedural in nature rather than preventative or prohibitive. Federal actions are generally seen to be beneficial to 'the many' while harmful to 'the few'. As such, if the agency follows proper procedure, it generally may proceed with the project regardless of direct impact to the resources (however defined).

Federal agencies generally regulate Indigenous heritage through a series of 'one-size-fits-all' laws that do not take into consideration the importance that heritage plays in Tribal cultures. The ways that federal laws and regulations force Tribal concepts into convenient Western ones separates a generally holistic perspective into artificial subsets. A broader concept of heritage—one that recognizes that the 'past' and present are inextricably intertwined—makes the separation of the various components of Tribal culture unseemly and unworkable.

Werkheiser, Brooks, and Chapman (this volume) note that there are increasingly models for preservation that do not rely on national or international legislative action, but rather rely on "increasing awareness of heritage issues, an evolving ethic of preservation, integrating cultural heritage into the risk management of multinational corporations and financial institutions, and growing the capacity of communities to articulate their heritage values" to fill the gaps in government regulations. Other actions, such as growing urbanization (as noted by Tang this volume) may also play an "important role in affecting people's attitudes towards cultural heritage" and its protection.

But in the United States, the federal approach to interacting with American Indians is incongruous. In spite of the fact that the Bureau of Indian Affairs exists specifically to 'manage' Indian issues, every agency in the federal government is tasked with interacting with Tribes regarding its specific programs. Heritage management is merely a reflection of this federal program of Indian (mis)management.

Notes

1 I use 'American Indians' and 'Native Americans' interchangeably, although some groups see political implications and aspects of each term. I was born an 'American Indian' but am now politically defined as 'Native American' by federal regulations.
2 Proposed for 2017 at the time of this writing.

References

Advisory Council on Historic Preservation 2011 Native American Traditional Cultural Landscapes Action Plan. Electronic document, www.achp.gov/docs/Native%20American%20Traditional%20Cultural%20Landscapes%20Action%20Plan%2011-23-2011.pdf, accessed April 12, 2016.

Ball, D., R. Clayburn, R. Cordero, B. Edwards, V. Grussing, J. Ledford, R. McConnell, R. Monette, R. Steelquist, E. Thorsgard, and J. Townsend 2015 A Guidance Document for Characterizing Tribal Cultural Landscapes. *Bureau of Ocean Energy Management*. OCS Study 2015–047.

Chilton, E. S., and R. Mason 2010 NSF White Paper: A Call for a Social Science of the Past. Submitted to SBE 2020: Future Research in the Social, Behavioral & Economic Sciences. Electronic document, www.nsf.gov/sbe/sbe_2020/submission_detail.cfm?upld_id=297, accessed April 12, 2016.

D'Errico, P. 2000 Sovereignty: A Brief History in the Context of U.S. "Indian Law". In *The Encyclopedia of Minorities in American Politics*, edited by J.D. Schultz, K. L. Haynie, A. M. McCulloch, and A. L. Aoki, pp. 691–693. Oryx Press, Phoenix, AZ.

Greer, O. J. 2013 Using Intellectual Property Laws to Protect Indigenous Cultural Property. NYSBA *Bright Ideas* 22(3):27–33.

Intellectual Property Issues in Cultural Heritage 2016 Intellectual Property Issues in Cultural Heritage: Theory, Practice, Policy, Ethics. "Project Description." Electronic document, www.sfu.ca/ipinch/about/project-description, accessed April 30, 2016.

King, T. F. 2008 *Cultural Resource Laws & Practice*, 3rd edition. AltaMira, Lanham, MD.

———. 2003 *Places That Count: Traditional Cultural Properties in Cultural Resource Management*. AltaMira, Lanham, MD.

Parker, P. L., and T. F. King 1998 Guidelines for Evaluating and Documenting Traditional Cultural Properties. *National Register Bulletin* 38. Washington, DC, National Park Service.

Shackel, P. A., and E. J. Chambers, editors 2004 *Places in Mind: Public Archaeology as Applied Anthropology*. Routledge, London.

Usher, P. J. 2000 Traditional Ecological Knowledge in Environmental Assessment and Management. *Arctic* 53(2):183–193.

Watkins, J., and J. Beaver 2008 "What Do We Mean by 'Heritage'? Whose Heritage Do We Manage, and What Right Have We to Do So?" *Heritage Management* 1(1):9–35.

12

THE NEW DATA MAKERS

Indigenous Innovations in Cultural Heritage Management

Pei-Lin Yu

Introduction

The creation, protection, organization, and retrieval of knowledge is at the heart of cultural heritage management (Meyer et al. 2007; Silberman 2010). Cultural heritage data, defined here as all forms of coded knowledge, comes in an ever-expanding variety of forms, from dusty notebooks to oral history recordings, museum collection databases, Geographic Information System layers, and material objects to precious traditional ways of knowing. Pooled in electronic clouds and oceans, cultural knowledge in the form of data can—and should—make the return migration to nourish descendant communities.

Of course, data are not perfect. Information can become corrupted or lost or fall into the wrong hands. Humans select information and assign value, which can result in bias or elitism (*sensu* Chilton this volume). But on our best days, cultural heritage data give voice to the past, bring meanings and values into sharper focus, provide compelling rationales for action, and shine a light into future solutions to emerging challenges.

Behind the data are the people who create it. Who are the data makers? In the cultural heritage sector, scholars, technicians, and program managers historically filled officially defined and funded roles: conducting interviews, reading original sources, measuring and documenting buildings, excavating archaeological sites—and generating data to further the aims of scholarly research, education, or government-mandated preservation. In colonialized countries, heritage data makers have historically been ethnically and culturally associated with colonizing powers: Western Europe, Japan, Russia, and so on. Indigenous cultures were studied by academics, and some Indigenous knowledge was collected and selected for conversion into data. Most was not deemed worthy of scholarly investigation.

Yet keepers of cherished Indigenous knowledge in descendant communities have maintained it in the face of an array of odds. The evolution of legislation and professionalization of community-based cultural preservation has—belatedly—begun to welcome Indigenous knowledge keepers into the 'formal' cultural heritage preservation enterprise. The practice of data making is slowly growing more diverse and reflexive, with growing capacity to preserve and express cultural heritage values through direct action of descendants (Chilton this volume; Smith this volume; Werkheiser et al. this volume; Watson this volume). The roles of Indigenous cultural experts have transformed from informants to consulting parties to professional researchers, crafters of policy, and program managers (Smith and Wobst 2005; Watkins this volume). This includes the development and management of cultural data in various forms. Government contracts and agreements for consultation and management have driven this process for decades, and small but growing private and nongovernmental sectors are showing promise (Werkheiser et al. this volume).

While in the past some might have agreed that Indigenous data making is a good thing 'when it's feasible', I will make a clear case that this is a *best practice* that should be formalized in policy objectives and implementation. The goals of this chapter are to

- highlight accomplishments of some tribal cultural heritage programs that I've been privileged to work with since the 1980s;
- describe emerging challenges and enumerate the mutual benefits of this approach, featuring a case study from Glacier National Park; and
- set forth actions to strengthen and normalize Indigenous data making to fully realize its potential in the cultural heritage enterprise as a whole.

I draw these goals from two statements in the Toronto Declaration (Appendix A, this volume): *enlist fiscal and human resources* of diverse parties to ensure that heritage is defined broadly and applied fairly and address the vested interests of *diverse stakeholders* in cultural heritage, with special emphasis on Indigenous and other descendant groups.

Some Selected Accomplishments in Indigenous Data Making

Rooted in cultural values and expertise, Indigenous cultural heritage programs, facilities, and data management systems are expanding rapidly in the new millennium. When I began my federal career in the mid-1980s, tribal cultural preservation offices were small and scarce, and staff often had to devote some of their time to nonrelated tasks (although see Watson this volume). Things have changed in 30 years: at the time of this writing, there are 167 Tribal Historic Preservation Offices (nathpo.org/wp/ accessed on 1/5/16). It's not unusual to walk into a busy tribal culture office and see an elder shoulder to shoulder with a 20-something whiz kid, pointing at a computer screen and talking excitedly. While working with three government agencies and two universities, I've been privileged to work alongside top-notch Tribal cultural heritage managers who tap into both traditional knowledge and modern skillsets to facilitate creative approaches to data making and management. Following are some successful case studies in Indigenous data collection and creation, management and protection.

Innovative Data Collection and Creation

The Confederated Salish and Kootenai Tribes of the Flathead Reservation (CSKT) have worked with the U.S. Forest Service and Bureau of Reclamation since the 1990s to collect detailed data at archaeological sites along the Hungry Horse Reservoir in northwest Montana. This process complements and minimizes collection and curation through extensive in-field documentation (site mapping and photography, artifact data on weight, maximum length, width, and thickness, and descriptives) that allow researchers to analyze commonly desired characteristics of lithic tools. Raw material types are assessed by trained technicians, and the advent of handheld X-ray fluorescence (XRF) devices will soon allow better accuracy. Artifact and site data are geo-referenced. Back in the office, HTML software is used to create a 'complete' virtual site package that combines scientific data with historic photos, elder interviews, GIS, and more. This leave-no-trace approach has strong support by tribal culture committees, as well as federal managers faced with a curation crisis. However, it should be noted that this approach requires well-trained crews with ample documentation time, equipment, and funds and is most practical for small surface sites.

Innovative Data Management

Looking west, the Confederated Tribes of the Colville Reservation (CCT) in central Washington State manage a large heritage program including an archaeological repository. This office has perfected a data-management strategy for efficient entry and queries in partnership with the Bureau of Reclamation, Corps of Engineers, Bonneville Power Administration, and other agencies. The CCT master catalog uses commonly available software, and the number of data fields is kept to the minimum needed for searching capability. If a researcher wishes to add more fields (such as an archaeologist listing detailed artifact or site attributes), s/he is provided with a stand-alone version of the database. After modifying the database, the researcher can provide the modified version to the CCT, who preserve it in the event that another researcher may wish to use similar fields. The repository's main database remains simplified and thus easy to query. This novel approach reduces the accumulation of 'clutter' and ensures that any misdiagnoses remain the responsibility of the researcher.

Innovations in Data Protection

Certain categories of cultural information, such as the location and characteristics of traditional cultural properties or sacred sites, are sensitive (Parker and King 1998). This can complicate matters when government or private entities contemplating an action that may have an impact request sensitive information from Tribes. In the United States, the location of archaeological sites on federal lands is protected, and locational data are exempt from the Freedom of Information Act. However, the Spokane Tribe of Indians in central Washington State (STI) have had bad experiences with looting and site desecration, and in the early 2000s were hesitant to share TCP information with federal land management agencies due to uncertainty about data security. The flow of data to my office came to a standstill.

To navigate to a mutually workable solution, I worked closely with tribal culture preservation staff and elders to establish specific criteria for physical security (e.g., lock and key) as well as encryption and password protection for electronic data. In 2004, the Spokane Tribe and the Bureau of Reclamation signed a Memorandum of Agreement for data security measures that were designed, vetted, and implemented by both parties. Since that time, the STI has shared data in a manner that maximizes the government's ability to discern if undertakings will harm cultural heritage resources and minimizes the risk of data finding its way into the wrong hands. Continuity is key here, and the terms of this Memorandum of Agreement need to be re-visited every five years.

Innovative Approaches to Locational Integrity

Every Tribe I have worked with has expressed a preference for leaving cultural heritage resources as near as possible to their place of origin. This approach can help federal managers to reduce the accumulation of curated archaeological collections. However, the 'protect in place' ethic potentially reduces availability to researchers, and if there is a high likelihood of looting or damage, it may be preferable to collect artifacts with high cultural significance and sensitivity. To address this, the CSKT and the Blackfeet Nation, in collaboration with Glacier National Park, have developed a unique protocol for protection in place in the backcountry. If sacred items, human remains, or other sensitive items are discovered, personnel protect the items for the amount of time it takes to document them (including location). A suitable alternative location is selected nearby (e.g., away from a busy hiking trail), and the items are hidden as well as possible. The 'protect in place' approach works best in areas where rediscovery is not likely or there are other protections available (such as tended cemetery grounds) and where cyclical monitoring is possible. In the United States and other countries where laws specify treatment of human remains and other highly sensitive objects, specific protocols are usually prescribed by regulations.

In the United States, the Native American Graves Protection and Repatriation Act (NAGPRA) covers items associated with human burials and sacred behaviors.

Typically, new discoveries require a waiting period for publication of newspaper notices and other procedures. In Washington state, elders of the Spokane Tribe expressed their wish that human remains and burial objects discovered on federal lands remain underground while mandated procedures for notification and documentation—some of them requiring weeks—are carried out. In 2004, the Spokane Tribe agreed with the Bureau of Reclamation and the National Park Service to use a special underground ossuary in the Tribal cemetery during the waiting period for NAGPRA procedures. The items can then be reburied properly. As with the Glacier Park protocol, detailed documentation of the items and discovery location ensures that data are updated, and areas with high probability of future discoveries can be monitored.

Innovations and Efficiencies

New challenges and demands on data management call for collaborative working relationships that make efficient use of the time and effort of Indigenous experts and managers (Vinyeta and Lynn 2013; Watkins this volume). Tribal culture preservation programs are often small—whereas federal and other consultation requests (meetings, phone calls, documentation) will continue to grow. In the Pacific Northwest, innovative agency/tribal working groups that meet on a regular basis to address emerging cultural heritage management issues leverage valuable time and energy. The Cooperating Groups in the Federal Columbia River Power System, the Wings and Roots Program in Southern Idaho, and the Glacier Cultural Management Group in Montana are all examples of such groups. Technical and planning actions are daylighted with ample notice, threats and opportunities are identified, and issues that require government-to-government consultation are referred up the chain of command. In addition, working relationships are forged and strengthened.

These cultural resource cooperating groups are also incubators for new data-management techniques, scoping and implementing many of the innovations discussed already. Sole source justifications for contracts or subcontracts with tribal culture offices can be based upon unique capacities of Indigenous groups to obtain, vet, and input unique cultural data as well as organize them. This results in a higher quantity and quality of cultural data, and unlike agency-centric data systems, the working groups distribute knowledge about cultural heritage data on broad, stable platforms that are duplicated physically, protected and safeguarded, and may be accessed efficiently by appropriate experts.

Emerging Challenges and Benefits of the New Data Makers

Innovative working relationships with Indigenous cultural data experts can help address the issue of obsolete data platforms. My own adventures in querying 'legacy data' began in 1988, and as late as 2004, my dissertation research on earth ovens required work on several platforms at three state historic preservation offices, a regional federal facility, and two tribal repositories. In the United States, new requirements for government accountability, shrinking budgets and staff, an indifferent Congress, the growing complexity of data, and the diversity of impacts to cultural heritage are hindering important tasks including

- Obtaining raw data (e.g., in the field or repository),
- Vetting, processing, and entering data,
- Securing data to protect cultural heritage resources and values,
- Accessing and querying data for management and research purposes,
- Analyzing and synthesizing data to identify patterning and trends, and
- Updating data and migration to new platforms.

Today's unpredictable financial and political climate, along with accelerating rates of impact to cultural heritage, call for multiple-platform data systems that are fast, flexible, and migratable. Indigenous data makers have a key role to play. One recent case study deserves special notice for using a Tribes–university–park partnership that bundles several innovative approaches into a coherent strategy.

The Glacier Ice Patch Project

In 2010, a team of cultural heritage experts from the National Park Service, the Confederated Salish and Kootenai Tribes, the Blackfeet Nation, the University of Wyoming, the University of Colorado Boulder, and the University of Arizona pioneered a survey strategy for ice patches in Glacier National Park to locate cultural heritage objects as well as paleobiological items. Climate change has been melting ancient ice patches in upper altitudes and latitudes across the world, and delicate organic objects are becoming exposed. The Glacier Team developed a winning proposal and was awarded a competitive grant under the NPS Climate Change Response Program for the project.

The Glacier Cultural Management Group was established, and our first order of business was culturally informed criteria for data collection, management, protection, and tracking (Glacier Cultural Management Group 2012). The protocols for fieldwork included Tribal experts as key members of the field team, capturing detailed provenience information using the latest GPS technology for in-field data loading into GIS files, and making entries for individual sites and artifacts that include ethnographic, archaeological, locational, and geographic data. Ice patches likely to contain cultural items were preidentified (using criteria such as routes that animals and people likely traversed and that surveyors could feasibly hike to during the limited field season). Aerial photographs of the park were orthorectified to assist in this task.

The decision to collect or leave cultural items was made in the field (Figure 12.1), with preference for leaving objects in place or nearby in a protected setting if possible. Paleobiological items with no evidence of cultural modification (wood, soil, animal remains, and ice) were agreed to be collectible and subject to analysis for paleoclimate

FIGURE 12.1 Ira Matt, left, and Don Sam, right, of the Confederated Salish and Kootenai Tribal Cultural Preservation Program Document Items Found Melting out of an Ice Patch

Source: Photo by Robert L. Kelly, used by permission.

and environmental indicators. The project resulted in some exciting discoveries that evoke ancient landscapes, plants, animals, and cultural behaviors in what is now Glacier National Park. Wood fragments indicate two major advances of the tree line upslope at c. 1,200 BP and 6,000 BP that included yew, Douglas fir, and pine species. This was corroborated by organic materials collected from ice cores. The ice patches themselves yielded animal remains from mountain goats, bighorn sheep, and a nearly complete skeleton of a young bull bison who climbed a high, steep mountain slope (for reasons we will never know) nearly 1,000 years ago. DNA and isotope analysis indicate the 'ice bison' was a hardy tourist from the grassy plains below.

These finds offer tantalizing insights into previously unknown bison behavior in subalpine regions—as well as reasons that ancient hunters might have made forays into this area. At the time of this writing, cultural items have not yet been discovered in Glacier's ice patches. Still, the absence of evidence presents an intriguing data contrast to Rocky Mountains National Park and others with evidence for Native presence in ice patch zones. Perhaps Glacier's ice patch country was being used differently, but additional surveys will be needed before absence of evidence can be argued as evidence for absence.

An intangible but significant benefit of the Ice Patch project is the reconnection of young Tribal experts from the Confederated Salish and Kootenai Tribes and the Blackfeet Nation with these remote, beautiful, and culturally meaningful alpine landscapes. To bring the ice patch data to life for students, Tribal communities, and larger publics, the project's ambitious education program included a thorough ethnographic study of cultural aspects of ice patches, a YouTube video (www.youtube.com/watch?v=w1Vgs9IMixY) and an interactive website (http://glaciericepatch.org/). The Cultural Protocols have been published in National Park Service reports and online at the website as an example of culturally informed scientific procedures. The Glacier Cultural Management Group will carry this collaborative approach forward to other planned cultural heritage management activities at the park.

The Future of the New Data Makers

Maximizing the benefits of working closely with Indigenous and other descendant groups to create, organize, store, protect, and disseminate cultural heritage data calls for a clear set of actions. Here, I offer some suggestions.

Agency or project proponents:

1. **'Bake in' Indigenous data-management partnering to agency cultural resource management policy and guidelines.**

This can be accomplished when agencies and other entities review and renew their cultural resources guidance, which usually occurs cyclically. Explicit guidance will increase the favorable climate for partnering with Indigenous data managers through federal business instruments like agreements and contracts wherever appropriate and lead the way for private and nongovernmental organizations to do the same.

2. **Modify Indigenous consultation guidance to include specific discussion of data-management practices and protocols.**

Consultation with Tribes traditionally happens 'after the fact' of planning, but clearly incorporating data-management practices in consultation offers partners a proactive arena for taking on specific responsibilities, making suggestions to others, and incorporating standards and criteria in agreement instruments (memoranda of understanding, etc.).

3. **Activate Indigenous participation on all forms of data creation and management through business instruments and agreements.**

In some cases, justification can be made for contracting directly with Indigenous partners to manage data. In others, partnerships can be worked out through cooperative agreements. Indigenous data managers can also participate meaningfully in data management conducted by other parties if that is explicitly included in contracting requirements.

4. **Train non-Indigenous cultural heritage managers, scholars, and students in consultation *and* data management, concurrently if possible.**

In my experience, training for Tribal consultation is easier to find than training in data management (cultural heritage staff are presumed to have expertise in spreadsheet database and mapping software, e.g., MS Excel, Geographic Information Systems). Heowever, receiving training or education in both areas concurrently would help managers identify areas in which mutual needs and capacities can be leveraged.

Actions for Indigenous cultural preservation programs:

1. **Invest in data management training, equipment, and software for cultural heritage staff, and ensure that qualifications and materials are kept up to date.**

Many Indigenous cultural programs have already taken these steps, so the main challenge is to maintain currency (also see Hassan this volume and Smith this volume). For new programs, an excellent resource is the National Tribal Historic Preservation website, nathpo.org/wp/. Training, conferences, and grant announcements can be found at http://nathpo.org/conferences/nathpo-conferences/.

2. **Invest in data-management and cultural heritage curricula in Tribal high schools and colleges.**

There is increased demand for data-management skillsets, including among Indigenous graduates. In the cultural sector, coursework, projects, and internships (in either Tribal or agency cultural heritage departments) are good mechanisms for acquiring these skills and education. Most Tribal colleges have curricula for informational technology and natural resources management, which are good starting places (see www.sipi.edu/). Salish Kootenai College is notable for having a cultural preservation bachelor of arts degree www.skc.edu/thp-program/. These valuable skillsets are transferable to a variety of other professions.

Discussion and Conclusion

Seemingly local solutions to cultural heritage data challenges they have global implications. Human societies face complex emerging threats of armed conflict (Stone this volume), looting (Burgess this volume), massive-scale development (Altschul this volume, Baram this volume), urbanization (Tang this volume), climate change (Douglas this volume), legal and political challenges (Soderland and Lilley this volume) and ideologically driven destruction of heritage (Stone this volume). Our hope for the future lies in active evolutionary management and protection of data that is informed by the latest technology and in partnership with communities.

The new Indigenous data makers are doing exactly this. As key stakeholders with unique connections to and information about cultural heritage, Indigenous cultural experts have enormous capacity and motivation to contribute to the coevolution of data and human societies. During the centuries of devastating cultural losses of Indigenous people in the era of colonization, the word 'data' did not exist. The Indigenous fight to save their cultural heritage is far from over—so the urgency of reliable, resilient data has special resonance. Everyone in the cultural community stands to benefit from growing Indigenous participation in cultural heritage data protection and innovation.

Acknowledgments

My thanks to the Wenner-Gren Foundation for supporting this workshop, and most heartfelt appreciation to Jackie Cook, Guy Moura, Adeline Fredin, Bryan Flett, Randy Abrahamson, Francis Auld, Kevin Askan, Ira Matt, Don Sam, and John Murray for everything you have taught me.

References

Glacier Cultural Management Group 2012 Cultural Protocol for Recovery of Items Found in Ice Patches. Report on file at Glacier National Park Headquarters, East Glacier, MT.

Meyer, É., P. Grussenmeyer, J. P. Perrin, A. Durand, and P. Drap, 2007 A Web Information System for the Management and the Dissemination of Cultural Heritage Data. *Journal of Cultural Heritage* 8(4):396–411.

Parker, P. L., and T. F. King 1998 Guidelines for Evaluating and Documenting Traditional Cultural Properties. *National Register Bulletin 38*. National Park Service, Washington, DC.

Silberman, N. 2010 Technology, Heritage Values, and Interpretation. In *Cultural Heritage in Contemporary Society*, edited by G. Smith, P. Messenger, and H. Soderland, pp. 63–74. Left Coast Press, Walnut Creek, CA.

Smith, C., and H. M. Wobst 2005 Decolonizing Archaeological Theory and Practice. In *Indigenous Archaeologies: Decolonizing Theory and Practice*, edited by C. Smith and H. M. Wobst, pp. 4–13. Routledge, New York.

Vinyeta, K., and K. Lynn 2013 Exploring the Role of Traditional Ecological Knowledge in Climate Change Initiatives. *U.S. Forest Service General Technical Report* PNW-GTR-879.

FIGURE 12.2 Consultation in Action: Ira Matt, foreground, Robert Kelly, and Deirdre Shaw Consider How to Protect Fragile Items in Transit from the Field.

Source: Photo: P. Yu.

13

CULTURAL HERITAGE MANAGEMENT IN DEVELOPING COUNTRIES

Challenges and Opportunities

Jeffrey H. Altschul

Countries use their pasts for all sorts of reasons, many of which are not explicit or intentional. Monuments to past glories on the battlefield, statues honoring achievements in the arts and letters, and state rituals and ceremonies speak to a sense of pride and social identity. Most countries declare in their constitutions or in their laws a commitment to safeguarding their past, although commonly these statements—however sincere—are not backed up with regulations or sanctions. Often, the desire to preserve the past is pitted against economic development, particularly natural resource exploitation, infrastructure improvements, and urban renewal that requires destroying or disturbing archaeological sites or replacing historic buildings with newer ones.

In most industrial societies, regulatory frameworks are in place that maintain a balance between cultural heritage and economic development. In many developing countries, however, these frameworks either do not exist or are ineffectual. This situation should not be construed to mean that people in developing countries have less pride in their heritage or less concern with their past or are less interested in using their past to chart a better future. Assisting developing countries to find an acceptable balance between preserving their heritage and economic growth is one of the greatest challenges facing the field of cultural heritage management (CHM) as well as one of the greatest opportunities to use cultural heritage to redress the social inequities of the past and to advance social well-being.

In this chapter, I focus on CHM in developing countries. I begin with a discussion of cultural heritage, arguing that heritage can only be defined within a social, political, and economic context. CHM is not a simple application of laws, regulations, charters, or conventions but must be adapted to the circumstances of a particular country and often to a specific case. Next, I examine the two prominent approaches to CHM: placing the burden of identification and treatment of heritage on the project proponent or vesting it with the government. I make the case for a holistic approach to CHM with a case study from Mongolia and end the chapter with some brief observations about the proper role of CHM specialists.

The Faustian Bargain

The World Bank classifies 135 countries in the world as 'developing economies' (The World Bank Group n.d.). In 2016, the World Bank defined 31 low-income economies that in 2014 had a gross national income (GNI) per capita of $1,045 or less. Another 51 countries were declared lower-middle income economies (GNI per capita between $1,046 and $4,125), with the 53 countries eligible for World Bank funding classified as upper-middle-income economies (GNI per capita between $4,126 and $12,735). Most lower-income countries are in sub-Saharan Africa, and the other two groups are dispersed throughout Africa, Asia, Latin America, and Eastern Europe.

All developing economies accept aid, grants, and loans from industrial countries and multilateral financial institutions (MFIs) that are supported by industrial countries. The premise underlying economic aid is that in exchange for allowing the growth and expansion of private enterprise and public infrastructure, the well-being of the people and society in that country will improve. This premise assumes that the country's leaders will act in the best interest of the population, that the money will be well spent, and that the benefits of economic development will outweigh the financial debt and the obligations placed on society by foreign governments and private entities. Skepticism with this premise is widespread in most developing economies. At every level—national, local, and individual—there is a belief that the benefits of development will be siphoned off by the powerful, leaving the costs of development to fall on those least able to shoulder them. To many, economic aid is no more a pact with the devil, a Faustian bargain to enrich the rich, paid for by the poor.

To give voice to their concerns, individuals and communities often mobilize around the belief that they are the 'true' owners of the place or resources threatened by economic development. Local communities contend that they should speak for the resource in question, not the government or private industry. Often, this belief is expressed in terms of saving their heritage, and frequently the fight is intense.

Cultural Heritage

Specialists like me use the term 'cultural heritage' to describe a community's assertion of rights to define who they are and what's important to them. Although often expressed as moral outrage when a community feels threatened, cultural heritage is more than *ad hoc* claims of ownership in times of conflict. Cultural heritage incorporates all aspects of social identity, including place, norms, and belief, that communities consider essential to defining who they are, how members are to behave, and what practices and places must be passed on to future members for the community to remain viable (see Chilton this volume). Buildings, monuments, and sites may be important in the history of a community, but they only become heritage when that community attaches meaning to the ways that those places inform members about how to live their lives and act toward others. These meanings are not inherent in the properties but are expressed in social behaviors, be they pilgrimages, rituals, feasts, parties, dances, concerts, sports, executions, or other acts that occur at these places.

Losing these places is an insult to a community not only in abrogating their control over their physical space but also in eliminating an anchor to their psychic and social identity. It is this latter loss that makes fights about cultural heritage so intense and fuels claims that cultural heritage should be treated as an inalienable human right (e.g., UN 2016; see Smith this volume; Soderland and Lilley this volume). In no small way, cultural heritage can be said to live in the space between local communities and outside entities that assert rights over that community and its resources.

It is important to recognize that cultural heritage is not static but evolves as the community changes (see Hassan this volume). Something or someplace can be mundane and then later become important or even sacred. The changeable nature of heritage is not, as some claim, a function of political expediency. Instead, it is a recognition that meanings, beliefs, and values attached to places are learned behavior. Places or events are given meaning through stories, festivals, and other familial or communal events, and these meanings can change as the community changes. With the exception of official recognition by government agencies, places may not be recognized as heritage outside of the community, much less given official status as heritage sites.

Cultural heritage is a statement about what a community stands for and how its members are to be seen by themselves and by outsiders. It is not a 'thing' but an assertion of a community's right to exist and to be respected. Cultural heritage experts are not simply passive agents receiving information from a community and submitting it to government decision makers but critical actors in a process of defining what constitutes a community's heritage and disseminating that pronouncement in ways that outside agencies can act appropriately. These actions and responsibilities distinguish cultural heritage specialists from social scientists, such as anthropologists, who by their own code of ethics are instructed to "do no harm" (Altschul et al. 2016:214). Often implicit, these concerns were made explicit in the preamble of the Declaration on the Need to Protect and Safeguard Cultural Heritage in the Americas and the Caribbean (Asociación Latinoamericana de Antropología 2016).

Protections of Cultural Heritage

Given the importance that people at all levels—local, national, and international—place on heritage, it is not surprising that there are myriad overlapping laws, regulations, conventions, and charters that protect different aspects of cultural heritage (see Tang this volume). Local government units, such as cities or counties, often have lists of protected sites and even local ordinances requiring the identification and consideration of heritage sites in development projects. Urban plans and resource land-use plans commonly discuss heritage sites and incorporate them in proposed developments. Heritage sites important to a nation will generally be found on the countrywide lists. Some such sites will be made into national monuments or incorporated in national parks, often with individually tailored site management plans that discuss anticipated conservation and restoration needs, maintenance requirements, infrastructure improvements, and tourism options.

At the international level, many countries have become state parties to conventions that protect, promote, and conserve cultural heritage adopted under the auspices of the United Nations Educational, Scientific and Cultural Organization (UNESCO). Such conventions include, among others, the World Heritage Convention of 1972, which created a list of sites of exceptional importance (i.e., sites that transcend local and national significance) and the Convention for the Safeguarding of Intangible Cultural Heritage of 2003, which expanded the definition and protection of cultural heritage beyond monuments, buildings, and sites. The International Council on Monuments and Sites (ICOMOS), an association dedicated to the conservation and protection of cultural heritage sites, has adopted more than a dozen charters and doctrines that cover a wide range of cultural heritage concerns. Such charters include the Athens Charter of 1931, which helped guarantee protections for cultural monuments; the Burra Charter of 1999, which expanded consideration of heritage beyond historical significance and into cultural realms; and the Charter for the Protection and Management of Archaeological Heritage in 1990.

MFIs have a large role in allowing economic development and infrastructure projects to proceed in developing countries. MFIs like the World Bank and the International Finance Corporation build cultural heritage safeguards into their loan process. Private financial institutions have followed the lead of the MFIs by adopting their own commitment to cultural heritage enshrined in the Equator Principles (www.equator-principles.com). Some industries have created their own statements, such as the International Council of Mining and Metals Sustainable Development Framework. A few multinational companies active in developing countries have issued their own cultural heritage guidance (e.g., Rio Tinto 2011).

With so much overlapping of safeguards, one might assume that cultural heritage is well protected. Sadly, nothing could be further from the truth. In 2010, the Global Heritage Fund (GHF) (2010:6) surveyed 500 global heritage sites and found that 200 were at elevated or extreme risk. GHF further estimated that 90% of the destruction of heritage sites in developing countries were due to five causes: economic development, unsustainable tourism, insufficient management, looting, and war and conflict. Of these causes, the one that is dominant, and the focus of most laws, regulations, charters, and conventions, is economic development. As GHF (2010:19) stated:

> A driving force of heritage loss in many developing countries is economic transformation; with it comes related changes in land use, population

distribution, and income levels. Here, the appeal of modernization often wins out over that of cultural heritage preservation, and even national-level heritage protection does not guarantee that a major cultural asset will survive.

If the importance of cultural heritage is recognized at local, national, and international levels, why are the protections so ineffective? To answer this question, we need to examine how cultural heritage is managed.

Cultural Heritage Management

CHM consists of those practices that identify a community's cultural heritage resources and the programs that ensure their transmittal to the next generation. In practice, countries generally adopt one of two approaches to CHM. The first I call the 'social license' approach, whereas the second I term the 'national patrimony' approach. It is important to note that the approaches are not mutually exclusive, and most countries adopt elements of both, although one usually predominates.

Social License

Many industrial and developing countries place the burden of complying with cultural heritage laws and regulations on the project proponent. The proposition underlying this approach is simple: the party responsible for causing potential damage, alteration, or destruction to a community's cultural heritage should bear the costs of determining what, if any part, of that cultural heritage is at risk and then pay for whatever mitigation the community and its authorities determine appropriate. Many refer to this scheme as the 'polluter pays' principle. I prefer the term 'social license' because 'polluter pays' has a pejorative connotation, suggesting that the project proponents are solely out for their own personal gain and that economic development has little or no public benefit. Further, by linking pollution with heritage, cultural heritage can be and often is viewed as an impediment to be overcome as opposed to a resource that the community values and wants to incorporate into plans for its future.

In contrast, 'social license' implies a community's acceptance of a project conditioned on the proponent agreeing to specific requirements, some of which may refer to protecting and conserving cultural heritage. A social license is composed of both sticks and carrots. Part of the license is complying with all laws, regulations, conventions, charters, and safeguards placed on the project proponent by government agencies and funding institutions, the sticks of CHM. Additionally, the proponent needs to gain the trust and confidence of local, indigenous, and descendant communities as well as national and international cultural heritage professionals and interested parties. To do so in developing countries, where CHM regulations are weak and weakly enforced, project proponents need to engage proactively with interested parties and to agree to conditions protecting cultural heritage that go beyond those protected in law. In contrast to most CHM compliance efforts, which tend to be 'one-time' actions (i.e., survey, excavation, building restoration, etc.), social licenses need to be maintained for the duration of a project, which, in the case of infrastructure or resource extraction projects, may be measured in years or even decades.

The social license approach has one major flaw: it is paid for by the project proponent. Given that most project proponents are seeking permission to do something else—build and operate a mine, construct a road or reservoir, put in sewers and water lines, and so forth—cultural heritage is viewed as something to do as quickly and cheaply as possible. Without strong or effective regulation, it is left to the project proponent to decide how much, if any, effort should be placed into identifying, evaluating, and treating cultural heritage resources. Given that the proponent has a vested interest in not finding things that will stop or impede their project, it should come as no surprise that their conclusion is often 'very little', if anything at all. Local and descendant communities are often cut out of the process and have little recourse if they choose to counter findings of studies funded by the proponent that conclude that significant heritage does not exist. It is not surprising, then, that when cultural heritage emerges as an issue, it is often hotly contested.

National Patrimony

Some countries view their cultural heritage as national patrimony and opt to have the government take responsibility for all aspects of CHM. These countries argue that their cultural heritage is too important to be treated as a commodity. Heritage resources must be protected from market forces and what many perceive to be an inevitable 'race to the bottom'. This position is often stated bluntly as, 'our heritage is not for sale'. In a national patrimony system, heritage is under government control: the government determines the proper balance between cultural heritage preservation and economic development; defines the financial and human resources needed to maintain this balance; allocates those resources; performs the necessary CHM services; and determines if the CHM services were adequately performed. As government employees, free of worries over job security, cultural heritage specialists should be able to focus on 'doing the job right', as opposed to consultants, who are constrained by budgets and schedules defined by entities with little interest in cultural heritage. In some cases, spectacular outcomes are achieved. Yet in other cases, the results fail to live up to expectations, and, occasionally, CHM projects fail catastrophically.

A national patrimony system makes CHM a government monopoly. Commonly, there is little incentive for government workers to meet budgets or schedules, and there is a genuine lack of accountability. Corruption is rife in many developing countries, and cultural heritage projects are not immune. Cultural heritage is sometimes ignored or downplayed on large infrastructure projects that are politically important. Far from being able to freely pursue their nation's past, cultural heritage specialists often are under political influence either to whitewash past sins or to validate and extol the virtues of those in power. By vesting the responsibility for cultural heritage with the government, CHM becomes a top-down activity, which often leads to the promotion of a national narrative at the expense of local and descendant community heritage. It is not uncommon for national patrimony systems to stifle consultation with local and descendant communities about heritage issues.

Cultural Heritage Programs

Regardless of whether a country's CHM system leans toward a social license or a national patrimony approach, the success of their CHM framework depends on meeting four criteria. The first is that CHM is adequately resourced both financially and with sufficient numbers of adequately trained cultural heritage specialists. Second, local and descendant communities are empowered to be part of the system and are integrated into CHM processes. Third, there are strong government regulations and oversight of CHM both in terms of the bureaucratic processes involved in identifying, evaluating, and treating cultural heritage resources and in monitoring actual CHM services, such as surveys, excavations, and consultations. And fourth, there is independent verification of the processes and services by experts who are adequately insulated from political pressure and authorized to make meaningful recommendations.

In some developing countries, successfully meeting the four criteria requires the establishment of a new CHM system. In what follows, we describe how one such country, Mongolia, did just this by using the opportunity provided by a major infrastructure project to develop a comprehensive cultural heritage program (CHP).

The Oyu Tolgoi CHP

At the turn of the 21st century, Oyu Tolgoi was the largest undeveloped copper-gold deposit in the world. The mine is located in Ömnögovi aimag, Mongolia's southernmost province, a part of the Gobi Desert that has been home to nomadic herders for millennia. Oyu Tolgoi, LLC (OT), a private company now led by Rio Tinto, was formed to develop the mine. In 2010, the Mongolian International Heritage Team (MIHT), a consortium of paired national and international experts representing all aspects of cultural heritage, was contracted by OT to design a CHP for Ömnögovi aimag that could provide a CHM framework for the mine and the province; it also was hoped that the CHP could serve as a model for other aimags and the nation.

Why was a CHP needed? Because the communities affected by OT and other infrastructure development in Ömnögovi aimag continually called out cultural heritage as a major concern in public meetings leading to the decision to build the mine (e.g., CPR and PTRC 2009). These concerns were echoed during the CHP design. At a risk analysis workshop during which participants were asked to list the major threats to cultural heritage posed by economic development together with the key opportunities to enhance cultural heritage presented by economic development, Mongolians from all walks of life responded in a relatively consistent manner (Table 13.1). Their major worry was that their way of life was threatened. The opportunities, in contrast, focused heavily on resource protection. In discussion, it became apparent that while most residents of the South Gobi viewed threats to their way of life as paramount, they did not see how CHP projects would do much more than protect places. The MIHT's greatest challenge, then, was to design a CHP that aligned threats to a way of life with opportunities to conserve that way of life.

After a year-long study (Gunchinsuren et al. 2011a) providing baseline information on all aspects of cultural heritage—tangible (archaeology, history, paleontology) and intangible (anthropology) resources, public policy, education, museum studies, heritage tourism, capacity building, compliance, and stakeholder interest and involvement—the MIHT presented a draft CHP design (Gunchinsuren et al. 2011b). The CHP focused on determining what people valued most, designing programs to meet those needs, and establishing regulatory processes and funding sources to make the CHP sustainable. CHP components included programs to protect tangible and intangible resources at risk from development, educational programs including teaching lessons and curricula for public schools as well as adult education, enhancement of provincial (aimag) and village (soum) museums and culture centers, development of heritage tourism sites and management plans, training opportunities for professional and nonprofessional cultural heritage specialists, and an implementation plan that included obtaining buy-in from all stakeholders and continuing engagement. A national meeting of all cultural heritage stakeholders was then held in Ulaanbaatar, where the CHP was presented to mining companies, government officials, nongovernmental organizations (NGOs), and so on, debated, and found general acceptance.

A key element of the CHP was restructuring the Mongolian cultural heritage framework from a Soviet-era system to one that embraced a market economy. The national law of cultural heritage was rewritten and then amended in 2014. Implementation of other aspects of the CHP, such as the development of heritage

TABLE 13.1 CHP Risk Analysis (Threats and Opportunities) Results Abstracted from Gunchinsuren et al. 2011a:247–253.

Threats to Cultural Heritage from Economic Development	*Opportunities to Enhance Cultural Heritage Afforded by Economic Development*
1. Loss of nomadic culture	1. Registration of cultural heritage and establishment of a CHM database
2. Destruction of archeological, historical, and paleontological sites	2. Improved research opportunities
3. Loss of customs and rituals	3. World Heritage List placements
4. Negative impact on traditional social order	4. New South Gobi museums and improved *soum* (village) museums
5. Loss of traditional animal husbandry	5. Enhancement of *soum* cultural centers

tourism in the Gobi, a functioning CHM system at OT, the protection of regional throat singing, and support for camel festivals and other social events, also have begun.

Discussion

The main ingredient for a successful CHP is desire. The population at all levels—local and descendant communities, municipal, provincial, and national—need to be proud of their heritage and concerned about preserving their way of life and important places. Without this interest, heritage compliance is little more than a checkbox for government bureaucrats and an impediment to be overcome by private entities focused on their self-interest.

Cultural heritage specialists have an important role in defining, evaluating, and treating cultural heritage. We are by no means passive agents who simply receive and pass on information for others to make decisions. Instead, our job is to mediate between stakeholders, shaping discussion about what is and what is not heritage, and to help formulate solutions. We give voice to those communities that are voiceless, at the same time that we respond to public policy that enables and supports economic development. Depending on the orientation of a country's heritage framework toward a social license or a national patrimony model, we may find ourselves employed by the state or by private consultants. Regardless, our ultimate responsibility must be to engage those whose heritage is at risk in ways in which they feel part of the decision-making process that defines their present and shapes their future.

Acknowledgments

I want to thank Pei-Lin Yu, George S. Smith, and Chen Shen for inviting me to participate in the Relevance and Application of Heritage in Contemporary Society workshop at the Royal Ontario Museum. This paper is an outgrowth of a Society for American Archaeology (SAA) Knowledge Series lecture under a different name presented in October 2015. I want to thank Maureen Malloy and Tobi Brimsek of the SAA for that opportunity as well as all those who commented on the lecture. I received valuable comments on this paper from Gerry Wait. Maria Molina and Pei-Lin Yu provided valuable technical edits. I alone am responsible for errors of fact or logic.

References

Altschul, J. H, I. Thiaw, and G. Wait 2016 *A Slave Who Would be King: Oral Tradition and Archaeology of the Recent Past in the Upper Senegal River Basin*. Archaeopress Publishing Ltd., Oxford, England.

Asociación Latinoamericana de Antropología 2016 Declaration on the Need to Protect and Safeguard Cultural Heritage in The Americas and The Caribbean. Electronic document, www.asociacionlatinoamericanadeantropologia.net/Campinasdeclaration_amended_final.pdf, accessed April 12, 2016.

Centre for Policy Research (CPR) & the Population Training and Research Center (PTRC) 2009 *Oyu Tolgoi Project Socio-Economic Impact Assessment: Final Report*. The Centre of Policy Research and the Population Training and Research Centre, School of Economic Studies, Mongolian National University for Ivanhoe Mines Mongolia, Inc., Ulaanbaatar, Mongolia.

Global Heritage Fund 2010 Saving our Vanishing Heritage: Safeguarding Endangered Vanishing Cultural Heritage Sites in the Developing World. Palo Alto, California. Global Heritage Fund. Electronic document, http://globalheritagefund.org/images/uploads/docs/GHFSavingOurVanishingHeritagev1.0singlepageview2b.pdf, accessed April 12, 2016.

Gunchinsuren, B, J. H. Altschul, and J. W. Olsen, editors 2011a *Protecting the Past, Preserving the Present: Report on Phase 1 Activities of the Oyu Tolgoi Cultural Heritage Program Design for Ömnögovi Aimag*. The Mongolian International Heritage Team for Oyu Tolgoi, LLC, Ulaanbaatar, Mongolia. Electronic document, http://ot.mn/media/ot/content/archive/reports/Oyu_Tolgoi_Cultural_Heritage_Programme_Design_EN_0.pdf, accessed April 12, 2016.

———. 2011b *The Oyu Tolgoi Cultural Heritage Program*. The Mongolian International Heritage Team for Oyu Tolgoi, LLC, Ulaanbaatar, Mongolia. Electronic document, http://ot.mn/media/ot/content/reports/communities/2011/Cultural_Heritage_Programme_proposal_EN.pdf, accessed April 12, 2016.

Rio Tinto 2011 Why Cultural Heritage Matters: A Resource Guide for Integrating Cultural Heritage Management into Communities Work at Rio Tinto. Electronic document, www.riotinto.com/documents/ReportsPublications/Rio_Tinto_Cultural_Heritage_Guide.pdf, accessed April 12, 2016.

United Nations Human Rights, Office of the High Commissioner (UN) 2016 Statement by Ms. Karima Bennoune, Special Rapporteur in the field of cultural rights, at the 31st session of the Human Rights Council. Electronic document, www.ohchr.org/EN/NewsEvents/Pages/DisplayNews.aspx?NewsID=18508&LangID=E, accessed April 12, 2016.

The World Bank Group n.d. World Bank Country and Lending Groups. Electronic document, http://data.worldbank.org/about/country-and-lending-groups, accessed April 12, 2016.

14

HERITAGE IN THE GLOBAL ECONOMY

Protecting Cultural Heritage through Nongovernmental and Voluntary Practices

Marion Werkheiser, Trace Brooks, and Ellen Chapman

Introduction

Advocates for the protection of cultural heritage are focusing much effort on new models for preservation that do not require national or international legislative action. These new models rely on increasing awareness of heritage issues, an evolving ethic of preservation, integrating cultural heritage into the risk management of multinational corporations and financial institutions, and growing the capacity of communities to articulate their heritage values. These efforts can fill the gaps in government regulations that leave certain classes of sites unprotected, encourage public appreciation for historic preservation, and pioneer tools that can safeguard heritage protection on both nonregulated and regulated projects.

This chapter discusses how voluntary guidelines and standards are filling gaps in the current legal frameworks to protect cultural heritage. Preservation advocates should become more involved in the development and implementation of these guidelines and standards, which have the potential to impact significantly how development and preservation are responsibly balanced.

Legal Regimes Fall Short

Almost every nation has a history of regulating the heritage it considers valuable; the UNESCO Database of Cultural Heritage Legislation lists 2,852 heritage protection laws enacted by hundreds of countries since the 19th century (UNESCO 2007). Yet legal regimes for the protection of cultural heritage frequently fall short by exempting certain classes of projects, emphasizing salvage and chance-find outcomes rather than early-stage planning and failing to provide resources for effective implementation. We can divide legal efforts into those that are proactive and reactive. Proactive regimes focus on identifying, interpreting, and protecting cultural resources. Reactive regimes call for identification, interpretation, and possible protection only when a resource is actively threatened by development. The United States, for example, has both proactive and reactive preservation laws.

The United States has relatively stringent cultural resources legislation, driven substantially by the federal historic preservation program created by the National Historic Preservation Act (NHPA), state environmental review regulations, and local historic preservation ordinances. At the same time, an examination of American legislation reveals that more national heritage is vulnerable than protected. Cultural heritage protection in the United States is largely reactive in nature and limited to the protection of federally associated resources. Section 106 of the NHPA requires federal agencies to review projects for possible impacts to cultural resources potentially eligible for inclusion on the National Register of Historic Places (ACHP 2013). Projects that affect eligible historic resources trigger a consultation process involving the agency, state historic preservation officers (SHPOs), the Advisory Council on Historic Preservation (ACHP), an independent federal agency, and applicable stakeholder groups. It has been estimated that more than 90% of the archaeology conducted in the United States has resulted from Section 106 reviews (Sebastian and Lipe 2010).

More proactive forms of heritage protection in the United States include Section 110 of the National Historic Preservation Act, which requires federal agencies to identify and catalog historic properties owned by the federal government. Yet chronic underfunding and insufficient staffing mean that most agencies have recorded only a small fraction of the sites they steward (NPS 2016). The Bureau of Land Management has recorded 278,000 historic sites—only a fraction of the 4 million sites estimated to exist on BLM-owned land (National Trust for Historic Preservation 2016). Similarly, though the National Forest Service identified more than 20,000 cultural resources between 2008 and 2011 (Preserve America 2011), only a small proportion of the almost 2 million heritage resources on National Forest land are being preserved (Layton 2008). A more successful form of protection has been the 1906 Antiquities Act, which has resulted in the creation of 123 national monuments that protect approximately 70 million acres of land with remarkable historic and scientific value (Squillace 2003). The Antiquities Act, however, can only be used to protect federally owned land.

We thus have a national legal regime that pays lip service to the protection of cultural resources on federal land but offers possible protection to sites on private land only when they are subject to threats from development projects that require a federal permit or use federal funds. Significant gaps exist, for example, where ground-disturbing activities like hydraulic fracturing and building of noninterstate pipelines occur on private land and require no assessment of impacts to cultural resources. Essentially, any type of private development that does not require permission from the government to proceed is immune from requirements to identify or protect cultural resources that may be affected by the development.

Expanding the legal regime to protect more cultural resources is a political nonstarter. The political climate for revision is more challenging today than it was in the mid-20th century, when many of these laws were established. Today, the regulatory system is perceived as inhibiting economic development with cumbersome, expensive processes that cause substantial project delays and even endanger some projects. This perception has a basis in truth, primarily because government agencies have not invested appropriately in tools and training to streamline the process. Even if these perceptions and realities could be overcome, the American emphasis on strong individual property rights and the poor legislative productivity of Congress in recent years (Desilver 2015) combine to create a difficult environment for expanding the protection of historic and cultural properties. As a result, the preservation advocacy community has focused in recent years on increasing funding to agencies to help streamline compliance with existing regulations and on opposing efforts by industry groups to create categorical exclusions from the NHPA for certain classes of federally permitted projects.

At the time of this writing, the Congressional authorization for the funding source for the federal preservation program—the Historic Preservation Fund—has expired. This modest funding provides the foundation for the budgets of SHPOs and tribal historic preservation offices, as well as some competitive grant programs. Without reauthorization and increased funding for the Historic Preservation Fund, the country's preservation program will grind to a halt. Even in other developed nations with different approaches towards land ownership, cultural heritage continues to face damage from private enterprise, transportation infrastructure, and energy projects. The specifics of these legal requirements and preservation structures vary; what does not change, however, is the fact that these protections are never complete.

International Legal Protections Similarly Fall Short

Legal protections at the international level are largely driven by organizations like UNESCO, the International Council on Monuments and Sites (ICOMOS), and the Council of Europe (COE), which have been primarily developed and maintained by Western countries. The 1972 passage of the Convention Concerning the Protection of the World Cultural and Natural Heritage by the UNESCO General Conference laid the foundation for the United Nations' cultural heritage protections. Though not directly binding on the private sector, the Convention has expansive reach through its many States Parties, representatives from nations that have ratified the World Heritage Convention. To facilitate implementation of the Convention, UNESCO formed the World Heritage Committee, the World Heritage Centre (WHC), and associated independent Advisory Bodies—the most relevant being the International Council on Monuments and Sites (ICOMOS) and the International Union for the Conservation of Nature (IUCN).

The administration of international cultural heritage standards occurs within a Western-dominated bureaucracy in which most of the representatives are state-appointed politicians rather than heritage professionals. While recent efforts seek to increase the representation of non-European sites on World Heritage lists, the assistance of UN experts to non-Western countries has been limited by a desire to avoid conflicts of interests in the site review process (Meskell 2013, 485–488). As a result, the existing international framework is considerably influenced by Western heritage principles (Brohman 1995; Samuels and Lilley 2015; Strasser 2002; Willems 2014:14–15). In recent decades, discomfort regarding the perceived imperialist, neoliberal, and bureaucratic nature of UNESCO heritage scholarship has been an obstacle to anthropological engagement with UNESCO regarding historical sites and cultural heritage topics (Smith 2006; Waterton 2010). While many prominent social scientists of earlier generations were closely involved with the UN, the discipline's ethical discomfort with a Western heritage bureaucracy has resulted in an evaporation of some of the scholarly expertise needed to develop new ways of managing cultural heritage (Meskell 2013).

Despite the misgivings between some academics and the UN network, international organizations play a critical role in protecting cultural heritage through committing their member nations to heightened protection standards. As with national legislation, however, international agreements do not always protect cultural heritage from destruction by private companies. For example, oil and gas development is frequently authorized in World Heritage Sites, and such concessions currently threaten 20% of World Heritage sites in some regions (Osti et al. 2011). In the last 15 years, companies like Shell Oil and Total, along with trade associations like the International Council on Mining and Metals (ICMM) have pledged not to develop in World Heritage sites (Timmons 2003; UNESCO 2016). These pledges highlight an alternative to national and international heritage protection systems: voluntary corporate practices.

Corporate Social Responsibility and Voluntary Practices

Voluntary practices, in which companies choose to meet certain ethical or environmental standards, are rooted in the corporate social responsibility movement that began in the 1950s (Carroll 1999). Corporate social responsibility can refer to any practice perceived to be reducing a company's negative impact or creating positive impacts—such as creating good employment conditions, low environmental impact, health-conscious products, greater social justice, and stronger local communities. Because of the lack of legal structures to ensure compliance, assertions of corporate social responsibility are assessed by a variety of nonprofit and activist groups, frequently including corporate shareholders themselves.

Environmental campaigns appealing to corporate social responsibility have enjoyed some success, particularly in conservation issues across multiple nations or where legal oversight for environmental protections is underdeveloped. At the same time, voluntary practices and disclosures often suffer from a lack of transparency, incomplete reporting, and unclear avenues for filing grievances (Othman and Ameer 2010). In one example, despite their pledge to avoid World Heritage sites, Shell Oil was recently criticized for owning a 50% stake in a liquid natural gas plant project impacting Australia's Great Barrier Reef (Coffey Environments 2012).

Currently, voluntary practices and guidelines for cultural heritage stewardship are much less common than those for environmental topics, but the potential and challenges in these sectors are similar. In an unwelcoming climate for new legislation and regulations, voluntary practices provide an avenue toward greater cultural heritage protections across industries. At present, voluntary standards and practices are emerging from two sources: (1) international development lenders and (2) corporations and trade associations.

Development Banks and Lenders

International development banks and other lenders are potentially an effective source of cultural heritage protection for projects that do not otherwise trigger international or national legal protections by requiring compliance with cultural heritage safeguards as a condition for financing. Developing countries often lack a sufficient government framework for the protection of cultural heritage; even in developing countries with robust legal protections for cultural heritage, adequate enforcement proves challenging (Eboreime 2009; GHF 2010). In borrower countries, lenders may catalyze the development of practices and standards. Lender-driven standards come from international financial organizations such as the World Bank Group (WBG), International Finance Corporation (IFC), the Inter-American Development Bank (IADB), and the International Monetary Fund (IMF).

The World Bank Group is comprised of 188 member countries who collaborate to decrease poverty and promote shared prosperity (World Bank 2016). The World Bank provides financial and technical assistance to developing countries and has recently developed environmental and social safeguards. These policies require that bank-financed projects include an environmental assessment of the risk and likely damage to cultural heritage and an environmental management plan to mitigate or avoid damages. Similar to Section 106 mitigation in the United States, World Bank processes include a consultation process with affected stakeholders. Such safeguards apply to World Bank–financed projects with an explicit heritage focus and others that generally are likely to impact cultural resources (Hankey 1999; Unit for Housing and Urbanization 1999; World Bank 2013). While the World Bank Safeguards have great potential for protecting currently vulnerable heritage, they heavily emphasize economic considerations in their determinations of value and therefore tend to focus more on establishing tourist attractions than on preserving less tangible forms of heritage (Hawkins and Mann 2007; Samuels 2008).

Another major international development lender with environmental sustainability requirements is the Inter-American Development Bank (IDB), which avoids overt orientation towards Western heritage typical of other large international organizations. The IDB seeks to reduce poverty and social inequalities, foster private sector development, and promote regional cooperation by providing loans and technical assistance to Latin American and Caribbean countries. The IDB is committed to socially inclusive, environmentally sustainable development through enforcing safeguards and a commitment not to "support operations that . . .

significantly convert or degrade critical natural habitats or that damage critical cultural sites" (IADB 2006). The IDB emphasizes local definitions of worthy heritage by maintaining a broad concept of cultural sites, including both those acclaimed by national and international governments but also areas recognized as protected by traditional local communities (IADB 2006:16).

While lender standards raise awareness of cultural heritage issues and spur development of national legal frameworks in borrower countries, more can be done. There is currently no organized cultural heritage–focused civil society group regularly engaging with international financial institutions, although the Society for American Archaeology should be applauded for regularly articulating archaeological concerns to the World Bank and IDB. Systematic engagement with these institutions could help reverse archaeological mitigation approaches that emphasize chance finds or salvage archaeology over early-stage planning that could avoid sensitive resources. Civil society organizations could also rally support for political leadership in developing countries, capacity building in developing countries to identify and resolve cultural heritage issues, and accountability mechanisms to ensure that cultural heritage concerns are appropriately addressed on projects.

Corporations and Trade Associations

In the corporate sphere, the growing awareness that companies need a social license to operate and manage risk has encouraged corporation and trade associations to take an active role in the preservation of cultural heritage. Even with full governmental and legal approval, corporations recognize that operating without strong community relations can lead to delays, protests, sabotage, and political challenges that produce financial and logistical damage to company interests. As a result, an increasing number of large corporations employ corporate social responsibility policies to provide internal guidance on their work (Samuels and Lilley 2015; Yates et al. 2013; Hoben et al. 2012).

A leading example of corporate social responsibility in cultural heritage management is Rio Tinto, a major international mining and metals production company. Through its resource guide *Why Cultural Heritage Matters*, Rio Tinto emphasizes the importance of cultural heritage management in its projects (Bradshaw et al. 2011; also see Altschul this volume). Rio Tinto requires significant stakeholder involvement, proper planning, continuous evaluation, and communication throughout a project's life cycle. The results of this cultural heritage commitment have included the development of heritage centers and museums in South Africa, collaborative traditional and scientific monitoring of fish and caribou well-being in the Northwest Territories, and the support of Aboriginal communities throughout Australia through the Rio Tinto Aboriginal Fund. Executives with Rio Tinto recognize a strong business incentive for such programs, which help reinforce community support for Rio Tinto in its areas of operations (Bradshaw et al. 2011).

Trade associations are also significant drivers of voluntary standards. In September 2015, IPIECA, API, and IOGP released their *3rd Edition of Guidance* for the oil and gas industry on voluntary sustainability reporting. The *Guidance* is a collaborative publication by the three largest oil and gas industry associations. The International Petroleum Industry Environmental Conservation Association (IPIECA) is the global oil and gas industry association for environmental and social issues and the lead organization on this Guidance. IPIECA's collective membership accounts for more than half of the world's oil production. The American Petroleum Institute (API) is the voice for America's oil and gas industry. The International Association of Oil & Gas Producers (IOGP), whose members produce more than half of the world's oil and more than a third of its gas, represents the global exploration and production industry. Collectively, these organizations have been publishing sustainability reporting guidance since 2005.

IPIECA's *Guidance* now includes the following reporting requirement when assessing local community impacts: "Describe assessment, consultation and preservation measures with regard to archaeological, historic and cultural sites of affected communities that could be impacted by the company's activities" (IPIECA 2015). This marks the first time that cultural heritage has been part of sustainability guidance for the oil and gas industry.

Public–Private Partnerships and the Emergence of Stakeholder Collaborations

Collaborative archaeological projects involving community-driven research design have become increasingly common since the 1990s but rarely include collaboration or cooperation with the companies whose projects threaten resources or who own the land occupied by heritage resources. To a certain extent, this reflects anthropological skepticism regarding capitalist enterprises and bureaucracy that has also characterized an anthropological withdrawal from UN objectives. However, corporate interests, particularly those associated with energy development, are also stakeholder interests. One way to align corporate social responsibility programs with heritage management and collaborative community archaeology is through public–private partnerships that are well positioned to intercede in spheres where governmental oversight is inadequate.

One prime example of this new collaborative model is Leaders in Energy and Preservation (LEAP). Its mission is to work collaboratively and pragmatically with the preservation community and the energy industry to identify and properly manage historic and cultural resources while encouraging efficient exploration and development of energy reserves. LEAP's board of directors includes representatives from Shell, Hess Corporation, Southwestern Energy, the Society for American Archaeology, and cultural resource management professionals. LEAP was formed initially to address the gap in cultural heritage protections for shale gas development on private lands. The Society for American Archaeology estimates that more than 200,000 heritage sites could be at risk from shale development.

LEAP works collaboratively to develop voluntary practices that can be incorporated into companies' existing business practices. As a result, LEAP's focus is on the planning stage of energy projects, when avoiding cultural resources is least expensive and least likely to cause delays to projects. A chief focus of LEAP's work is to identify challenges to cultural heritage protection in this sector and develop tools that will provide critical information about cultural resources to early-stage energy planners. For example, no national GIS database exists for energy companies to access information to help plan their projects in ways that limit impacts to historic and cultural resources. Rather, accessing spatial information about heritage resources is time consuming and challenging, with important data housed in multiple repositories or under restricted access. Available data is significantly incomplete because most of the United States has never been archaeologically surveyed.

To address these challenges, LEAP proposes to catalyze development of a national GIS-based screening tool that would allow energy companies to access critical information early in the planning process to help them manage risk from inadvertent disturbance of historic and cultural resources. This screening tool will use a predictive model to show areas where risk to cultural resource impacts is high, medium, or low, allowing planning in lowest-risk areas—or, if such planning is not possible, allowing for early development of risk-management plans (GAPP 2015). Once areas are slated for development, LEAP's site sensitivity tool can help energy companies understand which resources warrant preservation. The sensitivity score will inform company personnel when additional consultation with heritage professionals is required. LEAP has also developed a user guide that educates energy company personnel about cultural resources risk and also includes a chance-finds procedure, should sites be discovered after early-stage planning. The goal is to help energy companies avoid cultural resources and, when they are unavoidable, handle issues in a respectful way.

Recommendations for Future Progress

There are several potential avenues for innovative collaborations and approaches to heritage management outside the legal framework.

1. First, historical and archaeological academic and professional associations should unify to develop a preservation constituency that will advocate to key international players and provide expert guidance regarding best practices. Advocacy must also include proactive analysis of the practice of the many governmental, development bank, and voluntary corporate heritage projects operating worldwide.
2. Awareness must be raised within stakeholder groups involved in nongovernmental corporate practices. Local communities impacted by developments are often unaware of the collective influence they have in development areas or do not know how to navigate large corporate bureaucracies to get their interests heard. Multinational companies must be educated regarding the importance of adding cultural heritage guidance to their corporate social responsibility practices.

3. Partnerships between scholars, corporations, and governmental bodies should create tools that simplify understanding of cultural heritage impacts for corporations interested in avoiding significant sites and districts. It is easier for corporations to include cultural heritage protection and mitigation as standard elements of risk management than to deal with last-minute, costly obstacles when unexpected issues arise.

Community development projects like Statoil's Akassa project in Bayelsa State are accepted as successful best practices—even by skeptics of corporate social responsibility—because they have spent a considerable amount of time within local communities to identify regional needs, and they allow project outcomes to be substantially determined from local priorities (Frynas 2005:593–594). Voluntary cultural heritage practices and public–private partnerships provide both a risk and a potential improvement to heritage stewardship, and active participation by cultural heritage advocates is essential to closing the gap between responsible development and cultural heritage protection. Future developments in international heritage depend on flexibility within a variety of heritage management frameworks, increased collaboration and connectivity between heritage organizations, and willingness for heritage projects to be driven and led by local heritage practitioners and community members.

References

Advisory Council for Historic Preservation 2013 Section 106 Regulations Summary. Electronic document, www.achp.gov/106summary.html., accessed April 28, 2017.

Bradshaw, E., K. Bryant, T. Cohen, D. Brereton, J. Kim, K. Gillespie, and I. Lilley 2011 *Why Cultural Heritage Matters—A Resource Guide for Integrating Cultural Heritage Management into Communities Work at Rio Tinto*. Rio Tinto, Melbourne.

Brohman, J. 1995 Universalism, Eurocentrism, and Ideological Bias in Development Studies: From Modernisation to Neoliberalism. *Third World Quarterly* 16(1):121–140.

Carroll, A. B. 1999 Corporate Social Responsibility: Evolution of a Definitional Construct. *Business and Society* 38(3):268–295.

Coffey Environments 2012 Environmental Impact Statement: Arrow LNG Plant. Electronic document, http://eisdocs.dsdip.qld.gov.au/Shell Australia LNG (aka Arrow LNG Plant)/EIS/EIS Apr 2012/eis-01-introduction.pdf, accessed April 28, 2017.

Desilver, D. 2015 Congress's Productivity Improves Somewhat in 2015. Pew Research Center, December. Electronic document, www.pewresearch.org/fact-tank/2015/12/29/congress-productivity-improves-somewhat-in-2015/, accessed April 28, 2017.

Eboreime, J. 2009 Challenges of Heritage Management in Africa. In *Cultural Heritage and the Law: Protecting Immovable Heritage in English-Speaking Countries of Sub-Saharan Africa*, edited by W. Ndoro, A. Mumma, and G. Abungu, pp. 1–7. International Center for the Study of the Preservation and Restoration of Cultural Property, Rome.

Frynas, J. G. 2005 The False Developmental Promise of Corporate Social Responsibility: Evidence from Multinational Oil Companies. *International Affairs* 81(3):581–598.

Gas and Preservation Partnership (GAPP; now Leaders in Energy and Preservation). 2015 A National Screening Tool for Energy Projects. Unpublished Report on file.

Global Heritage Fund 2010 *Saving Our Vanishing Heritage: Safeguarding Endangered Cultural Heritage Sites in the Developing World*. Global Heritage Fund, San Francisco.

Hankey, D. 1999 Case Study Lahore, Pakistan: Conservation of the Walled City. South Asia. Washington, DC. Electronic document, http://www-wds.worldbank.org/external/default/WDSContentServer/WDSP/IB/1999/09/14/000094946_99052608150268/Rendered/PDF/multi_page.pdf, accessed April 28, 2017.

Hawkins, D. E., and S. Mann 2007 The World Bank's Role in Tourism Development. *Annals of Tourism Research* 34(2):359–361.

Hoben, M., D. Kovick, D. Plumb, and J. Wright 2012 *Corporate and Community Engagement in the Niger Delta: Lessons Learned from Chevron Nigeria Limited's GMOU Process*. Consensus Building Institute, Cambridge.

IADB 2006 Environment and Safeguards Compliance Policy.

IPIECA 2015 Sustainability Reporting Guidance for the Oil and Gas Industry, 3rd edition. Electronic document, www.ipieca.org/resources/good-practice/oil-and-gas-industry-guidance-on-voluntary-sustainability-reporting-3rd-edition/, accessed April 27, 2016.

Layton, L. 2008 Sites in National Forests at Grave Risk, Study by Preservation Group Indicates. *The Washington Post*, May 15.

Meskell, L. 2013 UNESCO's World Heritage Convention at 40: Challenging the Economic and Political Order of International Heritage Conservation. *Current Anthropology* 54(4):484.

National Park Service 2016 Section 110 of the National Historic Preservation Act. National Park Service Federal Preservation Institute. Electronic document, www.nps.gov/fpi/Section110.html, accessed April 28, 2017.

National Trust for Historic Preservation 2016 Federal Public Land Managing Agencies. National Trust for Historic Preservation. Electronic document, www.preservationnation.org/information-center/saving-a-place/public-lands/federal-agencies.html, accessed April 28, 2017.

Osti, M., L. Coad, J. B. Fisher, B. Bomhard, and J. M. Hutton 2011 Oil and Gas Development in the World Heritage and Wider Protected Area Network in Sub-Saharan Africa. *Biodiversity & Conservation* 20(9):1863–1877.

Othman, R., and R. Ameer 2010 Environmental Disclosures of Palm Oil Plantation Companies in Malaysia: A Tool for Stakeholder Engagement. *Corporate Social Responsibility and Environmental Management* 17:52–62.

Preserve America 2011 Report on the Progress of Identification, Protection, Enhancement, and Use of Historic Properties. Presented to the Advisory Council on Historic Preservation in fulfillment of Section 3 of Executive Order No. 13287. Electronic document, www.achp.gov/section3reports/2011/Preserve%20America%20Final.pdf.

Samuels, K. L. 2008 Value and Significance in Archaeology. Archaeology of Europe. *The 2007 EAA Archaeological Dialogues Forum* 15(1):71–97. doi: 10.1017/S1380203808002535

Samuels, K. L., and I. Lilley 2015 Transnationalism and Heritage Development. In *Global Heritage: A Reader*, edited by L. Meskell, pp. 217–239. John Wiley & Sons, Oxford.

Sebastian, L., and W. D. Lipe 2010 *Archaeology & Cultural Resource Management: Visions for the Future*. School for Advanced Research Press, Santa Fe.

Smith, L. 2006 *Uses of Heritage*. Routledge, London.

Squillace, M. 2003 The Monumental Legacy of the Antiquities Act of 1906. *Georgia Law Review* 37:473–610.

Strasser, P. 2002 'Putting Reform into Action'—Thirty Years of the World Heritage Convention: How to Reform Without Changing Its Regulations. *International Journal of Cultural Property* 11(2):215–266.

Timmons, H. 2003 Shell to Avoid Oil Drilling At Sites Listed By Unesco—NYTimes.com. *New Literary History*, August 31.

UNESCO 2016 UNESCO World Heritage Centre—Cement Giant Vows to Respect World Heritage in Joint Effort with IUCN and UNESCO. Electronic document, http://whc.unesco.org/en/news/1490, accessed April 29, 2017.

———. 2007 Database of National Cultural Heritage Laws. Electronic document, www.unesco.org/culture/natlaws/, accessed April 28, 2017.

Unit for Housing and Urbanization 1999 Case Study: Fez, Morocco—Rehabilitation of the Fez Medina. Electronic document, http://documents.worldbank.org/curated/en/1999/05/440861/case-study-fez-morocco-rehabilitation-fez-medina, accessed April 28, 2017 Waterton, E. 2010 *Politics, Policy, and the Discourses of Heritage*. Palgrave Macmillan, Hampshire.

Willems, J. H. W. 2014 The Future of World Heritage and the Emergence of Transnational Heritage Regimes. *Heritage & Society* 7(2):105–120.

World Bank 2016 Organization. Electronic document, www.worldbank.org/en/about/leadership, accessed April 28, 2017.

———. 2013 Q&A: Aynak and Mining in Afghanistan. Electronic document, www.worldbank.org/en/news/feature/2013/04/02/qa-aynak-mining-afghanistan, accessed April 28, 2017.

Yates, B. F., and C. L. Horvath 2013 Social License to Operate: How to Get It, and How to Keep It. Report prepared for Pacific Energy Summit 2013, manuscript on file.

15
HERITAGE, CLIMATE CHANGE, AND ADAPTATION PLANNING

Diane L. Douglas

Introduction

Climate change adaptation refers to the need for societies impacted by climate change to modify architecture and land-use practices in order to minimize the impact of future climate-induced disasters. This chapter reviews the importance of considering heritage resources in adaptation planning for three reasons:

1. The intrinsic value of tangible heritage resources in providing an enduring sense of community and a sense of identity in day-to-day life and contributing to the psychosocial well-being of survivors of climate-induced natural disasters;
2. The greater suitability of traditional architecture and traditional agricultural practices in creating resilience to climate-induced disasters, and
3. The value of indigenous knowledge in the identification of local ecological conditions that forewarn of impending climate-induced disaster risks and strategies to mitigate the impacts of these disasters.

Other contributors to this volume discuss related issues such as improving resilience to climate change by linking mitigation and adaptation measures with other social measures (see Fleming this volume); enhancing social cohesion and preservation of cultural heritage by fully involving indigenous communities in management of heritage they associate with (see Altschul, Yu this volume); garnering cultural pride among indigenous groups by fully engaging them as managers of their tangible and intangible heritage resources (see Stone, Watkins this volume); and reducing trauma associated with climate change–induced disasters by recognizing and valuing intangible heritage and traditional knowledge (see Chilton this volume).

What Are Heritage Resources?

Heritage resources reflect the ingenuity, inspiration, and imagination of humanity. Our heritage is expressed in a multitude of ways, from historical buildings, structures, and monuments to fine artifacts and paintings housed in museums; from cultural landscapes that reflect important historical themes in a region (e.g., Alto Douro Wine Region, Portugal) to historic industrial landscapes (e.g., Blaenavon Industrial Landscape, South Wales, UK; Falune Mine, Sweden) and historic cities (e.g., Melaka and George Town, Straits of Malacca, Malaysia; Historic City Centre of Kraków, Poland), as well as archaeological sites (e.g., Historic Sanctuary of Machu Picchu, Peru; Ban Chiang Archaeological Site, Thailand; and the Lascaux and Chauvet caves, France). All of these are inscribed on the United Nations Educational, Scientific and Cultural Organization (UNESCO) World Heritage List (WHL) for their outstanding universal value and meeting at least one of ten criteria required for inscription (UNESCO 2016). The majority of heritage sites are not inscribed on the WHL but have tremendous significance to local communities, and indeed nations. Locally significant sites can range from places of worship to historical government buildings or houses that belonged to community founders. Traditional gathering places such as historical pubs, town squares, and fountains can be imprinted on the minds and hearts of several generations as signature places that provide them with a sense of community and identity.

Heritage Resources and Community Resilience

Cultural heritage is not static but rather forms part of a living, breathing memory. From grandiose historical buildings to places of religious worship, town squares, and museums, tangible heritage resources reflect the lives and cultural identity of a community. For generations, people may gather in these places for national holidays or participate in important celebrations that bind us together, such as weddings, graduations, funerals, and historic events. These celebrations form a living memory shared from generation to generation and help bind a community together. The sense of shared identity provided by these places often serves as an allurement during or following natural disasters, perhaps in part because they reflect the resilience of humanity. Centers of culture that survive earthquakes, floods, and fires during previous generations perhaps give strength and hope to people who are traumatized by devastation and loss. For this reason alone, locally significant heritage resources should be protected from climate change. The fact that these resources have stood the test of time, remaining standing through previous natural disasters, should also not be lost upon engineers and planners. The traditional knowledge woven into the fabric of these structures may be harnessed and used in modern building designs and construction techniques that are better suited to the unique environmental and climate conditions in which this knowledge evolved.

The importance of tapping into the traditional knowledge often held by indigenous or local elders, craftsmen and -women, hunters, fishermen, and traditional healers has long been recognized by international financial institutions (IFI) like the World Bank Group that are vested in the sustainable development of nations. IFIs encourage governments, private enterprise and nongovernmental organizations (NGOs) to consult with indigenous peoples and local communities to identify issues and resources of local importance and help ensure these resources are considered in project designs and protected to the greatest degree possible.

More recently, UNESCO, the International Federation of Red Cross (IFRC), the United Nations International Strategy for Disaster Reduction (UNISDR) (Adger et al. 2013; IFRC 2014; Jigasu 2014; Nakashima et al. 2012; Vize and Seng 2013) have encouraged governments, private enterprise, and NGOs to work with indigenous peoples to identify and reintroduce traditional adaptive strategies and traditional technologies that were suppressed and/or supplanted during colonization and postcolonial assimilation and integration. Many working in the arena of disaster risk reduction (DRR) and climate change adaptation (CCA) recognize that resilience is best built at the local level; thus knowledge of local ecological systems and how they respond to varying climate stresses is critical.

Climate Change Risks to Heritage

Climate change is one of the most important and dangerous issues facing us today. For more than 20 years, scientists have argued that anthropogenic greenhouse gas (GHG) emissions and land use practices are the primary driving mechanism for extreme climate events observed worldwide since 1990. The widespread belief that CO_2 emissions from cars, industry, and tilling soil, combined with clear-cutting forests, are the primary causes of climate change is largely based on technical reports prepared by the Intergovernmental Panel of Climate Change (IPCC), an advisory body to the United Nations Climate Change Commission (UNFCCC). The IPCC reports synthesize scientific research by the world's leading climate and environmental scientists investigating how people are influencing global climate change patterns.

The IPCC reports indicate that anthropogenic GHGs are increasing the percentage of CO_2 in the atmosphere, which is warming the atmosphere at a faster rate than would occur under natural conditions (Forster et al. 2007; Jansen et al. 2007; Randall et al. 2007; Solomon et al. 2007). The reports state that if anthropogenic emissions of GHGs are not reduced and maintained at levels predating 1990, the earth could warm by up to 6.4°C by 2099 CE (Common Era), with an average estimate of 2.5°C (IPCC 2007:13, Table SPM3). In conjunction with the global rise in temperature, a 0.18 to 0.59 m (0.65 to 3.12 ft.) rise in sea level is estimated, associated with the expansion of oceans due to higher global temperatures (IPCC 2007:13, Table SPM3). Warming of 3 to 5°C in polar latitudes by 2099 would replicate temperatures that occurred during the last interglacial period, around 125,000 years ago (IPCC 2007:9). Sea level during this period was 4 to 6 meters higher than present (IPCC 2007:9). Clearly, a sea level rise of 6 m would devastate most coastal cities, inundate many coastal UNESCO WHL sites (e.g., Robben Island, South Africa), drastically change the ecosystem of coastal natural heritage sites (e.g., Galápagos Islands, Ecuador), and affect settlement and subsistence practices of communities reliant on marine and estuarine resources.

Familiar impacts of climate change through news reports include powerful and destructive storms, devastating droughts, and destructive wildfires. More subtle impacts, studied by scientists but less well reported, are the extinction of certain flora and fauna and a shift of others to higher latitudes and altitudes (e.g., Bradford and Warren 2014), including invasive species (e.g., Gonzalez-Muñoz et al. 2014). Changes in the distribution of species, especially the spread of invasives, can do irreparable damage to natural and cultural heritage sites. This also impacts the availability and abundance of species and natural resources (e.g., game, medicinal plants) important to cultural groups. New vectors (e.g., termites, see Tobin et al. 2014) that adversely affect natural and cultural heritage resources are also migrating to higher altitudes and latitudes. In addition to terrestrial impacts, changes in ocean temperatures are affecting the distribution of marine resources needed for subsistence. Table 15.1 provides examples of climate change effects to natural and cultural heritage resources and traditional cultural knowledge/practices. It is important to remember that for every tangible heritage resource lost (natural and cultural) to climate change, individuals and communities with ties to those resources often experience a deep sense of loss.

TABLE 15.1 Climate Change Impacts on Heritage Resources

Climate Condition	Climate Impacts	
	Tangible Heritage	*Intangible Heritage*
Oceanic impacts Sea level rise Saltwater intrusion into groundwater from rising sea level Changing oceanic currents from changes in temperature and salinity Changes in seasonality and distribution of sea ice	Loss of coastal sites from erosion, inundation Damage to natural heritage sites from topographic and ecosystem ecology changes Changing pH of buried coastal archaeological resources Physical changes to porous building materials, foundations of historic structures	Changes in coastal ecology—e.g., marshes traditionally exploited for flora and fauna, will change resource availability and abundance, affecting traditional economies and social networks, loss of rituals and ceremonies.
GHG emission impacts CO_2 increasing acidity of ocean SO_2 and NO_x causing acid rain	Changes in pH resulting in corrosion of metals and historic buildings/monuments (e.g., porous stone and brick)	Changes in distribution of marine life will change resource availability and abundance, affecting traditional economies and social networks.

(*Continued*)

TABLE 15.1 (Continued)

Climate Condition	Climate Impacts	
	Tangible Heritage	Intangible Heritage
Weather extremes More frequent and more intense typhoons, hurricanes, monsoons, El Niño events, flooding More frequent stationary low pressure systems causing intensive flooding in previously semiarid and arid regions Spread of vectors (e.g., termites) to northerly latitudes Increased seasonal temperature variance Increased aridity/ desertification	Weather changes impact archaeological sites, historical buildings, monuments, including destruction by flood/erosion/landslides, new vectors damage buildings, and increased aridity cracks structures, facades, murals, paintings.	Changes in distribution of traditional flora/fauna affect traditional subsistence strategies, ceremonies and rituals. Traditional architecture designed for historic conditions affected new climate conditions, requiring adopting new technologies/loss of traditional architecture.
Thawing permafrost	Subsoil instability, ground heave and subsidence Loss of Inuit village sites and burial grounds Loss of natural heritage sites	Changes in ground stability, surface water flows; Arctic communities must relocate/migrate to greater distances from traditional resources. Loss of Inuit burial grounds and villages in Arctic contributes to sense of loss, social-psychological stress.

Heritage, Climate Change, and Planning for Resilience

The IPCC estimates of climate change that will occur by 2100 would have devastating global impacts from reduced food security and insufficient potable water. Millions of people in low-lying coastal communities and along rivers affected by sea level and tidal surges will need either to move to higher ground, adopt new technologies to raise houses and other buildings above water levels, or build protective infrastructure (e.g., dikes and berms). In an effort to help governments plan for climate change impacts and other types of disasters (e.g., earthquakes and tsunamis), in 2005, the UNISDR began holding World Conferences on disaster risk reduction (DRR). In 2011, 2013, and 2015, the International Council for Monuments and Sites (ICOMOS), International Scientific Committee (ISC) for Risk Preparedness

(ICORP), participated in the UNISDR World Conferences on DRR in an effort to raise awareness of the role that heritage can play in building resilience to climate change (e.g., Jigasu et al. 2013). Through the efforts of ICOMOS/ICORP and several others (e.g., UNESCO, International Centre for the Study of the Preservation and Restoration of Cultural Property [ICCROM], UNISDR, Blue Cross Blue Shield, etc.), cultural heritage resources were recognized in the Sendai Framework for DRR 2015–2030. Through this framework, the UNISDR encourages all governments (local to national) to evaluate how traditional cultural knowledge contributes to building resilience in their community or nation (UNISDR 2015:Article 24(i)). The Sendai Framework is a 15-year voluntary, nonbinding agreement for local governments, the private sector, and other stakeholders to help national governments reduce disaster risk. The framework further acknowledges the need to consider tangible cultural heritage in DRR planning, stipulating that governments and agencies should "[p]rotect or support the protection of cultural and collecting institutions and other sites of historical, cultural heritage and religious interest" (UNISDR 2015:Article 30(d)).

At the highest level of international governance, the Sendai Framework provides guidance for governments to consult with local communities and indigenous groups to identify their concerns regarding climate change as well as actively engage them in planning for resilience. Other international organizations (e.g., UNESCO, ICOMOS, ICCROM) work with local communities and conduct trainings and workshops with government agencies, educational institutions, and private enterprise to "mainstream heritage in disaster risk management and development sectors for effective mitigation, response and recovery actions before, during and after disasters" (Jigasu 2014:41). The Making Cities Resilient Campaign, led by the UNISDR and supported by multiple partners, also promulgates the consideration of heritage resources and local knowledge in DRR planning (UNISDR 2016).

Successful DRR planning identifies the potential risks of natural disasters caused by geologic forces (e.g., earthquakes, rockslides, tsunamis, etc.) and climate-induced disasters (drought, flooding, tornadoes, hurricanes, typhoons, etc.) impacting a community's critical infrastructure (e.g., hospitals, schools, roads, utilities, dams, etc.). As encouraged by the UNISDR and some emergency management agencies (e.g., Federal Emergency Management Agency, USA), heritage resources should be incorporated into DRR plans. Through tourism, World Heritage List–inscribed resources and locally significant heritage resources can contribute significantly to the economy and provide a sense of cultural identity and, if protected, can serve as places of refuge during disaster recovery and response. More recently, the UNISDR has encouraged governments to incorporate climate change adaptation (CCA) in their DRR plans. Researchers and planners have found that traditional ecological knowledge (TEK), as well as traditional architecture can contribute to CCA and DRR.

A critical measure in incorporating heritage resources and TEK into disaster-resilient development planning is involving local community groups (e.g., elderly, women's groups, men's groups) as well as local heritage professionals (museums, archives, archaeologists, historians; see for example Altschul this volume). While the environmental and social laws and regulations of many countries often require stakeholder consultation as a part of development planning, this is often not participatory. In other words, while community members and local experts may be provided an opportunity to comment on projects, they are not invited to the planning table. Often, community and stakeholder comments are addressed in an addendum to development plans and environmental reports but not incorporated into the body of the plan or report. As a result, important insights these groups or individuals might contribute to make a development plan more resilient are not shared with the planning committee.

Further to development planning, an important aspect to be considered by the ministries of agriculture, forestry, fisheries, and water resources globally is consideration of TEK in resource and land-use plans. Indigenous groups who have been living in an environment for generations and often relying on natural landscape and ocean resources for survival have an intimate knowledge of species ecology and know how to interpret environmental stress based on natural signs (e.g., Huntington 2000; see Watkins this volume). These insights can be used by planners and resource managers to identify sustainable measures for CCA (e.g., Ford et al. 2006; Naumann et al. 2013).

Traditional Knowledge and Climate Change Adaptation

Several previous investigations have identified the ingenious ways that traditional cultural and technology help make communities resilient to climate change. There are too many examples of how TEK has contributed to the resilience of communities worldwide to discuss here (e.g., Adger et al. 2013; Ford et al. 2006; Leonard et al. 2013, etc.). Table 15.2 provides a summary of the results of some of these

TABLE 15.2 Cultural Adaptive Strategies to Climate Change

Climate Impact	Cultural Adaptive Strategy	Citation
Studies summarized from Shaw and Baumwoll 2008.		
River flooding and erosion	To reduce flood impacts, Gifu Prefecture in Japan continues to build traditional ring dykes (Waju) to protect houses and cultivated land. Special village committees maintain ring dykes, which strengthens community ties. Raised houses (Mizuya) store important belongings above flood zones. The hijiri-ushi, an ox-bow looking structure traditionally made of wood and more recently of concrete, is placed at key points along the river to minimize erosion during flood events.	Takeuchi, Yukiko, and Rajib Shaw 2008

Climate Impact	Cultural Adaptive Strategy	Citation
River flooding	In eastern Terai of Nepal and Chitral District of Pakistan, people reduce impacts of flooding on traditional communities by piling mud against the walls of their buildings/structures and constructing flood-control fences of bamboo and mud, and elevated platforms and storage areas to protect food, important belongings, livestock, and people.	Dekens, J., 2008.
Mudslides and landslides	In the Bardiya, Chitwan, Syangja, and Tanahu Districts of Nepal, traditional methods to protect villages from landslides and mudslides include building stone walls and/or planting shrubs to stabilize the slopes above the villages. For greater food security, a mixed variety of crops is planted in different microclimates to help ensure success of at least some of the crops during extreme climate events.	Thapa, Man B., Youba Raj Luintel, Bhupendra Gauchan and Kiran Amaty 2008.
Seasonal drought	The Karez irrigation system in Northwestern China is a proven and effective indigenous drought-reduction technology that is still in use. Irrigation canals are excavated through sandstone several meters below the ground surface to carry water from the highlands to the lowlands. Gravity irrigation brings water to agricultural fields and settlements. Underground canals prevent evaporation and provide a steady water supply to this traditionally dry region.	Fang, Weihua, Fei He, Jingning Cai and Peijun Shi 2008
High winds and typhoons	In the Batanes region of the Philippines, unique traditional house architecture is of stone instead of wood, bamboo, and nipa palm thatch. Ivatan homes are built with limestone walls 2 to 4 feet thick and roofed with layers of reeds and cogon grass. The windward wall is windowless, and the remaining walls are narrow built. These structures withstand typhoons and are built using locally available materials.	Uy, Noralene and Rajib Shaw 2008.

(*Continued*)

TABLE 15.2 (Continued)

Climate Impact	Cultural Adaptive Strategy	Citation
Selected samples of traditional knowledge and CCA from other sources		
Drought and water stress from industrial development	Traditional agricultural practices in the Sudano-Sahelian region of southeastern Senegal help people respond to short-term periods of drought as well as to maximize crop production for food security. A wide variety of crops are planted in rotation to take advantage of seasonal rains. Lower river terrace farming takes advantage of floodwater recession; dry farming on colluvial slopes relies on rains. Farming at the toeslopes relies on rainfall and runoff accumulation at the base. Traditional farming tools are used to minimize erosion. Goats and sheep graze shrubs and lower branches of trees to create light for crops grown in forested areas, and they provide protein. Traditional social networks and farming practices help ensure food security for the entire community.	Douglas, D., J. Homburg and M. Vendrig 2017
Drought impacts on agriculture	In the Sahel, farmers rotate crops and plant at different times based on local predictions of climate and cultural models of weather. Adaptation strategies include the use of emergency fodder during droughts, multispecies composition of herds to survive climate extremes, and culling of weak livestock for food. Pastoralists' nomadic mobility reduces the pressure on low-carrying-capacity grazing areas through circular movement from dry northern areas to moist southern areas.	Nyong A., F. Adesina, B. Osman Elasha 2007

studies and demonstrates the range of traditional knowledge/technology that can be either sustained or adopted to create resilience. In some regions, communities have implemented climate-resilient technology for generations and continue to do so. Elsewhere, traditional technologies that had been adapted to climate stresses were lost during colonization and assimilation (e.g., Peruvian highland agriculture, Raymondi et al. 2012) and needed to be reintroduced to reduce local vulnerability to climate change risks.

The Sri Lanka Case: Traditional Water Conservation and Farming Technology

Over the generations, traditional Sri Lankans devised a way to conduct large-scale irrigation, including irrigating hilly areas, help keep wildlife outside villages, and capture sediment before it enters irrigation networks (Bandara and Madduma 2008). To accomplish this, a series of water tanks was built in different geographic settings with specific functions. To reduce human–animal conflict, Sri Lankans built water tanks in forested areas to provide water for wildlife so that animals would not venture into the village for water during dry years. In dry regions, the people constructed large reservoirs to capture rainwater that could be used during the dry season and developed a 'cascade system' of irrigation technology in the dry zone. For several generations, they have maintained a system of 'small-tank' irrigation technology that is a signature feature of the "undulating landscapes of the North Central, North Western, and southern Regions" of Sri Lanka (Bandara and Madduma2008:68–72). Bandara and Madduma (2008) note that this irrigation system is an important part of Sri Lankan cultural identity, and the tanks (Wewa), rice fields (Wela), and religious monuments (Dagaba) form a well-known cultural trinity.

In recent years, traditional agricultural practices have come under threat in Sri Lanka as a result of poor land-use management, resulting in deforestation, runoff, and erosion resulting in oversiltation of irrigation networks. Changes in the nation's economic objectives and a breakdown in the old social order have thus degraded the environment, creating stresses on biodiversity, diminished water quality for consumption, a reduction in water conserved for use in the country's dry zone, and reduced capacity for small-tank hydraulic irrigation of rice fields. All of these impacts can be mitigated by adopting different environmental, forestry, and agricultural policies, as well as land-use management plans that minimize risk to forest and water resources. If these policies included aspects of the country's old social order and traditional technologies for managing forests, water, and agriculture, Sri Lanka could revitalize its culture while enhancing agricultural productivity and managing its biodiversity for future generations.

Highland Agriculture Case: Reinvigorating Incan Agricultural Technology

The highlands of South America experience climate extremes that challenge productive agriculture. Prior to Spanish conquest, however, the Incas devised ingenious irrigation agriculture that helped their civilization thrive in the extreme mountain environment. The Incan Waru Waru agricultural methods rely on raised soil platforms surrounded by canals. Water in the canals helps to moderate temperature and protect the crops from frost damage and the cold nighttime temperatures of the High Andes as well as provide moisture during periods of drought (Raymondi et al. 2012). Seasonally, nutrient-rich sediment from the canals was used to fertilize the raised soil platforms, helping ensure a rich harvest. The Incas also grew more than 2,700 varieties of potatoes, with different varieties grown in different microclimates on the mountains. This wide variety of food crops grown at different elevations and varying aspects (east-, west-, north-, or south-facing slopes), helped ensure that at least some of the crops would succeed if others failed due to extreme climate events. Harvests were shared, enhancing food security. In addition to this, group construction and maintenance of the Waru Waru canal systems provided an opportunity for communities to create strong social networks.

The comprehensive irrigation systems of the Inca were lost after Spanish conquest, and during more recent assimilation into a global market economy, many farmers stopped growing the hundreds of potato varieties that they had depended on traditionally, only farming a few potato varieties for sale at market. The Agriculture Network Organization (2011) explained that the commercialization of farming in Peru encouraged the introduction of high-yielding varieties and the use of agrochemicals to protect them from pests. This process has not only led to the loss of genetic diversity but reduced pesticide resistance of crops. In addition farmers have also been confronted with health problems associated with use of toxic pesticides (see Osorio and Travaglini 1999:58). Abandoning ancient technical and social methods of controlling the way resources are used has also contributed to soil erosion, overgrazing, and firewood shortage. Having to face the various challenges that put the sustainability of their production systems at stake, farmers have been forced to find new ways out of their environmental and economic problems (Agricultures Network Organization 2011).

With the impacts of climate change and the market-driven reduction in the varieties of potatoes farmed, many Peruvians lost their food security, and childhood malnutrition became a serious threat. In the early 1990s, scientists and NGOs began working with the Quechua people to revitalize traditional farming and increase food security in the region. The International Potato Center (ICP) and NGO ANDES began working with Quechua people in the Cuzco Region to reintroduce more than 400 varieties of potato that had been stored in seed banks for 50 years (Anstett 2015). Old social networks are being revitalized, and communities living at different altitudes are exploring the variety of potatoes and other vegetables that can be grown successfully within different microclimate niches. Farmer groups working in the highlands can rely upon farmers in the lowlands (and vice versa) to help support their families if their crops fail due to climate stress: in this way, communities across ecological zones are working together to build resilience to climate change.

Conclusion

Indigenous and other traditional communities can achieve greater resilience to climate change and potentially help the community at large through identification and protection of heritage resources that are important to them and engaging in the management of these resources. In conjunction with this process, TEK should be identified that can be tapped to enhance food and water security as well as make communities safer from flood risks and other climate-induced disasters. Conceivably, cultural pride may be enhanced and traditional knowledge passed on to youth, better ensuring survival of this knowledge over time.

References

Adger, W. N, J. Barnett, K. Brown, N. Marshal, and K. O'Brien 2013 Cultural Dimensions of Climate Change Impacts and Adaptation. *Nature Climate Change* (3):112–117. doi: 10.1038/NCLIMATE1666.

Agricultures Network Organization 2011 Peru Programme. Electronic document, www.agriculturesnetwork.org/magazines/global/finding-common-ground/peru-programme, accessed April 11, 2016.

Anstett, S. 2015 The Potato Park: Indigenous Knowledge and Agricultural Success in Peru. Electronic document, http://innovatedevelopment.org/2015/07/13/the-potato-park-indigenous-knowledge-and-agricultural-success-in-peru, accessed April 11, 2016.

Bandara, C. M. Maddduma 2008 Village Tank Cascade Systems: A Traditional Approach to Drought Mitigation and Rural Well-being in the Purana Villages of Sri Lanka. In *Indigenous Knowledge for Disaster Risk Reduction: Good Practices and Lessons Learned from Experiences in the Asia-Pacific Region*, edited by Rajib Shaw, Noralene Uy, and Jennifer Baumwoll, pp. 68–72. UNISDR, Geneva, Switzerland.

Bradford, M. A., and R. J. Warren II 2014 Terrestrial Biodiversity and Climate Change. In *Global Environmental Change*, edited by Bill Freedman, pp. 355–361. Springer Science and Business Media. Dordrecht, Netherlands. doi: 10.1007/978-94-007-5784-4_13.

Dekens, Julie 2008 Local Knowledge on Flood Preparedness: Examples from Nepal and Pakistan. In *Indigenous Knowledge for Disaster Risk Reduction: Good Practices and Lessons Learned from Experiences in the Asia-Pacific Region*, edited by Rajib Shaw, Noralene Uy, and Jennifer Baumwoll, pp. 35–40. UN/ISDR, Geneva, Switzerland.

Douglas, Diane L., Jeffrey Homburg and Mark Vendrig ca. 2017 Agricultural Sustainability in the Sudano-Sahelian Region: Climate Change and the Application of Traditional Knowledge to Enhance Agricultural Productivity and Sustainable Development. In *Proceedings of the 13th Congress-PanAfrican Archaeological Association for Prehistory and Related Studies-PAA 20th Meeting-Society of Africanist Archaeologists-SFA Preserving African Cultural Heritage UCAD II, University Cheikh Anta Diop, Dakar, Senegal, November 1–7, 2010*, edited by Ibrahima Thiaw and Homody Bocoum, pp. 475–486. MÉMOIRES DE L'IFAN—C. A. DIOP, No. 93, Dakar, Senegal, 2017.

Fang, Weihua, Fei He, Jingning Cai and Peijun Shi 2008 Karez Technology for Drought Disaster Reduction in China. In *Indigenous Knowledge for Disaster Risk Reduction: Good Practices and Lessons Learned from Experiences in the Asia-Pacific Region*, edited by Rajib Shaw, Noralene Uy, and Jennifer Baumwoll, pp. 1–4. UN/ISDR, Geneva, Switzerland.

Ford, James, Tristan Pearce, Barry Smit, Johanna Wandel, Mishak Allurat, Kik Shappa, Harry Ittusujurat, and Kevin Qrunnut 2006 Reducing Vulnerability to Climate Change in the Arctic: The Case of Nunavut, Canada. *Arctic* 60(2):150–166.

Forster, P., V. Ramaswamy, P. Artaxo, T. Berntsen, R. Betts, D. W. Fahey, J. Haywood, J. Lean, D. C. Lowe, G. Myhre, J. Nganga, R. Prinn, G. Raga, M. Schulz, and R. Van Dorland 2007 Changes in Atmospheric Constituents and in Radiative Forcing. In *Climate Change 2007: The Physical Science Basis. Contribution of Working Group I to the Fourth Assessment Report of the Intergovernmental Panel on Climate Change*, edited by S. Solomon, D. Qin, M. Manning, Z. Chen, M. Marquis, K. B. Averyt, M. Tignor, and H. L. Miller. Cambridge University Press, Cambridge.

Gonzalez-Muñoz, N., J. C. Linares, P. Castro-Diez, and U. Saas-Klaassen 2014. Predicting Climate Change Impacts on Native and Invasive Tree Species Using Radial Growth and Twenty-First Century Climate Scenarios. *European Journal of Forest Research* 133(6):1073–1086.

Huntington, Henry P. 2000 Using Traditional Ecological Knowledge in Science: Methods and Applications. *Ecological Applications* 10(5):1270–1274.Intergovernmental Panel on Climate Change 2007 *Climate Change 2007: Synthesis Report. Contribution of Working Groups I, II and III to the Fourth Assessment Report of the Intergovernmental Panel on Climate Change*, edited by Pachauri, R.K. and Reisinger, A. IPCC, Geneva, Switzerland.

International Federation of Red Cross 2014 *World Disasters Report: Focus on Culture and Risk*, edited by Terry Cannon and Lisa Shipper. International Federation of Red Cross and Red Crescent Societies. Geneva, Switzerland.

Jansen, E., J. Overpeck, K. R. Briffa, J.-C. Duplessy, F. Joos, V. Masson-Delmotte, D. Olago, B. Otto-Bliesner, W. R. Peltier, S. Rahmstorf, R. Ramesh, D. Raynaud, D. Rind, O. Solomina, R. Villalba, and D. Zhang 2007 Palaeoclimate. In *Climate Change 2007: The Physical Science Basis. Contribution of Working Group I to the Fourth Assessment Report of the Intergovernmental Panel on Climate Change*, edited by S. Solomon, D. Qin, M. Manning, Z. Chen, M. Marquis, K. B. Averyt, M. Tignor, and H. L. Miller. Cambridge University Press, Cambridge.

Jigasu, Rohit 2014 Reducing Disaster Risks and Building Resilience in Small Island Developing States. In *Safeguarding Precious Resources for Island Communities*, edited by Haraguchi, S. and Ron van Ders, pp. 38–45. World Heritage Paper 38. UNESCO, Paris, France.

Jigasu, Rohit, Manas Murthy, Giovani Boccardi, Chris Marrion, Diane L Douglas, Joseph King, Geoff O'Brien, Glenn Dolcemascolo, Yongkyun Kim, Paola Albrito, and Mariana Osihn 2013. *Heritage and Resilience: Issues and Opportunities for Reducing Disaster Risks*. United Nations International Strategy for Disaster Risk Reduction, Geneva, Switzerland. Electronic document, www.unisdr.org/we/inform/publications/33189

Leonard, Sonia, Meg Parsons, Knut Olawsky, and Frances Kofod 2013 The Role of Culture and Traditional Knowledge in Climate Change Adaptation: Insights from East Kimberley, Australia. *Global Environmental Change* (1088):623–632. doi: 10.1016/j.gloenvcha.2013.02.012

Nakashima, D. J., K. Galloway McLean, H. D. Thulstrup, A. Ramos Castillo, and J. T. Rubis 2012. *Weathering Uncertainty: Traditional Knowledge for Climate Change Assessment and Adaptation*. UNESCO, Paris, France and United Nations University, Darwin, Australia.

Naumann, Sandra, McKenna Davis, Richard Munang, Jesica Andrews, Ibrahim Thiaw, Keith Alverson, Musconda Mumba, Levis Kavagi, and Zhen Han 2013 *The Social Dimension of Ecosystem Based Adaptation*. UNEP Policy Series Ecosystem Management, Policy Brief 12–2013. Nairobi, Kenya.

Nyong, A., F. Adesina, and B. Osman Elasha 2007 The Value of Indigenous Knowledge in Climate Change Mitigation and Adaptation Strategies in the African Sahel. *Mitigation and Adaptation Strategies for Global Change*, 12:787–797. doi: 10.1007/s11027-007-9099-0, accessed April 12, 2016.

Osorio, Luis Gomero, and Alfonso Lizárraga Travaglini 1999 Pesticides in Peru's Highlands. *ILEIA Newsletter*, 58–59. Electronic document, http://edepot.wur.nl/79872, accessed April 12 2016.

Randall, D. A., R. A. Wood, S. Bony, R. Colman, T. Fichefet, J. Fyfe, V. Kattsov, A. Pitman, J. Shukla, J. Srinivasan, R. J. Stoufer, A. Sumi, and K. E. Taylor 2007 Climate Models and Their Evaluation. In *Climate Change 2007: The Physical Science Basis. Contribution of Working Group I to the Fourth Assessment Report of the Intergovernmental Panel on Climate Change*, edited by Solomon, S., D. Qin, M. Manning, Z. Chen, M. Marquis, K. B. Averyt, M. Tignor, and H. L. Miller. Cambridge University Press, Cambridge and New York, NY.

Raymondi, Ann Marie, Sabrina Delgado Arias, and Renée C. Elder 2012 Technological Solutions for Climate Change Adaptation in the Peruvian Highlands. In *Human and Social Dimensions of Climate Change*, edited by Netra Chhetri, pp. 3–30. In TECH.doi: 10.5772/3242, accessed April 11, 2016.

Solomon, S., D. Qin, M. Manning, Z. Chen, M. Marquis, K. B. Averyt, M. Tignor, and H. L. Miller, editors 2007 *Contribution of Working Group I to the Fourth Assessment Report of the Intergovernmental Panel on Climate Change*. Cambridge University Press, Cambridge and New York, NY.

Takeuchi, Yukiko, and Rajib Shaw 2008 Traditional Flood Disaster Reduction Measures in Japan. In *Indigenous Knowledge for Disaster Risk Reduction: Good Practices and Lessons Learned from Experiences in the Asia-Pacific Region*, edited by Rajib Shaw, Noralene Uy, and Jennifer Baumwoll, pp. 23–26. UN/ISDR, Geneva, Switzerland.

Thapa, Man B., Youba Raj Luintel, Bhupendra Gauchan and Kiran Amaty 2008 Indigenous Knowledge on Disaster Mitigation: Towards Creating Complementarity between Communities' and Scientists' Knowledge. In *Indigenous Knowledge for Disaster Risk Reduction: Good Practices and Lessons Learned from Experiences in the Asia-Pacific Region*, edited by Rajib Shaw, Noralene Uy, and Jennifer Baumwoll, pp. 30–34 UN/ISDR, Geneva, Switzerland.

Tobin, Patrick C., Dylan Parry and Brian H. Aukema 2014 The Influence of Climate Change on Insect Invasions in Temperate Forest Ecosystems, In *Challenges and Opportunities for the World's Forests in the 21st Century*, edited by Trevor Fenning, pp. 267–293. Forestry Sciences Series Vol 81, DOI 10.1007/978-94-007-7076-8_1, Springer Netherlands.

United Nations Educational, Scientific and Cultural Organization 2016 UNESCO World Heritage Centre, 1992–2016. World Heritage List. UNESCO, Paris, France. Electronic document, http://whc.unesco.org/en/list/, accessed April 11, 2016.

United Nations International Strategy for Disaster Reduction 2016 Making Cities Resilient: My City is Getting Ready. Toolkit for Local Governments, Sea Level Rise With Vertical Land Movement for Cities App. http://slr-cities.climsystems.com/, accessed April 26, 2016.

———. 2015 Sendai Framework for Disaster Risk Reduction 2015–2030. March 18, 2015. A/CONF/224/CRP.1. UN/ISDR, Geneva, Switzerland.

Uy, Noralene, and Rajib Shaw 2008 Shaped by Wind and Typhoon: The Indigenous Knowledge of the Ivatans in the Batanes Islands, Philippines. In *Indigenous Knowledge for Disaster Risk Reduction: Good Practices and Lessons Learned from Experiences in the Asia-Pacific Region*, edited by Rajib Shaw, Noralene Uy, and Jennifer Baumwoll, pp. 59–63 UN/ISDR, Geneva, Switzerland.

Vize, Sue, and Denis Chang Seng 2013 *Traditional Knowledge for Adapting to Climate Change: Safeguarding Intangible Cultural Heritage in the Pacific*. UNESCO and International Information and Networking Centre for Intangible Cultural Heritage in the Asia-Pacific (ICHCAP), Republic of Korea.

16

THE FUSION OF LAW AND ETHICS IN CULTURAL HERITAGE MANAGEMENT

The 21st Century Confronts Archaeology

Hilary A. Soderland and Ian A. Lilley

As contemporary society becomes increasingly interconnected and the geopolitical reality of the 21st century poses new threats to protecting archaeological sites and the integrity of the archaeological record during armed conflict and insurgency, law has fallen short or has lacked necessary enforcement mechanisms to address on-the-ground realities. A changing global order shaped by human rights, Indigenous heritage, legal pluralism, neocolonialism, development, diplomacy, and emerging nonstate actors directs the 21st-century policies that shape laws and ethics. Archaeologists in the field today work within a nexus of domestic and international laws and regulations and must navigate increasingly complex ethical situations. Thus, a critical challenge is to realign approaches to current dilemmas facing archaeology in a way that unifies the 'legal' and the 'ethical' with a focus on human rights and principles of equity and justice. With examples from around the world, this chapter considers how law and ethics affect professional practice and demonstrates how engagement with law and awareness of ethics are pivotal to archaeologists in the field.

Introduction

The vestiges of 20th-century wars, imperialism, and colonial encounters present contemporary society with contested ownership disputes, repatriation/restitution claims, and other complex questions of law and ethics. Iconic examples are the Parthenon/Elgin Marbles, Nazi-looted artwork, the Kennewick Man/Ancient One, the destruction of the Mostar Bridge—only exemplars, yet history is replete with such instances. Recent decades have seen a proliferation of global, regional, national, and local attempts to safeguard increasingly threatened cultural heritage and to offer remedy for loss or destruction (see Altschul, this volume; Burgess, this volume; Fleming, this volume; Stone, this volume; and Werkheiser et al., this volume). Laws or ethics have been the first resort, perceived as the key to the puzzle. Yet neither has proved sufficient. As the 21st century unfolds, the search for effective remedies and equitable resolutions to complex situations only intensifies as the precepts embodied in law and ethics often fall short and the archaeologist in the field is left to grapple with the uncertainty of real-world dynamics. The discourse of legal pluralism, despite ongoing criticism for harboring the very hegemonic undercurrents it espouses to shed, has made important inroads into how intangible mores of culture can be balanced with juridical norms (e.g., among many, see the recent work of Anker 2014; Berman 2014; Carpenter and Riley 2014; Darian-Smith 2013; Klabbers and Piiparinen 2014). However, the processes of globalization are accelerating and present new urgent challenges to archaeology (Biehl et al. 2015). It is evident that addressing collective global issues will require collaborative action on a broad scale—from the individual archaeologist in the field to national governments, professional societies, and international bodies. The disciplinary trajectory of archaeology on a global level can itself be instructive as to how past practice inflects present challenges, which in turn frame our future.

Archaeology and Ethics

A strong 'postcolonial' ethical concern for the dignity and autonomy of local, Indigenous, and non-Western communities, peoples, and nations has developed in the context of accelerating post–World War II decolonization. In archaeology, this was most tellingly witnessed by the creation of the World Archaeological Congress (WAC) in 1986 (see Okamura this volume, for a discussion on how WAC has developed over the last 30 years). WAC was created as a break-away from the UNESCO-affiliated International Union of the Pre- and Proto-historic Sciences (IUPPS), when the latter refused to sanction scholars from South Africa during the time of global anti-Apartheid protests. In addition to routine professional duties concerning "the exchange of results from archaeological research—and the conservation of archaeological sites", WAC is dedicated to "professional training and public education for disadvantaged nations, groups and communities; the empowerment and support of Indigenous groups and First Nations people" (WAC 2010). WAC's "One World Archaeology" book series was central in establishing this scope and tone, and early volumes featured titles such as *Domination and Resistance*, *Who Needs the Past? Indigenous Values and Archaeology*, *Conflict in the Archaeology of Living Traditions*, *The Politics of the Past*, *The Excluded Past*, and *Social Construction of the Past: Representation as Power*.

The ethos of such works became a touchstone for archaeologists and heritage managers negotiating fieldwork that many found to be caught up in the reality of turbulent and indeed deeply threatening social and political waters. Influential as it was, WAC was not alone in addressing such issues. National discourse was also shaped. This is clearly evident in Australia, to take a leading example. Before WAC burst onto the scene, pioneering Australian archaeologist Isabel McBryde in 1985 edited *Who Owns the Past?* McBryde was an influential figure in the same Antipodean milieu that sensitized WAC founder Peter Ucko to the issues. As Principal of the then Australian Institute of Aboriginal Studies (now Australian Institute of Aboriginal and Torres Strait Islander Studies [AIATSIS]), Ucko helped foster wider under-standing that Australia has two Indigenous populations: Aboriginal people and Torres Strait Islanders.

Since that time, the themes addressed by McBryde's contributors have been repeatedly revisited around the world but especially in the Anglophone settler societies mentioned in Bruce Trigger's well-known 1984 paper, namely Australia, Canada, New Zealand, and the United States, with interesting material also emerging from southern Africa (Trigger 1984; cf. Lilley 2000). One crucial result of the changes in the attitudes and approaches of archaeologists and heritage practitioners, charted in the foregoing literature, has been the emergence of codes of ethical professional conduct focused on the decolonization of the discipline(s). These codes all have their own histories but often trace their ultimate origins to developments in Australia such as the resolutions concerning Aboriginal ownership of Aboriginal archaeological heritage passed at the 1982 annual conference of the Australian Archaeological Association. At that meeting, Tasmanian Aboriginal activist Ros Langford eloquently expressed her people's right to control and share their culture and history (Langford 1983). As detailed by Jim Allen, one of the protagonists in those and later events in Tasmania, the two salient motions were:

1. That this conference acknowledges Aboriginal ownership of their heritage. Accordingly, this conference calls on all archaeologists to obtain permission from the Aboriginal owners prior to any research or excavation of Aboriginal sites . . . [and]
3. That in acknowledgement of the debt owed to the Aboriginal people by the archaeological profession this conference calls on all archaeologists to actively support the Aboriginal land rights campaign through whatever means they have at their disposal (Allen 1983:7).

As Allen remembers it, neither of these motions was passed unanimously, but each was passed, signaling a groundbreaking shift in Australian archaeology and heritage practice (see also *Commonwealth v. Tasmania*). This shift saw the creation of the Association's Code of Ethics. The last of the four Principles Relating to Indigenous Archaeology endorses and directs members to the AIATSIS guidelines for ethical research with Indigenous people. This link explicitly highlights the overlap and other close ties between the membership of the Association and that of the AIATSIS and, indeed, the personal influence of Peter Ucko on Australian archaeology when he was at the Institute and later (e.g., Ucko 1983).

These upheavals in Australia were not restricted to the discipline of archaeology alone, nor of course to Australia as a nation, even if the profession in that country has long been at the cutting edge of the global decolonization process as it continues to unfold. In Australia today, all research disciplines must comply with strict ethical requirements for clearance to work with Indigenous individuals and communities, with the AIATSIS guidelines often forming a central plank in institutional research-ethics frameworks. This sort of compliance framework is familiar to colleagues in other Anglophone settler societies if not so much in other parts of the world. Globally, WAC adopted the Vermillion Accord on Human Remains in 1989 and the First Code of Ethics the following year. Unsurprisingly, given the formative role of Australian experience in the development of WAC, the language and intent of the latter is similar to that in Australian codes and guidelines. Around the world, other professional archaeological and heritage organizations as well as museums and their representative bodies also have developed ethical codes and guidelines. The Canadian Archaeological Association, for example, has strong specific guidelines for Indigenous research as well as a separate code of ethics. Most, though, are not nearly as explicitly 'decolonizing' of professional practice as those of WAC or those in widespread everyday use in Australia and Canada.

The Society for American Archaeology (SAA), for instance, has a repatriation policy, Concerning the Treatment of Human Remains, as well as a set of Principles of Archaeological Ethics. Both are less postcolonial in their specific concerns about issues of decolonization than Australian, Canadian, and WAC equivalents. The same can be said of the New Zealand Archaeological Association's Code of Ethics. This is surprising given the very strong role Indigenous Maori (and in the Chatham Islands, Moriori) people play in New Zealand life today, including in archaeology and cultural heritage (cf. Lilley 2000). On the other side of the world, despite (or perhaps because of) the very long-term involvement of European archaeologists in what Trigger (1984) would call colonialist and imperialist archaeologies around the planet, the European Association of Archaeologists (EAA) Code of Practice contains almost nothing about working with communities, local, Indigenous, or otherwise.

In the same vein, museums, at both the individual and overarching representative levels, also have developed codes of ethics, standards, and best practices (see Burgess this volume). Museums' continued difficulties with repatriation issues and regular scandals regarding connections with looting and cultural resource trafficking indicate this sector occupies a fraught position in a decolonizing world (cf. Luke and Kersel 2008). Yet on a positive note, the UN-linked International Council of Museums (ICOM) has a Code of Ethics that recognizes the close collaboration museums have with the communities from which their collections originate as well as those they serve:

> Principle: museum collections reflect the cultural and natural heritage of the communities from which they have been derived. As such, they have a character beyond that of ordinary property, which may include strong affinities with national, regional, local, ethnic, religious or political identity. It is important therefore that museum policy is responsive to this situation.
>
> *(ICOM 2004)*

This principle—or at least the general ethical sentiments behind it—is recognized increasingly in international agreements regarding museums and matters of repatriation and the illicit trafficking of cultural resources (e.g., Luke and Kersel 2013b).

Plainly, such ethical codes—and, increasingly, formal laws and regulations flowing from them or reinforcing them—have an impact on field archaeology, especially as it is connected with national museums as official state repositories or with laboratories that need to import excavated materials for technical analysis. While such regulation might constrict the free flow of scientific knowledge and at least temporarily impede field or related laboratory research, it is consonant with both the values of 'engaged archaeology' and a deepening emphasis on human rights in archaeology and especially cultural heritage.

Engaged Archaeology

The term 'engaged archaeology' is most commonly used to refer to equitable decolonized collaboration between archaeologists or heritage specialists and local, Indigenous, or other descendent communities (and so is often seen to be synonymous with 'community archaeology'; e.g., Agbe-Davies 2010; cf. Chilton this volume for an excellent assessment of engagement and collaboration in heritage projects). In this chapter, the term extends to include not only the legal and legislative communities but also other crucial audiences such as the popular media, heritage bureaucracies (e.g., the international World Heritage system, including the statutory advisory bodies ICOMOS and IUCN, as intimated in the discussion of Ian Lilley's projects, as well as national and subnational agencies), the World Bank and other development lenders, and the transnational extractive industries sector. We maintain that developing productive relationships with these sectors will be fundamental to how 'engaged archaeology' will evolve in the 21st century (Willems 2014) and thus to how archaeology will be practiced in the field.

Conventional public or community outreach is of course absolutely critical to archaeology's and heritage management's social license to operate in a world that does not necessarily see their activities as a self-evident public good, worthy of funding and moral support. Our reasoning, though, is that the other interest groups just mentioned directly or indirectly create and pay for the vast bulk of archaeological and heritage management work carried out around the planet and thus should be seen by these discipline(s) as absolutely vital publics as well as the subjects of critical scholarly scrutiny (cf. Lafrenz Samuels and Lilley 2015; Welch and Lilley 2013).

Within this context, Claire Smith, as WAC president, attempted to bring WAC into an arrangement during the mid-2000s with the mining corporation Rio Tinto to help the company meet its corporate social responsibility goals in relation to cultural heritage. This effort resulted in a meeting in Melbourne, Australia, in 2007 between selected WAC members and Rio Tinto staff. The endeavor ended badly for both parties, as partially captured by Shepherd and Haber (2011; see Smith's 2011 measured response). The furor shows that going down the path of corporate engagement faces hurdles from within the archaeological and cultural heritage communities as well as hurdles erected by publics or audiences not well informed about or naturally sympathetic to our disciplines' interests. Nonetheless, we believe such initiatives are worth pursuing and, at the very least, are not severable from 'engaged archaeology' in the 21st century.

For this reason, one of us (Ian Lilley) has continued to work with Rio Tinto after the WAC debacle as well as to engage with the World Bank, particularly through the formation of the nongovernmental International Heritage Group (IHG) in 2011. Prior to the Oxford workshop that led to IHG's creation, Lilley played a central role in the Rio Tinto project on "Why Cultural Heritage Matters". This project saw the corporation approach the University of Queensland's Centre for Social Responsibility in Mining (CSRM) to produce A Resource Guide for Integrating Cultural Heritage Management into Communities Work at Rio Tinto. The aim was to formulate one set of global corporate standards and values regarding heritage that was sufficiently adaptable to accommodate "the unique needs and aspirations of the communities that host [. . .] [Rio Tinto] operations" (Rio Tinto 2010:2). A consortium of colleagues (later involved in IHG) followed principles consistent with these guidelines in the course of cultural heritage work on Oyo Tolgoi, Rio Tinto's project in Mongolia. These corporate guidelines are now publicly available in English and other major languages including French, Portuguese, and Spanish (Rio Tinto 2010).

While the Rio Tinto guide is intended particularly for situations in which archaeological and heritage management capabilities need strengthening, its requirements also apply in developed nations such as the United States, where the ability of government agencies to modify what archaeologists and heritage practitioners would see as substandard behavior on the part of private interests is restricted not by lack of financial and human resources, as in less-developed countries, but by statutes protecting private property and individual and corporate freedoms. In jurisdictions such as the United States, binding corporate guidelines such as Rio Tinto's can require 'reluctant' business units in, or working for, international corporations to comply with globally acceptable standards. This is not a trivial matter in a country where private interests are sacrosanct and, in certain instances, the destruction or looting of heritage sites on private property is difficult or impossible to prosecute.

In addition to engaging corporations such as Rio Tinto, IHG members recently have encouraged the major professional archaeological bodies such as the AIA, SAA, WAC, and the Indo-Pacific Prehistory Association (IPPA) to comment on the cultural heritage guidelines of the Inter-American Development Bank (IDB) and on the first draft revisions of the World Bank's Environmental and Social Framework, which includes the Bank's 'safeguard' policy on archaeology and cultural heritage. Several of the foregoing organizations have submitted detailed comments to the World Bank's review team and in some cases also to the Bank's Committee on Development Effectiveness, which has overall responsibility for the review process.

While the World Bank has engaged periodically with selected members of the profession in the past, to our knowledge, the foregoing submissions to the 2014 revisions of the Bank's safeguard framework are the first ever to come from the profession in this globally coordinated way. Despite such opportunities to engage as the joint biannual World Bank–International Monetary Fund (IMF) Civil Society

Policy Forum, again to our knowledge, no professional archaeological or cultural heritage body previously had made representations to any part of the World Bank Group, including the International Finance Corporation (IFC). This is astounding, given the great impact that the activities of the Bank and similar institutions, such as the IDB, have on field archaeology and cultural heritage management around the world (e.g., Lafrenz Samuels and Lilley 2015).

In 2016, a delegation led by Lilley under the auspices of the Society for American Archaeology (SAA) attended the Civil Society Policy Forum in Washington, DC, linked with the joint World Bank–IMF Spring Meetings. As part of this overall effort, in 2014, the SAA also held meetings with staff from the World Bank, IDB, and other Latin American development banks, along with archaeological and cultural heritage colleagues and civil society representatives, in Lima, Peru, in association with the SAA's 2nd Conferencia Intercontinental. Similar meetings are scheduled in conjunction with the SAA's 83rd Annual Meeting in Washington, DC, in 2018.

It is hoped that the engagement processes currently emerging in this sector will bear fruit in the not-too-distant future. In certain circumstances, collaboration with corporate and/or multilateral entities may raise ethical implications should that engagement simply be a fulfilment of corporate social responsibility rather than a genuine commitment to archaeology or cultural heritage. On balance, we consider that in principle it is better to engage than not—particularly given that this sector represents a vital and enduring public with a substantial impact on archaeological and other heritage resources.

Practicing 'engaged archaeology' with a broad, diverse, and/or nontraditional audience is challenging both from a disciplinary and an individual perspective. Yet the audiences of the 21st century are broader, more diverse, and increasingly nontraditional. Pluralist discourse is not solely a legal metric. For archaeology, 'engaged pluralism' will prove a valuable resource for field archaeologists and heritage managers irrespective of geographical, chronological, or subfield specialization. Moreover, 'engaged pluralism' presents great capacity to promote and to advance a broader understanding of cultural rights and human rights.

Archaeology and Human Rights

Although few if any of the foregoing developments have been couched explicitly in terms of human rights, the disciplinary processes entailed have been playing out in the wider global dynamics of post-Holocaust human rights discourse, central aspects of which are discussed by scholars such as Brysk and Jimenez (2012) and Mazower (2004). Only a handful of archaeologists and heritage practitioners have engaged closely with this discourse, as examined in this chapter. Such scant connection is unsurprising. International human rights agendas have until very recently completely ignored archaeology and heritage and indeed cultural issues more generally, despite unambiguous UNESCO interest in the matter dating back nearly half a century (Meskell 2010:840). As noted elsewhere (Welch and Lilley 2013:475–476), this is clear in UN declarations concerning the Millennium

Development Goals (MDGs), the original formulations of which did not mention culture or heritage.

The absence of culture (and heritage) in the MDGs is now seen as a major oversight. The UN General Assembly has passed resolutions seeking to remedy this situation, at least some of which deploy the language of rights regarding intellectual property (IP) and cultural heritage. Farida Shaheed's 2011 UN Report of the Independent Expert in the Field of Cultural Rights has figured prominently as it focuses on the "right of access to [,] and enjoyment of [,] cultural heritage" (Shaheed 2011:1). Although this recent UN activity coincides with an upswing in professional interest in heritage and human rights, heritage lawyers such as Patrick O'Keefe (2000) have been writing about such matters for almost two decades. Lawyerly interest in the field persists, for instance through Janet Blake's contributions (e.g., 2011), though she notes that the topic "has not been sufficiently examined in the literature, particularly by human rights specialists" (Blake 2011:199).

Among cultural heritage specialists and archaeologists rather than lawyers (though Blake originally trained as a classicist), Helaine Silverman and Fairchild Ruggles (2007a) published the first collection to deal expressly with these issues. However, it is the research of William Logan at Australia's Deakin University that since then has stood out globally. A geographer by training, Logan is heavily involved in international and especially UNESCO work on heritage and human rights and has written extensively on the question (e.g., 2014, 2013, 2012, 2009) following his 2007 chapter in Silverman and Ruggles's ground-breaking volume.

A significant dimension of Logan's work, and a matter raised by Silverman and Ruggles's introduction (2007b:4) as well as more recently by scholars such as Lynn Meskell (e.g., 2013), is the question of intangible heritage. Owing to its focus on living culture, this concept is held up as a counter to the long-standing universalizing focus in heritage management on tangible (e.g., physical and usually monumental) remains. With UNESCO's 2003 Convention for the Safeguarding of the Intangible Cultural Heritage and the associated List of Intangible Cultural Heritage in Need of Urgent Safeguarding, Representative List of the Intangible Cultural Heritage of Humanity, and Register of Best Safeguarding Practices, expressions of intangibility and cultural practice attained global stature. Intangible cultural heritage is now recognized, or 'inscribed', insofar as it is "compatible with existing international human rights instruments" (Article 2). However, the concept of intangible heritage is difficult to operationalize (e.g., Meskell 2013:157) and, in Logan's view, even more than tangible heritage, is susceptible to the sort of debasement for political ends that was characterized in the *Journal of Field Archaeology* by Meskell (2012) as "the rush to inscribe". Interestingly in this profoundly conflicted context, and relevant to this chapter's discussion of archaeology in the 21st century, Logan (2014:166) points out that while those with global responsibility for cultural heritage face continuing difficulties implementing rights-based approaches, the global body for natural heritage, the International Union for the Conservation of Nature (IUCN) "by contrast is already well advanced in developing a rights-based approach" (e.g., Oviedo and Puschkarsky 2012; see also Blake 2013; Blake and

Boer 2009). Logan asserts that the International Council on Monuments and Sites (ICOMOS, IUCN's cultural equivalent) should find IUCN's effort useful vis-à-vis "Cultural sites [sic] and Cultural Landscapes" (2014:166). Innovative work linking nature conservation and cultural heritage on this basis recently has been published by New Zealand archaeologist Richard Walter and his colleague Richard Hamilton of the Nature Conservancy (Walter and Hamilton 2014; see also Watkins this volume; and Douglas this volume regarding traditional ecological knowledge and plants as 'heritage').

A related but different angle has been taken by Canadian archaeologists and heritage practitioners in Simon Fraser University's seven-year international project on Intellectual Property Issues in Cultural Heritage: Theory, Practice, Policy, Ethics (IPinCH) (see Watkins this volume, for further description of IPinCH). Led by George Nicholas, this recently completed endeavor is

> ultimately concerned with larger issues of the nature of knowledge and rights based on culture—how these are defined and used, who has control and access, and especially how fair and appropriate use and access can be achieved to the benefit of all stakeholders in the past.
>
> *(IPinCH 2016)*

This is not to say that project members take an uncritical approach to rights in heritage or culture. Legal anthropologist Rosemary Coombe, for instance, argues that "we have seen little by way of sustained dialogue between critics of rights or conversations between rights critics and theorists of culture" (Coombe 2010:230). She proposes greater attention be paid to developing appropriate theoretical and methodological tools to deal effectively with "a global policy environment that has put increasing emphasis upon cultural identity and cultural resources in both rights-based practices and neoliberal governmentalities" (Coombe 2010:230). In a broadly similar vein, Meskell (2010:840) uses a South African example to suggest that "heritage practitioners might be more effective and ethically responsible by being attendant to pragmatic approaches that enhance human capabilities and human flourishing" rather than succumb to "the desire to harness the urgency of human rights discourse" to solve heritage and other ethical conflicts and dilemmas.

Meskell (2010:847) asks, "very specifically, what does the mantle of universal human rights bring to heritage?" That same question must be asked in relation to field archaeology. Meskell (2010:847–848) thinks that, owing to "our disciplinary inexperience . . . [with such matters], deferring to rights discourse and determinations may in fact attenuate our daily negotiations and obligations, passing those responsibilities further up the chain to an ever-increasing transnational bureaucracy and governance". Instead, Meskell proposes that "being more conversant with the scope and limitations of human rights and other alternatives, on the ground, can forge more pragmatic solutions" (2010:855).

Although Lilley shares Coombe's and Meskell's questioning attitudes, he recently has brought two separate new projects together to determine whether explicit attention to human rights issues can help enhance what World Heritage listing might deliver to associated Indigenous communities. The issue of what costs and benefits World Heritage listing brings to Aboriginal Australians is the subject of a three-year study examining the matter in a sample of sites designed to capture the range of ways in which Aboriginal interests are managed in the Australian World Heritage system.

The research team is studying three kinds of World Heritage property: those sites nominated solely for their natural heritage values but where Aboriginal interests are nonetheless considered by site managers through formal advisory mechanisms (case studies Fraser Island and Purnululu); sites nominated (eventually if not initially) for Aboriginal cultural values as well as natural values and now comanaged by government authorities and local traditional owners (case study Uluru-Kata Tjuta); and, properties nominated for Aboriginal archaeological values, as defined by archaeologists, without formal recognition of the values living Aboriginal people invest in the area, though Aboriginal interests are to some extent accommodated by management authorities (case study Southwest Tasmania). Key Aboriginal and non-Aboriginal figures connected with these properties as well as staff in relevant state and federal government World Heritage management agencies (and when possible the politicians responsible for those agencies) are being interviewed, with the ultimate aim of developing tools or instruments to measure in Indigenous terms the effectiveness of management policies and procedures concerning Indigenous interests.

Owing to his involvement with recent joint efforts to integrate better the approaches of ICOMOS and IUCN to the management of World Heritage, the leaders of a now-funded Swiss proposal entitled "Understanding Rights Practices in the World Heritage System: Lessons from the Asia Pacific" approached Lilley to head an Australian project node. This multisite study investigates the question "What are the major factors shaping, preventing or enhancing human rights–based approaches in the World Heritage system?" in Australia, the Philippines, Nepal, and Vietnam. In the Australian case, the project 'piggybacks' on the Aboriginal World Heritage project described earlier, in a way that allows the researchers to compare and contrast responses regarding human rights with replies to earlier questions regarding Indigenous interests in World Heritage more generally. While still exploratory, these sorts of projects and those described by scholars such as Logan and Meskell show how the discourse of human rights is influencing the field and how far archaeology and heritage management have come since the difficult days of the 1980s. Such developments coincide with those in international and domestic law, as considered in this chapter.

Archaeology and Law

Alongside ethics, law has become customary and integral in archaeological field practice and scholarship as well as in cultural heritage management. One would be hard pressed to name a country that has not promulgated some sort of legal framework—at least 'law on the books'—governing archaeological activity and cultural heritage management and earmarking ownership rights over the past. A growing list of countries face ongoing disputes over the rightful ownership of archaeological resources and cultural property that were once, but are no longer, within their possession or jurisdiction or are being claimed by Indigenous people as part of their heritage. Any archaeologist working in the field—irrespective of nationality, geographic focus, or chronological or subfield specialization—will have had to navigate sometimes thorny national or local regulations and laws, many of which have been influenced by principles, norms, and customs of international law. Yet few practitioners have the legal training to help in charting a course through these regulatory frameworks. Given the interconnection of law and archaeology, this can constitute an omission in the practitioner's toolkit.

The application of international law's norms to modalities of archaeological heritage at the national or local level has been the subject of significant scholarship, particularly in the spheres of armed conflict, the (il)licit trade in antiquities, restitution/repatriation, and, more recently, intangible heritage and Indigenous rights (e.g., Disko and Tugendhat 2013; Gerstenblith 2009, 2010; Lixinski 2013; Luke and Kersel 2013a; O'Keefe 2006; Soderland 2013; Willems 2014). While the literature is vast, of significance here is the fact that international law during and since the 20th century has become integral to the discipline of archaeology, and its precepts are entwined in national legal frameworks worldwide (see Stone this volume). In so doing, law has instilled a rights-based discourse that has directed how the past has been studied, protected, managed, and regulated.

As international law developed throughout the 20th century, archaeological practice—especially but not exclusively vis-à-vis cultural heritage—steadily came within its purview and, correspondingly, the concept of 'customary international law' has gained relevance to archaeologists' daily activities. Customary international law "consists of rules of law derived from the consistent conduct of States acting out of the belief that the law required them to act that way" (Rosenne 1984:55). Thus, customary international law rises from and subsequently depends upon the practice of states. A fundamental aspect is that a state is typically 'bound' as a member of the global community of nations by customary international law regardless of whether the state has ratified a convention or effected implementation of such in domestic law. For the purposes of this chapter, customary international law can be defined as general practice among states that is accepted as law.

The shortcomings of multilateral treaties have long been recognized and so, while noted (in relation to World Heritage, see what follows), the focus here highlights customary international law in order to provide archaeologists with a further understanding of the reaches of law. Since the application of customary international law still remains largely untested in archaeology and heritage management, the general practice of states can hold substantial implications for these fields as the 21st century progresses. This can be seen clearly in dynamics surrounding the 2007 United Nations Declaration on the Rights of Indigenous Peoples (hereafter the Declaration).

The Declaration is predicated on the principles of international human rights law, including justice, equality, nondiscrimination, democracy, good faith, and good governance and has impacted legal pluralism on a worldwide scale. When representatives of the world's 370 million-plus Indigenous peoples advocated within the United Nations, they did so using a rights-based framework, deploying the discourse of human rights.

Akin to the movement in archaeology since the 1980s, the institutionalization of action at the United Nations to promote Indigenous peoples' rights has been historic and monumental, particularly for a group that prior to 1982 had virtually no presence within the United Nations institutional framework. Recognition at the United Nations accorded Indigenous peoples a platform that unsettled the autonomy of the nation-states in which these people live and significantly provided the institutional presence necessary to exert influence upon national governments. To traditional norms of human rights and fundamental freedoms, Indigenous peoples brought their concerns based upon a belief in their collective rights as peoples and their struggles to maintain their unique cultural identities, traditions, and institutions—including association to land and values of spirituality, sacredness, and religion—in the face of the discriminatory practices and development pressures imposed by national governments.

The Declaration's preamble and 46 articles draw from jurisprudence and numerous prior treaties and conventions (such as the United Nations International Convention on the Elimination of All Forms of Racial Discrimination, adopted in 1965, and the International Labour Organization No. 169 Indigenous and Tribal Peoples Convention, adopted in 1989). Article 1 of the 2007 Declaration states that Indigenous peoples have the right, on an individual or collective level, to "all human rights and fundamental freedoms as recognized in the Charter of the United Nations, [in] the Universal Declaration of Human Rights, and [in] international human rights law". The rights recognized in the Declaration constitute the "minimum standards for the survival, dignity, and well-being of the indigenous peoples of the world" (Article 43).

The Declaration construes self-determination as a human right of an individual, of a collective, or of a people. Without discrimination, self-determination represents the right to collective ownership; to a spiritual connection to traditional lands, territories, and natural/cultural resources; to the ability to participate through "free, prior, and informed consent" in state action that may adversely affect their livelihood, traditional land, and/or resources; to the ability to establish and control their own educational systems; to retain their linguistic heritage; and, to appoint their own representatives and establish and control their own institutions, from health care to the judiciary. In relevant jurisprudence, courts and case law have recognized that the right of self-determination—both in cultural and spiritual integrity and in the right to the land—is essential to the very survival of Indigenous peoples (particularly in light of modern development and, in many regions across the globe, state grants to third-party contractors for land exploitation and/or mineral extraction). As a result of the Declaration, the values of Indigenous rights are ensconced within the United Nations system and within global human-rights jurisprudence. This includes the spiritual connection to land (Case of *Yatama v. Nicaragua*), the right of self-determination (*Saramaka People v. Suriname*), and the right to own and use traditional land and natural resources (*Maya Indigenous Cmty. of Toledo Dist. v. Belize*).

The Declaration represents global consensus—at least on paper—and, in turn, may in fact become customary international law. However, regardless of current state signatory status, the Declaration has yet to attain the standard of customary international law because its principles are not widely followed by states based on the belief that general custom requires them to do so. The Declaration's limits mirror the well-documented constraints of international 'soft law' and domestic noncompliance. On September 13, 2007, the United Nations General Assembly adopted the Declaration by a majority of 144 states in favor, with 11 abstentions. The four votes against were by the Anglophone settler societies: Australia, Canada, New Zealand, and the United States. In the intervening years, countries that originally abstained have indicated their support for the Declaration. More significantly, by 2010, Australia, New Zealand, and Canada reversed their original position of opposition, leaving the United States as the sole nonsignatory in that group.

In April 2010, the United States announced it would revisit the Declaration and review its position. As part of the review process, the United States Department of State and federal agencies held consultations with federally recognized Indian tribes and other interested stakeholders, including NGOs. On December 15, 2010, President Obama announced at a White House Tribal Nations Conference that the United States would 'lend its support' to the Declaration. Even though the Declaration is the basis for the international human rights law of Indigenous peoples, it is a nonbinding instrument and remains aspirational—and not only in the United States. Nation-state support or endorsement does not equate or amount to implementation in domestic legal regimes or adoption of all principles set forth in the Declaration. Canada, prior to becoming a signatory, restricted its support for the Declaration to those clauses that are wholly consistent with domestic law and the Canadian Constitution.

The United States has yet to issue details on how its newfound 'support' will manifest if or when it signs the Declaration. Opponents to endorsement or 'support' advocate that the United States should not relinquish nation-state sovereignty in order to move beyond existing law, particularly when their conviction considers existing Indigenous cultural heritage to be ethically managed and sufficiently governed by current jurisprudence. Thus, uncertainty persists as to how the United States will become a signatory given the actual and potential conflicts between the Declaration's articles and United States law and constitutional norms. Perhaps it will follow Canada's lead. Signing the Declaration would then have the effect of recognizing Indigenous rights only so far as those rights are consistent with established United States law and policy.

A clear reflection of the United States' position vis-à-vis Indigenous rights is the 1990 Native American Graves Protection and Repatriation Act (NAGPRA). NAGPRA departs from previous decades of law governing archaeology that did not accord legal standing to Native Americans or, for the most part, associate archaeological landscapes, sites, or artifacts with Native American culture, past or present (but see the 1979 Archaeological Resources Protection Act [ARPA] permit process acknowledging cultural beliefs and practices as recognized by the 1978 American Indian Religious Freedom Act; see Watkins this volume). Until 1990, Native human remains and grave sites on federal and tribal lands were property of the United States government. Premised on 'cultural affiliation', NAGPRA granted proprietary rights to certain Natives ('lineal descendants', federally recognized 'Indian tribes' (25 C.F.R. § 83.7), and Native Hawaiian organizations, encompassing certain classes of Native Hawaiians and Alaska Natives) to claim certain remains of their past. NAGPRA is limited to federally recognized Natives with formalized roles and vested rights specified in the law's procedure and implementation; 'Native Americans' *per se* do not have legal standing or recourse.

NAGPRA is predicated upon 'lineal descent' or 'cultural affiliation' based on "a relationship of shared group identity that reasonably can be traced historically or prehistorically between a present day [group] . . . and an identifiable earlier group" (25 U.S.C. §3001 (2)). The law determines appropriate disposition options for 'human remains' and statutorily defined 'cultural items' ('associated funerary objects', 'unassociated funerary objects', 'sacred objects', 'cultural patrimony'; 25 U.S.C. §3001 (3)(A-D)), irrespective of age, found or excavated on federal or tribal land since the statute's enactment. NAGPRA requires consultation among Natives and non-Natives (including archaeologists) in a variety of contexts. Other provisions include the establishment of repatriation protocols, the protection of Native grave sites, and the prohibition against trafficking in Native 'human remains' or 'cultural items'. The implementation of NAGPRA altered the manner in which archaeology is practiced in the United States in a different way than prior legislation. All institutions receiving federal funding (including museums and universities) as well as federal agencies (with the exception of the Smithsonian Institution) became subject to specific compliance requirements. This impelled the opening of NAGPRA offices throughout the United States. A national NAGPRA program was launched to assist the federal government with particular duties in implementation, adherence, and enforcement and to support the responsibilities of the NAGPRA Review Committee.

NAGPRA is considered by many to be human rights legislation and is perceived to redress "part of a larger historical tragedy: the failure of the United States Government, and other institutions, to understand and respect the spiritual and cultural beliefs and practices of Native people" (Trope and Echo-Hawk 2001:32). In so doing, it addresses race relations, tribal sovereignty, historical marginalization, past injustices (including the denial of civil liberties, citizenship, and religious freedom), and human and constitutional rights (see Richman 2003 on the constitutional adequacy of NAGPRA.) The attainments championed by NAGPRA are generally situated within such a rights-based discourse.

What unquestionably remains the most iconic test of NAGPRA came with the 1996 discovery of an approximately 9,300-year-old skeleton near Kennewick in Washington State. One of the oldest and best-preserved New World skeletons ever discovered, it was coined the 'Ancient One' by Native Americans and 'Kennewick Man' by scientists. Native Americans claimed 'cultural affiliation' under NAGPRA. Archaeologists and physical anthropologists disputed this claim in order to avert repatriation and allow scientific study. After nearly eight years of litigation, in 2004, the United States Court of Appeals for the 9th Circuit held that no 'cultural affiliation' to modern-day 'Indian tribes' could be established, and thus NAGPRA did not apply. This meant that scientists were granted access to study the remains (*Bonnichsen v. United States*, 367 F.3d 864 (9th Cir. 2004); Owsley and Jantz 2014). The *Bonnichsen* decision underscored "the power—and potential ambiguity—of legal definitions, and the importance of examining the minutiae of statutory and regulatory wording . . . [particularly when] attempting, within a legal framework, to define terms with strong (and varied) cultural, political, and individual interpretations" (Bruning 2006:507).[1]

The *Bonnichsen* ruling is often cited as upholding the letter rather than the intent of the law. Numerous attempts to amend NAGPRA, written in direct response to the judicial interpretation in the Kennewick Man/Ancient One case, were introduced in Congress. None succeeded in becoming law. In the 20 years since the remains of Kennewick Man/Ancient One were unearthed, no comparable litigation has contested conceptions of cultural human rights, Indigenous heritage, intangibility, professional ethics, and legal interpretation.

In 2010, NAGPRA's implementing regulation on 'culturally unidentifiable human remains' added additional ambiguity in standing by creating a new hierarchy of claimants among Indigenous groups not 'recognized' in federal law. Still, however, not all Native Americans are able to assert claims under NAGPRA—a stark departure from the ideals embraced in the 2007 United Nations Declaration on the Rights of Indigenous Peoples. It is difficult to determine how such issues will be remedied if or when the United States fulfills its support of the Declaration. Yet it is apparent that even the outlier United States is influenced by how social values, ethics, and law have united toward acknowledging Indigenous peoples' rights not only as human rights but also as customary norms.

Since 2007, the jurisprudence of Indigenous peoples across the globe has been fortified by the UN Declaration and the acknowledgement of Indigenous populations as distinct 'peoples' with collective identity and unique cultural integrity. Whether, in 2016, the Declaration meets the elements of customary international law is not as important as the question of whether the ethical mores articulated in the Declaration are, should, or will become customary international law. Given that the Declaration has been in force for less than a decade, perhaps it is premature to forecast. Nevertheless, it is evident that Indigenous peoples' rights set forth in the

Declaration will continue to affect the discourse of global legal pluralism and, in turn, the ethics of archaeology and the practice of archaeologists in the field.

Another UN covenant that profoundly influences professional practice is UNESCO's 1972 Convention Concerning the Protection of the World Cultural and Natural Heritage (hereafter the Convention). The Convention's preamble states that it

> is incumbent on the international community as a whole to participate in the protection of the cultural and natural heritage of outstanding universal value . . . [and to establish] an effective system of collective protection of the cultural and natural heritage of outstanding universal value, organized on a permanent basis and in accordance with modern scientific methods.

The Convention, which entered into force on December 17, 1975, is almost universally accepted. There were 193 signatory States Parties as of January 2017, and the Convention's ratification, acceptance, approval, or accession has resulted in implementation in domestic legal systems across the globe. The World Heritage Convention effected a widespread and internationally agreed-upon standard of 'outstanding universal value'. Precise criteria set forth by the World Heritage Committee assess whether heritage nominated by a State Party exhibits 'outstanding universal value' and thereby warrants inscription to the World Heritage List (UNESCO Operational Guidelines for the Implementation of the World Heritage Convention 2013:20–21). Only States Parties may propose natural and cultural heritage within their national borders to be considered for inscription on the World Heritage List. Moreover, only States Parties are eligible for international assistance, including expert review, training, loans, equipment, and, most crucially, fiscal allocation from the World Heritage Fund.

The Convention also authorizes the World Heritage Committee to define precise criteria to determine how World Heritage sites are evaluated for inclusion on the List of World Heritage in Danger. As of March 2018, 54 properties were so listed. Notably, six inscribed in 2013 were in Syria and five inscribed in 2016 were in Libya, signifying the drastic degree to which contemporary geopolitical factors affect and jeopardize heritage (as discussed in what follows). The World Heritage Convention not only offers a universal standard of assessing heritage, but also the Convention in and of itself symbolizes a universal standard. It is a supranational legal instrument championing cultural heritage in terms of endorsement as well as in operation over the past four decades. States have pledged to protect their natural and cultural heritage under the Convention and the Convention's ethos, and the 'World Heritage Values' it imbues have been implemented into domestic law worldwide. As the most widely accepted global conservation treaty (indeed one of the most widely accepted treaties), the World Heritage Convention embodies international consensus on heritage even though signatory status does not necessarily translate into domestic adherence or address the political dimensions of ratification.

This international consensus must, however, be balanced with the reality that the World Heritage Convention is not immune from the trappings of treaty-based regimes, or 'soft law'. International instruments such as the World Heritage Convention are structured as responsibilities and obligations between and among nation-states, a status not held by Indigenous peoples by definition. Moreover, the Convention does not bind nonstate actors who pillage, destroy, or otherwise assail World Heritage sites. In 2001, the Buddhas of Bamiyan were a singular flash point but just over a decade later, numerous other World Heritage sites have succumbed to a similar fate. Militants' attacks on World Heritage sites in Mali, Libya, Iraq, and Syria (see the following) are recent and highly visible instances of nonstate actors without regard for heritage values, laws, or ethics. The lack of (already tenuous) enforcement mechanisms in the World Heritage Convention makes it difficult, if not impossible, to effect remedy if the treaty is contravened by a State Party. Nonstate actors that disregard universal mores and ideals of global heritage protection are virtually untouchable.

The terms of the World Heritage Convention limit effective enforcement of violations or sanctions for noncompliance. No dispute settlement mechanism is expressly identified, and monitoring, management, and periodic reporting reside with States Parties. Moreover, the Convention does not include mechanisms for addressing noncompliance (such as trade sanctions, liability, warning) or violations, other than the ability to suspend the privilege of the violating party from World Heritage Committee membership. The power of the World Heritage Committee is limited, so the loss of a vote on the World Heritage Committee is not a true deterrent. First, if the violating State Party already is ineligible for World Heritage Committee membership (e.g., if the State Party utilized Article 16 to avoid the compulsory fiscal obligation), then this exclusion rings hollow. Second, in general, the loss of voting rights has not proved to be an effective deterrent on the international stage. Thus, one State Party has little avenue for redress against another State Party and no redress against outlaw actions of Nonstate Parties.

It may seem somewhat paradoxical that non- or extralegal means reflect the method of choice to enforce the violation of, or to address noncompliance with, a United Nations legal instrument—particularly the World Heritage Convention, to which almost all nation-states are party (see Werkheiser et al. this volume for consideration of how cultural heritage is protected through voluntary practices and nongovernmental channels). From conventional modes of diplomatic channels to NGO advocacy and outcry from Indigenous peoples and professional societies, public awareness that spawns international condemnation (or 'shaming') is perhaps the most effective way to alter the behavior of a State Party or to deter noncompliance. Adverse publicity for a World Heritage site or for a State Party could have material economic effect, primarily by reducing tourist numbers. Inscription on the World Heritage List secures international recognition of national heritage of 'outstanding universal value' from which flow global recognition and prestige that, in turn, attract tourist monies as well as other financial and philanthropic contributions.

Neither as legal instrument nor as ethical *raison d'être* has the World Heritage Convention—an expression of international unity, ostensibly rising to customary international law—proved infallible in providing remedy to protect cultural heritage. Nor has the Convention met its potential to engender an engaged archaeology with Indigenous and other local and descendent communities (see Pulitano 2012; Disko and Tugendhat's 2013 Report: International Expert Workshop on the World Heritage Convention and Indigenous Peoples). Furthermore, recent destruction of World Heritage sites by nonstate actors during armed conflict offers a sobering reminder of the limitations of the World Heritage apparatus.

Archaeology and Conflict: New Threats from Nonstate Actors

The emergence and rapid spread of political and/or ideological extremism poses an unprecedented and urgent challenge for archaeologists and heritage practitioners. This represents a severe threat to the fundamental principles underpinning the human rights regime that took shape in, and were shaped by, the 20th century. Existing frameworks of international heritage management are ill-equipped to address the threat from a nonstate actor operating within and/or across national boundaries with blatant disregard for conventional ethics, domestic and international law, and global 'norms' (see Fleming this volume). The rise of militant groups that target cultural heritage and endorse the industrial-scale plunder and trafficking of antiquities is already a 'clear and present danger' to the archaeological record, the cultural rights of local communities (e.g., access to and enjoyment of their cultural heritage), and indeed to individual working archaeologists. It reflects the broader dilemma that confronts governments and policy makers in the struggle to devise 'global solutions' to the varied but often interlinked contemporary 'global problems' that stretch across national boundaries.

Communities living in the new zones of conflict have suffered from widespread actions by extremist groups that seemingly reject any notion of or adherence to the principles of human rights law and international legal norms. For archaeology, the issue is particularly salient in light of reports that militant groups may be engaged in the looting and smuggling of antiquities as a source of funding. This accentuates the nexus of ideology and capital in destroying ancient sites, religious monuments, and holy places and extinguishing the cultural heritage rights of minority groups and other local and descendent communities under militants' territorial control.

During armed conflict and insurgency, it is difficult to assess directly the full impact of hostilities on the historical and cultural heritage of an occupied area, often owing to prolonged violence (for a discussion of the 2003 Iraq War, see Rothfield 2008 and Stone and Bajjaly 2008; for analysis of the post-2011 civil war in Syria, see Casana and Panahipour 2014). Access to sites is restricted by the overlapping conflicts between competing forces, and information on the condition of specific sites often is gleaned from secondhand accounts or through the use of remote sensing imagery (e.g., see Parcak 2009 and Boyle 2014 for the role of remote sensing in documenting the extent of damage over time in Egypt and how that information can be used as evidence for the need to legislate to combat the systematic looting and international trafficking of antiquities).

In Syria, for instance, in 2012, it was estimated that up to 90% of heritage sites lay within the borders of battlefields, and all six Syrian World Heritage sites suffered direct or collateral damage or both (Erciyes 2014; Cunliffe 2012:4). In September 2013, ICOM issued an Emergency Red List of Syrian Cultural Objects at Risk following reports of widespread damage and looting. In June 2014, a set of financial accounts appeared to indicate a profit of up to US$36 million from the trafficking of antiquities from the al-Nabuk area alone (Chulov 2014), though subsequent media reports on the scale of antiquities looting in Syria have been disputed and are difficult to verify (Felch 2014).

In Iraq, the Ministry of Tourism and Antiquities reported that by August 2014, up to 4,500 historical monuments had been stolen or damaged, spanning 6,000 years of human history dating back to the Sumerian and Assyrian eras (Erciyes 2014). Multiple sites across northern Iraq holy to the country's Shia, Turkmen, Christian, and other minority communities were damaged or destroyed in July and August 2014, as were a number of Sunni religious sites such as the Tomb of the Prophet Jonah in Mosul. In addition, the displacement of some 200,000 Yazidis, who represent one of the last concentrations of Aramaic speakers in the world, was described as "a cultural and linguistic emergency of historic proportions" (Perlin 2014).

While the pillaging of cultural heritage during war is an age-old practice, the rise of militant groups stresses the urgency to rethink approaches to the protection of cultural heritage in conflict zones. The international community first enacted treaties more than a century ago that specifically addressed the protection of cultural property (and, by implication acknowledging cultural rights) during armed conflict. The 1899 and 1907 Hague Conventions with Respect to the Laws and Customs of War on Land were updated by the 1954 Convention for the Protection of Cultural Property in the Event of Armed Conflict (hereafter the Hague Convention). The Hague Convention defined the rights and duties of states relating to cultural property before, during, and after armed conflict. Each state is required to protect its cultural property and respect other states' cultural property by not targeting or using such property for military purposes. Yet the Hague Convention, the 1970 UNESCO Convention on the Means of Prohibiting and Preventing the Illicit Import, Export, and Transfer of Ownership of Cultural Property and the 1972 World Heritage Convention (see earlier), among others, are firmly grounded in the principle of statehood, as expressed through the language of 'States Parties', which does not encompass the reality of contemporary geopolitics.

Insofar as international treaties face enforcement (compliance and sanction) difficulties, no equivalent framework exists to address the current situation posed by nonstate actors operating within and across national boundaries. Archaeology, cultural heritage, and local people's cultural rights are in peril, and it is likely that extremist group action in the context of the breakdown of state authority will continue to pose a substantial threat to heritage interests for years to come. The incompatibility of current governance arrangements is a microcosm of a larger, systemic difficulty with an institutional architecture that has failed to keep pace with rapid changes to the global order. State-based approaches to international governance notably have struggled to adapt to two of the most significant emergent trends in the highly interdependent 21st-century landscape. First is the shift in the types of conflict and disorder as violence within societies has become far more common than wars between or among states (Williams 2008:1115; Forrest 2014). Second is that the inherently transnational element of 'global problems' no longer can be resolved by any one nation-state alone. Instead, as political science advocates, the geopolitics of the 21st century require a restructuring of the core concepts of sovereignty, territoriality, and legitimate political authority that underpinned the 20th century states-based international system (Held 2008).

The challenge facing archaeology is profound. The damage to cultural heritage and archaeological resources—and therefore also to human rights in heritage—is irreversible and likely to continue unabated unless a new approach is developed that better equips both archaeologists and policy makers to address the snowballing impacts of state failure and the actions of nonstate actors, whether in Iraq, Syria, or elsewhere across the globe. The outlook in such cases certainly seems bleak. These nonstate actors lack respect for widely agreed-upon domestic and international codes, ethical mores, human rights, and universal norms built up over the last century. While the loss of access to fieldwork locations impacts archaeologists on an individual level, the collective threat to archaeology, heritage, and cultural human rights is magnified when neither law nor ethics, or a fusion of the two, impels nonstate actors to adhere to common principles and the global good.

Conclusion

Ethics inform law and law informs ethics. The power of ethics and the force of law are situated within a social context and, as all field archaeologists are acutely aware, context matters. As the new global order unfolds through the 21st century, this social context will gain increasing significance, and law and ethics—already symbiotic as this chapter illustrates—will become even more integrated with the study of the archaeological record and within schemes of heritage management. As practitioners in the field face a range of new threats and challenges, it is more important than ever that law and ethics coalesce to assist the discipline in adapting to continually evolving uncertain circumstances.

The outlook for law and ethics in archaeology and heritage management is good in parts. While room for improvement remains in all the varied areas of activity discussed, significant progress has been made in decolonizing the discipline(s) and dealing ethically with the cultural human rights of those among and with whom we work to advance our understanding of the past. Relations with Indigenous and other local and descendent communities are thus in general much improved in comparison with the situation even a decade ago and embrace tenets of an 'engaged pluralism'.

The engagement of the profession with the corporate sector and the multilateral development banks usually seems to take at least one step backward for every step forward, whether because of disagreement within the discipline(s) or the shifting agendas (and finances) of the corporations and institutions in question, or both. Yet if practitioners understand the need to persist and think very deliberately long term in relation to this and the other matters addressed in this chapter, the profession(s) can look back over the last few decades and see unquestionable progress on most fronts, which augurs well for the future.

Also good in parts is the outlook of legal, legislative, and self-regulatory ethical action to moderate the impacts of looting and illegal trafficking in cultural resources. True, the policies and practices of some major national and domestic heritage agencies and professional bodies still fall short, but in most cases colleagues involved do recognize that there are serious issues to be addressed even if operationalizing this recognition remains a work in progress.

The growth of violent nonstate actors in recent years, however, has placed those in the field—whether archaeologists and heritage managers or members of affected communities—in unprecedented danger. The rise of extremist groups emphasizes further the difficulty or impossibility of engaging with actors, whether individuals or organizations, who fundamentally reject globally accepted legal norms and values concerning cultural heritage and human rights and operate without any adherence to generally understood concepts of 'law' and/or 'ethics'. The changing dynamics of conflict in the 21st century have at once hastened the collapse as well as taken advantage of fragile and failing states. The simultaneous acceleration of transnational and nonstate processes threatens to render obsolete the 20th-century state-led architecture that evolved to manage national and international frameworks of governance. This is, of course, a much broader phenomenon, but for archaeology, it calls into question the relevance of any rules- or ethics-based system when nonstate actors refuse to acknowledge, let alone play by, those rules. This holds serious implications for human rights, cultural rights, and achieving effective remedies and equitable resolutions to contemporary exigencies in cultural heritage management.

Acknowledgments

This chapter was published originally as an article in the 40th Anniversary Issue of the *Journal of Field Archaeology* (Volume 40, Issue 5, October 2015, pages 508–522; www.tandfonline.com). The authors thank Christina Luke, then editor-in-chief of the *Journal of Field Archaeology*, for her invitation to write this piece for the 40th Anniversary Issue, and four anonymous referees who helped improve our text. We appreciate this opportunity to think broadly about the field, how it has developed, and what challenges lie ahead. The article is reprinted here with permission. Minor modifications and additions have been made to the text to maintain up-to-date information, cross-reference other chapters in this book, and format for this volume's requirements. For the invitation to participate in the October 2016 Relevance and Application of Heritage in Contemporary Society Workshop held at the Royal Ontario Museum and in this book, we thank Pei-Lin Yu, George S. Smith, and Chen Shen.

Note

1 At the time of publication of this volume, remains associated with the Ancient One have been determined through DNA analysis to be related to modern Native Americans. The remains were repatriated and reburied in 2017.

References

Agbe-Davies, A. 2010 An Engaged Archaeology for Our Mutual Benefit: The Case of New Philadelphia. *Historical Archaeology* 44(1):1–6.
Allen, J. 1983 Aborigines and Archaeologists in Tasmania. *Australian Archaeology* 16:7–10.
Anker, K. 2014 *Declarations of Interdependence: A Legal Pluralist Approach to Indigenous Rights*. Ashgate, Aldershot.
Berman, P. 2014 *Global Legal Pluralism: A Jurisprudence of Law Beyond Borders*. Cambridge University Press, Cambridge.
Biehl, P., D. Comer, C. Prescott, and H. Soderland, editors 2015 *Identity and Heritage: Contemporary Challenges in a Globalized World*. Springer Press, New York.
Blake, J. 2013 UNESCO/World Heritage Convention—Towards a More Integrated Approach. *Environmental Policy and Law* 43(1):8–17.
———. 2011 Taking a Human Rights Approach to Cultural Heritage Protection. *Heritage & Society* 4(2):199–238.
Blake, J., and B. Boer 2009 Human Rights, the Environment and the Tehran Declaration. *Environmental Policy and Law* 39(6):302–307.
Boyle, K. 2014 Egypt Turns to Technology in Effort to Protect Ancient Treasures From Looters. *The Washington Post*, June 1.
Bruning, S. 2006 Complex Legal Legacies: The Native American Graves Protection and Repatriation Act, Scientific Study, and Kennewick Man. *American Antiquity* 71(3):501–521.
Brysk, A., and A. Jimenez 2012 The Globalization of Law: Implications for the Fulfillment of Human Rights. *Journal of Human Rights* 11(1):4–16.
Carpenter, K., and A. Riley 2014 Indigenous Peoples and the Jurisgenerative Moment in Human Rights. *California Law Review* 102(1):173–234.
Casana, J., and M. Panahipour 2014 Satellite-based Monitoring of Looting and Damage to Archaeological Sites in Syria. *Journal of Eastern Mediterranean Archaeology and Heritage Studies* 2(2):128–151.
Chulov, M. 2014 How an Arrest in Iraq Revealed ISIS's $2bn Jihadist Network. *The Guardian*, June 15.
Coombe, R. 2010 Honing a Critical Cultural Study of Human Rights. *Communication and Critical/Cultural Studies* 7(3):230–246.
Cunliffe, E. 2012 Damage to the Soul: Syria's Cultural Heritage in Conflict. *Global Heritage Fund*, May 16:4.
Darian-Smith, E. 2013 *Laws and Societies in Global Contexts: Contemporary Approaches*. Cambridge University Press, Cambridge.
Disko, S., and H. Tugendhat 2013 *Report: International Expert Workshop on the World Heritage Convention and Indigenous Peoples*. The International Work Group for Indigenous Affairs, Copenhagen.
Erciyes, C. 2014 Islamic State Make Millions from Stolen Antiquities. *Al-Monitor*, September 2.

Felch, J. 2014 Danti's Inference: The Known Unknowns of ISIS and Antiquities Looting. *Chasing Aphrodite*, November 18.
Forrest, C. 2014 Safeguarding Cultural Heritage in Times of War. *World Politics Review*, July 29.
Gerstenblith, P. 2010 The Obligations Contained in International Treaties of Armed Forces to Protect Cultural Heritage in Times of Armed Conflict. In *Archaeology, Cultural Property, and the Military*, edited by L. Rush, pp. 4–14. Boydell and Brewer Press, Woodbridge.
———. 2009 Increasing Effectiveness of the Legal Regime for the Protection of the International Archaeological Heritage. In *Cultural Heritage Issues: The Legacy of Conquest, Colonization, and Commerce*, edited by J. Nafziger and A. Nigorski, pp. 305–322. Brill Publishers, Boston.
Held, D. 2008 Global Challenges: Effectiveness and Accountability. *Open Democracy*, January 17.
Intellectual Property Issues in Cultural Heritage: Theory, Practice, Policy, Ethics 2016 Project Description. Electronic document, www.sfu.ca/ipinch/about/project-description, accessed March 19, 2018.
Klabbers, J., and T. Piiparinen 2014 *Normative Pluralism and International Law*. Cambridge University Press, Cambridge.
Lafrenz Samuels, K., and I. Lilley 2015 Transnationalism and Heritage Development. In *Global Heritage: A Reader*, edited by L. Meskell, pp. 217–239. Blackwell, Oxford.
Langford, R. 1983 Our Heritage—Your Playground. *Australian Archaeology* 16:1–6.
Lilley, I. 2000 Professional Attitudes to Indigenous Interests in the Native Title Era: Settler Societies Compared. In *Native Title and the Transformation of Archaeology in the Postcolonial World*, edited by I. Lilley, pp. 99–119. Oceania Publications, Sydney.
Lixinski, L. 2013 *Intangible Cultural Heritage in International Law*. Oxford University Press, Oxford.
Logan, W. 2014 Human Rights—Avoidance and Reinforcement. *Heritage & Society* 7(2):156–169.
———. 2013 Australia, Indigenous Peoples and World Heritage from Kakadu to Cape York: State Party Behaviour under the World Heritage Convention. *Journal of Social Archaeology* 13(2):153–176.
———. 2012 Cultural Diversity, Cultural Heritage and Human Rights: Towards Heritage Management as Human Rights-based Cultural Practice. *International Journal of Heritage Studies* 18(3):231–244.
———. 2009 Playing the Devil's Advocate: Protecting Intangible Cultural Heritage and the Infringement of Human Rights. *Historic Environment* 22(3):14–18.
———. 2007 Closing Pandora's Box: Human Rights Conundrums in Cultural Heritage Protection. In *Cultural Heritage and Human Rights*, edited by H. Silverman and D. Ruggles, pp. 33–52. Springer Press, New York.
Luke, C., and M. Kersel 2013a *U.S. Cultural Diplomacy and Archaeology: Soft Power, Hard Heritage*. Routledge Press, New York.
———. 2013b Archaeological Heritage and Ethics. Editorial Introduction. Memoranda, Markets, and Museums in Mesoamerica. *Journal of Field Archaeology* 38(3):263.
———. 2008 Archaeological Heritage and Ethics. Editorial Introduction. *Journal of Field Archaeology* 33(4):461–462.
Mazower, M. 2004 The Strange Triumph of Human Rights, 1933–1950. *The Historical Journal* 47(2):379–398.
McBryde, I., editor 1985 *Who Owns the Past? Papers from the Annual Symposium of the Australian Academy of the Humanities*. Oxford University Press, Melbourne.

Meskell, L. 2013 UNESCO and the Fate of the World Heritage Indigenous Peoples Council of Experts (WHIPCOE). *International Journal of Cultural Property* 20(2):155–174.

———. 2012 The Rush to Inscribe: Reflections on the 35th Session of the World Heritage Committee, UNESCO Paris, 2011. *Journal of Field Archaeology* 37(2):145–151.

———. 2010 Human Rights and Heritage Ethics. *Anthropological Quarterly* 83(4):839–859.

O'Keefe, P. 2000 Archaeology and Human Rights. *Public Archaeology* 1(3):181–194.

O'Keefe, R. 2006 *The Protection of Cultural Property in Armed Conflict*. Cambridge University Press, Cambridge.

Oviedo, G., and T. Puschkarsky 2012 World Heritage and Rights-based Approaches to Nature Conservation. *International Journal of Heritage Studies* 18(3):285–296.

Owsley, D., and R. Jantz, editors 2014 *Kennewick Man: The Scientific Investigation of an Ancient American Skeleton*. Texas A&M University Press, College Station.

Parcak, S. 2009 *Satellite Remote Sensing for Archaeology*. Routledge Press, New York.

Perlin, R. 2014 Is the Islamic State Exterminating the Language of Jesus? *Foreign Policy*, August 14.

Pulitano, E., editor 2012 *Indigenous Rights in the Age of the UN Declaration*. Cambridge University Press, Cambridge.

Richman, J. 2003 NAGPRA: Constitutionally Adequate? In *Legal Perspectives on Cultural Resources*, edited by J. Richman and M. Forsyth, pp. 216–231. Altamira Press, Walnut Creek.

Rio Tinto 2010 Why Cultural Heritage Matters. A Resource Guide for Integrating Cultural Heritage Management into Communities Work at Rio Tinto. Electronic document, www.riotinto.com/documents/ReportsPublications/Rio_Tinto_Cultural_Heritage_Guide.pdf, 1–132, accessed March 19, 2018.

Rosenne, S. 1984 *Practice and Methods of International Law*. Oceana Publications, New York.

Rothfield, L., editor 2008 *Antiquities Under Siege: Cultural Heritage Protection after the Iraq War*. Altamira Press, Walnut Creek.

Shaheed, F. 2011 *Report of the Independent Expert in the Field of Cultural Rights*. Report A/HRC/17/38 of the UN Human Rights Council to UN General Assembly, March 21, pp.1–24.

Shepherd, N., and A. Haber 2011 What's up with WAC? Archaeology and 'Engagement' in a Globalized World. *Public Archaeology* 10(2):96–115.

Silverman, H., and D. Ruggles, editors 2007a *Cultural Heritage and Human Rights*. Springer Press, New York.

———. 2007b Cultural Heritage and Human Rights. In *Cultural Heritage and Human Rights*, edited by H. Silverman and D. Ruggles, pp. 3–29. Springer Press, New York.

Smith, C. 2011 Errors of Fact and Errors of Representation: Response to Shepherd and Haber's Critique of the World Archaeological Congress. *Public Archaeology* 10(4):223–234.

Soderland, H. 2013 Heritage Values, Jurisprudence, and Globalization. In *Heritage in the Context of Globalization: Europe and the Americas*, edited by P. Biehl and C. Prescott, pp. 9–15. Springer Press, New York.

Stone, P., and J. Bajjaly, editors 2008 *The Destruction of Cultural Heritage in Iraq*. Boydell and Brewer Press, Woodbridge.

Trigger, B. 1984 Alternative Archaeologies: Nationalist, Colonialist, Imperialist. *Man New Series* 19(3):355–370.

Trope, J., and W. Echo-Hawk 2001 The Native American Graves Protection and Repatriation Act: Background and Legislative History. In *The Future of the Past: Archaeologists, Native Americans and Repatriation*, edited by T. Bray, pp. 9–34. Garland Publishing, New York.

Ucko, P. 1983 Australian Academic Archaeology: Aboriginal Transformation of its Aims and Practices. *Australian Archaeology* 16:11–26.

Walter, R., and R. Hamilton 2014 A Cultural Landscape Approach to Community-based Conservation in Solomon Islands. *Ecology and Society* 19(4): Article 41.

Welch, J., and I. Lilley 2013 Beyond the Equator (Principles): A Forum on Community Benefit Sharing in Relation to Major Land Alteration Projects and Associated Intellectual Property Issues in Cultural Heritage Held at the Meeting of the Society for American Archaeology, Honolulu, 5 April 2013. *International Journal of Cultural Property* 20(4):467–493.

Willems, W. 2014 The Future of World Heritage and the Emergence of Transnational Heritage Regimes. *Heritage and Society* 7(2):105–120.

Williams, M. 2008 The Coming Revolution in Foreign Affairs: Rethinking American National Security. *International Affairs* 84(6):1115.

World Archaeological Congress 2010 About the World Archaeological Congress. Electronic document, www.worldarchaeologicalcongress.org/about-wac, accessed on March 19, 2018.

Cases Cited

Bonnichsen v. United States, 367 F.3d 864 (9th Cir. 2004).
Commonwealth v. Tasmania (1983) 158 CLR 1.
I/A Court H.R., *Case of Yatama v. Nicaragua*. Preliminary Objections, Merits, Reparations, and Costs. Judgment of June 23, 2005. Series C No. 127.
I/A Court H.R., *Saramaka People v. Suriname*. Preliminary Objections, Merits, Reparations, and Costs. Judgment of November 28, 2007. Series C No. 172.
Maya Indigenous Cmty. of Toledo Dist. v. Belize. Case 12.053, Report No. 40/04, Inter. Am. C.H.R., OEA/Ser.L/V/II.122 Doc. 5 rev., (2004).

Statutes, Conventions, and Regulations Cited

The American Indian Religious Freedom Act of 1978, 42 U.S.C. § 1996.
The Archaeological Resources Protection Act of 1979, 16 U.S.C. § 470aa-mm.
The Charter of the United Nations, signed on June 26, 1945. Electronic document, www.un.org/en/documents/charter/index.shtml, accessed March 19, 2018.
The Convention for the Protection of Cultural Property in the Event of Armed Conflict with Regulations for the Execution of the Convention 1954, First Protocol, The Hague, May 14, 1954, Second Protocol, The Hague, March 26, 1999. Electronic document, http://portal.unesco.org/en/ev.php-URL_ID=13637&URL_DO=DO_ TOPIC&URL_SECTION=201.html, accessed March 19, 2018.
The Convention Respecting the Laws and Customs of War on Land and Its Annex: Regulations Concerning the Laws and Customs of War on Land, The Hague, October 18, 1907. Electronic document, www.icrc.org/applic/ihl/ihl.nsf/385ec082b509e76c41256739003e636d/1d1726425f6955aec125641e0038bfd6, accessed March 19, 2018.
The Convention with Respect to the Laws and Customs of War on Land and Its Annex: Regulations Concerning the Laws and Customs of War on Land, The Hague, July 29, 1899. Electronic document, www.icrc.org/ihl/INTRO/150?OpenDocument, accessed March 19, 2018.
The International Council of Museums Code of Ethics for Museums, adopted 1986, as amended 2001 and retitled and revised 2004. Electronic document, accessed March 19, 2018.
The International Labour Organization No. 169 Indigenous and Tribal Peoples Convention, adopted 1989. Electronic document, http://icom.museum/fileadmin/user_upload/pdf/Codes/code_ethics2013_eng.pdf, accessed March 19, 2018.

The Native American Graves Protection and Repatriation Act of 1990, 25 U.S.C. §3001 *et seq.*

Native American Graves Protection and Repatriation Act Regulations—Disposition of Culturally Unidentifiable Human Remains; Proposed Rule, 72 Fed. Reg. 199: 58582–58590 (Oct. 16, 2007) (to be codified at 43 C.F.R. pt. 10).

Native American Graves Protection and Repatriation Act Regulations—Disposition of Culturally Unidentifiable Human Remains; Final Rule, 75 Fed. Reg. 49: 12378–12405 (Mar. 15, 2010) (codified at 43 C.F.R. pt. 10).

The United Nations 2007 Declaration on the Rights of Indigenous Peoples. Electronic document, http://un.org/esa/socdev/unpfii/documents/DRIPS_en.pdf, accessed March 19, 2018.

The United Nations Educational, Scientific, and Cultural Organization (UNESCO) 2013 Operational Guidelines for the Implementation of the World Heritage Convention. Electronic document, http://whc.unesco.org/archive/opguide13-en.pdf, i—vii, 1–167, accessed March 19, 2018.

The United Nations Educational, Scientific, and Cultural Organization (UNESCO) 2003 Convention for the Safeguarding of the Intangible Cultural Heritage. Electronic document, http://unesdoc.unesco. org/images/0013/001325/132540e.pdf, accessed March 19, 2018.

The United Nations Educational, Scientific, and Cultural Organization (UNESCO) 1972 Convention Concerning the Protection of the World Cultural and Natural Heritage. Electronic document, http://whc.unesco.org/en/conventiontext, accessed March 19, 2018.

The United Nations Educational, Scientific, and Cultural Organization (UNESCO) 1970 Convention on the Means of Prohibiting and Preventing the Illicit Import, Export, and Transfer of Ownership of Cultural Property. Electronic document, http://portal.unesco.org/ en/ev.php-URL_ID=13039&URL_DO=DO_TOPIC&URL_ SECTION=201.html, accessed March 19, 2018.

The United Nations International Convention on the Elimination of All Forms of Racial Discrimination, adopted 1965. Electronic document, www.ohchr.org/EN/ProfessionalInterest/Pages/ CERD.aspx, accessed March 19, 2018.

The United Nations Universal Declaration of Human Rights, adopted 1948. Electronic document, www.un.org/en/documents/udhr/indexshtml, accessed March 19, 2018.

The United States Department of the Interior, Bureau of Indian Affairs. Tribal Government, Procedures for Establishing that an American Indian Group Exists as an Indian Tribe—Mandatory Criteria for Federal Acknowledgement, 25 C.F.R. § 83.7.

17

CULTURAL HERITAGE STEWARDSHIP

Global Challenges and New Approaches for an Uncertain Future

Arlene K. Fleming

Introduction

The record of human habitation on earth includes civilizations obliterated and cultures destroyed as a result of conflict, natural disasters, and the inability to accommodate environmental, technological, or economic change. We are now challenged by scientific predictions and irrefutable evidence of profound global climatic developments with the potential for physical, social, and economic upheaval. Changes in ocean composition, coastline configuration, drought and precipitation patterns, and other environmental disruptions have ramifications including mass movements of people and conflict stimulated by scarce natural and financial resources as well as erosion of governmental stability and authority.

Attention to climatic changes and their potential socioeconomic effects will be necessary to assess the implications for cultural heritage protection and management. We must acknowledge the basic assumptions of the current global framework for managing cultural heritage and assess their viability in the context of international agreements regarding climate, armed conflict, migration, and potential effects on governance at all levels. Current and future challenges require vigilance, realism, and practicality, aided by flexibility, ingenuity, and imagination.

Current Approaches to Heritage Stewardship

Following the massive destruction of World War II, recognition and valuation of cultural heritage advanced considerably, especially regarding its material 'tangible' manifestations. Recently, the 'intangible' or nonmaterial aspects of culture are acknowledged as essential for understanding and appreciating the scope and value of heritage. Standards and provisions for heritage identification, documentation, protection, conservation, management, and economic use have proliferated through legal, professional, and public initiatives within governmental frameworks at international, national, subnational, and local levels. Nongovernmental, professional, and civic participation, as well as private-sector enterprises, including tourism, have increased the awareness, care, and use of historic sites, structures, objects, and cultural practices globally.

Although the post–World War II era was not without conflict, and the strength and viability of nation-states varied, the prevailing construct for protection and management of cultural heritage is based on international consensus and the responsibility of governments at national and subnational levels. The conceptual and administrative framework of national 'ownership' and custodial responsibility for cultural heritage continues even after the World Heritage Convention of 1972, wherein States Parties of the United Nations Educational, Scientific and Cultural Organization (UNESCO), recognized 'outstanding universal value'. This designation confers a place on the World Heritage List of sites with global significance (UNESCO 1972).

Following the establishment of UNESCO in 1945, constituent States Parties have created Recommendations and Conventions containing procedures and standards for protecting and managing cultural heritage (UNESCO 2017a). The International Council on Monuments and Sites (ICOMOS), an organization of heritage professionals established in 1965, has constituent national committees and several standard-setting charters for conservation and management of material cultural heritage (ICOMOS 2017; Australia ICOMOS 2013). Regional advisory standards are contained in conventions for archaeology, architecture, and landscapes created by constituent members of the Council of Europe (COE 2017). Most countries have national legislation and regulations for material cultural heritage, and many have legal and regulatory requirements at subnational levels, as well as zoning regulations affecting cultural and historic property (UNESCO 2017b; Messenger and Smith 2010). Several countries have private, public, or quasi-public trusts for heritage conservation, and a plethora of private organizations operate at international, national, and local levels. In recent decades, cultural heritage concepts, standards, and practices throughout the world have evolved in important respects, including accommodation of varying cultural norms, the relationship and interdependence of cultural and natural heritage, the role of cultural heritage in sustainable development, equitable sharing of resources, and human rights (UNESCO 2005, 2015).

Increasing ease of travel, leisure time, and disposable income have vastly increased tourism and appreciation of cultural heritage, bolstering economies of national governments, local communities, and commercial enterprises. The relationship between cultural heritage and social and economic development is recognized by inclusion in Environmental and Social Impact Assessment (ESIA) as reflected in policies of public and private international, regional, national financial development institutions (World Bank 2006, 2016). Thus the relatively stable period after 1950 and continuing into the early 2000s witnessed huge gains in the recognition, appreciation, valuation, and management of cultural heritage at international, national, and local levels. However, the changing nature of armed conflict in parts of the world and the focus on cultural heritage as contentious religious symbolism and territorial claims results in deliberate destruction of internationally valued heritage icons. Moreover, the supranational threat of climate change portends dangerous sea level rise, ocean acidification, changing weather patterns, and natural disasters, threatening agricultural production and water resources. These conditions are expected to stimulate huge migrations and, potentially, economic stress and cultural conflict. Predictive evidence is provided by experts and events, but the actual progression and timetable are unknown; thus uncertainty is exacerbated by the interrelationship between these threatening, challenging developments.

To protect heritage and preserve memory, we must consider that the framework may shift from relatively stable international and national entities to a more unpredictable, uncontrollable situation in which national political and economic power may be diminished and priorities for basic human needs may eclipse investment in heritage protection and management. Brief observations on international provisions for managing climate change, armed conflict, migration, government authority, and financing, as well as evidence for the interrelationship of these factors, are followed by suggestions for a viable approach to cultural heritage stewardship in an uncertain and challenging future. Current practice and emerging initiatives are also considered.

Climate Change

In 2015, representatives from 195 nations convened in Paris at the United Nations Framework Convention on Climate Change (UNFCCC) Conference of the Parties (COP21) to create a landmark treaty establishing a course for global action that significantly strengthened the UN climate regime dating to 1992. Provisions of the Paris Agreement (the CMA) and an accompanying COP decision include reaffirming the goal to limit global temperature increase below 2 degrees Celsius above preindustrial levels, binding commitments by all nations to renew contributions every five years, and reaffirming developed countries' support for efforts by developing countries, including voluntary contributions. Following the treaty signing in April 2016, the government of each signatory country must formally accept the agreement and implement required actions (UN 2015; C2ES 2015).

The UNFCCC's work over four years was informed by a series of Assessment Reports; the most recent, AR5, was issued in 2014 (IPCC 2014a, b). A Summary for Policymakers (in a separate Synthesis Report) summarizes AR5 as follows (IPCC 2014c): Climate changes have impacted human and natural systems on all continents and across all oceans, with changes unprecedented in past decades and even millennia. The atmosphere and ocean are warmer, amounts of snow and ice are diminished, and the sea level has risen. Observations since the mid-20th century include an increase in cold and warm temperature extremes and heavy precipitation. It is extremely likely that human actions—termed *anthropogenic*—have been the major cause of warming in the 20th century. Increasing greenhouse gas (GHG) emissions since the preindustrial era have created atmospheric concentrations of carbon dioxide, methane and nitrous oxide, unprecedented in the past 800,000 years.

Continued GHG emissions will result in further warming and long-lasting climatic changes, with increased likelihood of severe, pervasive, and irreversible effects on ecosystems and humans. Substantial reductions in GHG emissions, accompanied by adaptation to climate change, will be necessary. While projections vary widely and depend on climate policy and socioeconomic developments, a rise in surface temperature is projected during the 21st century under all emission scenarios. Thus an increase in frequency and duration of heat waves and extreme precipitation events is predicted for many regions, and the oceans are expected to warm and acidify. New risks for natural systems and humans will be unevenly distributed but are predictably greater for poor and disadvantaged communities. Even with decreasing GHGs, many impacts of climate change will continue for centuries, and risks of abrupt or irreversible changes will intensify with the magnitude of warming (IPCC 2014c).

Prospects for reducing and managing effects of future climate change depend on complementary strategies of *adaptation* and *mitigation*. By the late 21st century, even with strengthened mitigation and adaptation, warming is expected to result in "high to very high risk of severe, widespread and irreversible impacts globally" (IPCC 2014c). Adaptation has limited potential to reduce risks of impacts; effectiveness

FIGURE 17.1   Flooding and Wind in Jacksonville, Florida, during Hurricane Irma in 2017

Source: Photo by Beth Rucker. Used by permission.

depends on long-term sustainable development. Mitigation actions likely to hold warming below 2 degrees Celsius relative to preindustrial levels would necessitate substantial reductions in emissions over the next few decades followed by near-zero carbon dioxide and other long-lasting GHGs by the late 21st century. Such reductions would require considerable economic, social, and technological adjustments. A wide variety of adaptation and mitigation measures must be integrated with other societal objectives and actions, for example: effective governance, innovation and investments in environmentally respectful technology and infrastructure, and changes in human behavior and livelihood. Adaptation strategies will vary within sectors and regions, likely becoming more challenging as the negative effects of climate change increase. Mitigation measures will be most effective if accompanied by reduced energy use. Climate change challenges us to link mitigation and adaptation measures with other societal objectives in an integrated response (see Douglas this volume).

The nature, dimensions, and time frame of climate changes are under intense investigation, and predictions are constantly revised. Two studies published in 2016 question the generally accepted goal of holding global warming below 2 degrees Celsius above preindustrial levels (Hansen et al. 2016; DeConto and Pollard 2016). Analysis of ancient warm eras and ice melt in Antarctica suggest increasing speed and severity of sea level rise. With continued high GHG emissions, the Antarctic effect could range from a rise of about 2 feet in some parts of the world by 2100 to several meters over 50 to 150 years. Heritage sites in coastal areas and river valleys will be especially vulnerable.

Armed Conflict: Destruction of Cultural Heritage

The United Nations emerged in 1945 from the trauma and destruction of World War II with 51 nations committed to a framework for international governance that included UNESCO. The devastation of the built environment, including significant cultural and historic places, and the massive loss of cultural objects during the war stimulated the States Parties of UNESCO to create the Convention for the Protection of Cultural Property in the Event of Armed Conflict, signed at The Hague in 1954 (UNESCO 1954a, b). This Convention, and its accompanying Protocol, reflect military practice and technology of the era, and concern conflict between nations. A Second Protocol, created in 1999, was intended to make the Convention applicable to developing modes of conflict such as those in the Balkans, Iraq, Afghanistan, and Israel/Palestine during the late 20th century (UNESCO 1999).

The Geneva Convention of 1949 (administered by the International Committee of the Red Cross or ICRC) forbids intentional damage to undefended cultural heritage by armed combatants or occupying forces and prohibits pillage (ICRC 1949). Two supplementary treaties, the Additional Protocols I and II of 1977, incorporate the 1954 Hague Convention with specific provisions for cultural property protection (ICRC 1977a, b). They prohibit attacks against cultural property, use of cultural property in support of military effort, and its designation as an object of reprisal without exception for military necessity. Additionally, Protocol II mandates protections during intrastate armed conflict.

The UNESCO Convention on the Means of Prohibiting and Preventing the Illicit Import, Export and Transfer of Ownership of Cultural Property, created in 1970, applies during armed conflict, occupation, and peacetime but requires bilateral agreements between nations and has had limited effectiveness in preventing the illicit antiquities trade (UNESCO 1970). In 1995, the UNIDROIT Convention on Stolen or Illegally Exported Cultural Objects addressed some of the same issues (International Institute for the Unification of Private Law 1995).

Despite cultural property destruction during conflict or occupation, until the 1990s, there were no prosecutions under the 1954 Hague Convention. In 1993, the Statute of the International Criminal Tribunal for the Former Yugoslavia (ICTY) defined as a war crime the "seizure of, destruction or willful damage done to institutions dedicated to religion, charity and education, the arts and sciences, historic monuments and works of art and science" and, on this account, convicted the commanders of an attack on the Old Town of Dubrovnik (Forrest 2010:123). Subsequently, charges against Radovan Karadzic, president of the Republika Srpska from 1992 to 1996, who was convicted in 2016, included "intentional and wanton destruction of religious and cultural buildings of the Bosnian Muslim and Bosnian Croat communities including, but not limited to, mosques, churches, libraries, educational buildings and cultural centres" (Ibid.). Ratko Mladic, the former Bosnian Serb military leader indicted in 1995 whose trial continued in 2016, was similarly charged, as was Slobodan Milosevic, former Serbian president, who died in 2006 while on trial at The Hague.

The 1998 Rome Statute of the International Criminal Court (ICC), states that "[i]ntentionally directing attacks against buildings dedicated to religion, education, art, science or charitable purposes, historic monuments, hospitals and places where the sick and wounded are collected, provided they are not military objectives" is a war crime, based on customary international law (UN General Assembly 1998; Forrest 2010:123). In 2015, the ICC began prosecution for attacks against historic religious monuments and buildings, including nine mausoleums and one mosque in Timbuktu, Mali, during 2012. Ahmad Al Faqi Al Mahdi, a member of Ansar Dine, the Tuareg militia linked to al-Qaeda, was convicted at The Hague in 2016 (ICC 2016a, b).

Conflicts during the post–World War II era had not produced alarming reports of damage to cultural heritage prior to news of looted provincial museums in Iraq in the aftermath of the First Gulf War in 1991, an early event in a series of internationally publicized deliberate attacks on cultural heritage. Intentional erasure of cultural heritage was a strategic aim in the conflict between Serbs, Croats, and Bosniaks during the 1990s.

In Afghanistan, intentional destruction of the Bamiyan Buddhas and pre-Islamic artifacts in the national museum by the Taliban in 2001, although not a result of armed conflict, aroused international indignation, as did the sack of the Iraq Museum during the invasion by the United States in 2003, followed by large-scale illicit excavation and looting in Iraq. Existing international agreements for heritage protection during conflict and occupation, as well as national laws of the combatants, proved useless in these instances. Destruction as 'collateral damage' during fighting continues in the Middle East and Africa, with additional deliberate, provocative actions by the Islamic State of Iraq and Syria (ISIS), who have destroyed artifacts in the Mosul Museum and demolished the entire archaeological site of Nimrud in Iraq during 2015, followed in 2016 by the obliteration of major ancient structures in Palmyra, Syria, documented by satellite imagery.

Looting and illicit trade in antiquities continue during conflict and chaotic conditions in Afghanistan, Iraq, Syria, Egypt, Yemen, and Libya (see Burgess this volume). Changes in the nature of armed conflict include participation of 'non-state actors', fluctuating alliances of militia groups, terrorists, criminal gangs, global recruiting, ethnic cleansing, religious extremism, and factionalism. Cultural heritage also is subject to destruction from advanced weaponry used by government forces.

International attention from cultural heritage organizations, professionals, the media, and the public has been reactive, focused on single incidents, remote data gathering and analysis, 'no-strike lists', numerous informal discussions and meetings, and, where possible, training for custodians of the heritage in conflict areas (for activities of the Blue Shield, see Stone this volume). Initial response in some cases is to reconstruct destroyed historic structures, as in the case of Stari Most, the renowned Ottoman-era bridge in Bosnia and Herzegovina, demolished by Croat forces in 1993.

Migration

The challenge of accommodating displaced people following World War II led in 1951 to the Convention Relating to the Status of Refugees, administered by the United Nations Refugee Agency (UNHCR), and amended in 1967 with a Protocol Relating to the Status of Refugees, which broadened the convention's applicability to include areas outside of Europe (UNHCR 1951, 1967). These remain the key international agreements. However, the circumstances stimulating population movements in the 21st century are diverse and complex, creating numerous categories of migrants not covered by the Convention and Protocol. These include asylum seekers; economic migrants; and internally displaced persons (IDPs). The international agreements exist in combination with national laws, regulations, and fluctuating political and economic decisions. Moreover, the Convention and Protocol do not address the *causes* of migration, such as human rights violations, political repression, armed conflict, economic disparities, natural disasters, or environmental degradation.

The International Organization for Migration (IOM), also established in 1951, is an intergovernmental organization with 162 member states and offices in more than 100 countries. IOM's mission is to promote humane and orderly migration by providing services and advice to governments and migrants through work in four areas: migration and development, facilitating migration, regulating migration, and forced migration (IOM 2015).

During 2014–2016, international media focused on the drama of migrants streaming into Europe escaping conflict in the Middle East—mainly in Syria and Iraq—as well as from sub-Saharan Africa. In 2015, Germany alone accepted 1 million refugees. The UN identified nearly 60 million persons forcefully displaced either externally or internally in 2016, indicating that one person of every 122 in the world had fled home. UNHCR has warned of "an unchecked slide into an era in which the scale of global forced displacement as well as the response required is now clearly dwarfing anything seen before" (UNHCR 2014b).

A UNHCR report based on information from the first half of 2015 revealed worsening indicators. The number of refugees who could safely return home was the lowest in more than three decades, with habitation impossible due to continuing conflicts or severe damage to infrastructure, social services, and other necessities. As the population stuck in exile increases, political, economic, social, and cultural pressures on host countries worsen (UNHCR 2015). While the international media highlighted the influx into Europe, most refugees locate in neighboring countries, with global distribution heavily skewed toward poorer nations. In 2014, almost 9 of 10 refugees were in economically less developed countries (UNHCR 2014a).

Figures from 2014 indicate that 19.3 million IDPs in 100 countries were forced to flee their homes by disasters including earthquakes, volcanic eruptions, floods, and storms (IDMC 2015a and b). Often the displacement from natural disasters is protracted, especially in low- and middle-income countries (Bohra-Mishra et al. 2014). The scale and continuing increase in external migration and internal displacement due to conflict and environmental conditions constitutes a huge hidden economic and humanitarian crisis with no solution in sight. It is a potential threat to the political, social, cultural, and economic viability of affected countries, perpetuating or even creating 'failed states'.

Government Authority and Financing: Weakened States

Although climate change is a global phenomenon, the burdens will likely fall disproportionately on the poor, especially those living in weaker states. 'Fragile, failed, or failing states' defines countries unable to provide basic requirements of education, housing, health, welfare, employment, justice, governance, security, and human rights. The 2015 Fragile States Index (FSI) of the Fund for Peace lists 25 countries (F25) in this category based on social, economic, and political indicators including: poverty and economic decline; demographic pressures; legitimacy; security; human rights; rule of law; fractionalized elites; and external intervention (Chamie and Mirkin 2016). Four of the F25 countries are categorized as 'Very High Alert': South Sudan, Somalia, Central African Republic, and Sudan. Twelve in the 'High Alert' category include the conflict countries of Afghanistan, Iraq, Syria, and Yemen. Sixty percent of the F25 countries have been among the top 10 on the index since its inception in 2005. Despite dire conditions, the population growth rate of F25 countries is 10 times that of developed countries (Ibid.).

With young populations and poor prospects for livelihood, F25 countries are the largest source of refugees and IDPs. Failing states may have a destabilizing effect on neighboring countries and constitute a global challenge. In 2016, millions of refugees from the ongoing Syrian conflict were severely straining the budgets and the health, education, and infrastructure systems in neighboring Turkey, Lebanon, and Jordan; the fragile economy and social service network of Greece—the gateway to Europe for refugees—was further stressed. Profound physical, economic, social, psychological, and cultural damage in Syria resulted in an estimated US$1.3 trillion in lost economic growth as of 2016. While it is difficult to gauge reconstruction costs during continuing intense conflict, they have been projected at nearly $US200 billion in future decades, with priority for basic infrastructure (World Vision International 2016).

The Nexus: Climate Change, Conflict, and Migration

The dire long-term consequences of climate change are punctuated by major sudden-onset weather events, increasingly frequently. Scientists' warnings are borne out by warming temperatures and changing patterns within ecosystems. The gradual loss of areas suitable for habitation by humans and other species, including for agriculture and aquaculture, and immediate effects of dramatic weather events are expected to vastly increase population movement in the quest for security and livelihood (Werz and Conley 2012). A projected global population of 8.5 billion by 2030 will be vying for resources, increasing the potential for conflict and for the flow of migrants (UNFPA 2015). This *nexus of climate change, conflict, and migration* may be difficult to control and stressful to existing economic, political, social, and legal systems at all levels of society. The dual recommendation of the UNFCCC for addressing climate change—*adaptation* and *mitigation*—must be considered within this broader physical, social, economic, and cultural context. Specific characteristics and dynamics of situations in which climate change, conflict, and migration are interrelated may vary widely.

Challenges and New Approaches

During the past few decades, numerous international, regional, national, and local cultural heritage organizations, as well as individual scholars and practitioners, have recognized potential threats to cultural heritage sites, structures, and objects from the effects of climate change, natural disasters, armed conflict, and, to a lesser extent, migration and diverse cultural norms. Discussions, meetings, declarations, policies, conventions, recommendations, and studies in the heritage field have been accompanied by practical action in the form of new organizations and alliances, technical assistance, training, and enhanced conservation and management techniques (Berenfeld 2015; ICOMOS/ICORP 2013; Sabbioni et al. 2012; UCS 2015). But the pace and complexity of observable and predicted developments are accelerating.

Clearly, the issue is not simply a concern for the survival of cultural heritage *vis-à-vis* the effects of changes in the climate and physical environment, but in the context of related ramifications, including the potential for conflict, population movements and dislocation, and the stress these events place on global, national, and subnational governance and economies.

How do we supplement the post–World War II construct for cultural heritage stewardship with new concepts and approaches suitable for the threats and uncertainties ahead while utilizing available technologies, modes and patterns of communication, means of collecting, organizing, and presenting information, and broad public participation? New approaches are buttressing and enhancing the existing international, national, and subnational administrative and legal frameworks for cultural heritage protection, management, and appreciation. Our challenge is to assess and scale up efforts to augment the existing regime for heritage management and compensate for gaps and weaknesses exposed by radically and rapidly changing conditions.

New approaches will build on concepts evolved over the past half century, including the recognition of heritage as a global public good while also an integral aspect of local community identity, responsibility, and socioeconomic benefit. Technological advances in survey and spatial analysis, vast data management, enhanced image creation, virtual reality, three-dimensional replication, and instantaneous global communication will be essential.

A practical system for documentation, protection, and management of cultural heritage in anticipation of future conditions and challenges could focus on specific heritage places and practices in a three-part approach including awareness, assessment, and action.

Awareness

- Follow and understand developments, indicators, and effects of climate change, conflict, population movements, and their potential impact on tangible and intangible cultural heritage.
- Factor this information into all policies, planning, management, and monitoring schemes.

Assessment

- Determine, on a continuing basis, the type and degree of vulnerability of cultural heritage places, objects, and practices to climate change and its ramifications.
- Define the value and importance, including the unique characteristics, of the tangible and intangible heritage:
  - as a guide for protection, conservation, and management.
  - as a guide for conserving memory if physical survival is rendered impossible.
- Identify optimal skills, technologies, methods, and participants for stewardship, including documentation, conservation, monitoring, and reporting.

Action

- Integrate heritage with general management and protection strategies, plans, and activities in localities, and collaborate with relevant authorities (e.g., disaster preparedness, first responders, development proponents).
- Enlist local communities in the care, monitoring, and reporting on cultural heritage places, objects, and practices, including the gradual and cumulative effects of climate change (see Altschul and Chilton this volume).
    - Establish systematic information exchange between local communities and heritage experts.
    - Use social media and crowd sharing for timely training, observation, documentation, and communication.
- Establish a robust source of funding and an administrative structure to enable sharing of successful techniques demonstrated at specific cultural heritage places and scale up to a worldwide effort.
- Generate a global audience and support network for cultural heritage.
    - Stimulate wide public interest and appreciation.
    - Educate using appropriate technologies and communication (see Smith and Hassan this volume).
    - Use electronic communication for public involvement.

Uncertainties and serious threats on massive scales require a conceptual change and new approaches to cultural heritage documentation, protection, conservation, and management commensurate with the challenges. Fortunately, a strong base of interest and practice, established during recent decades, together with new and emerging technologies, should support this urgent and compelling endeavor.

References

All electronic documents were accessed on February 7, 2017.

Australia ICOMOS 2013 *The Australia ICOMOS Charter for Places of Cultural Significance, The Burra Charter.* Electronic document, http://australia.icomos.org/publications/burra-charter-practice-notes/.

Berenfeld, M. L. 2015 Planning for Permanent Emergency: "Triage" as a Strategy for Managing Cultural Resources threatened by Climate Change. *The George Wright Forum* 32(1):5–12.

Bohra-Mishra, P., M. Oppenheimer, and S. M. Hsiang 2014 Nonlinear permanent migration response to climatic variations but minimal response to disasters. *Proceedings of the National Academy of Sciences* 111(27).

Center for Climate and Energy Solutions (C2ES) 2015 Outcomes of the U.N. Climate Change Conference in Paris: 21st Session of the Conference of the Parties to the United Nations Framework Convention on Climate Change (COP 21), November 30–December 12, 2015.

Chamie, J., and B. Mirkin 2016 In an Age of Global Terror, Do Failed States Endanger You, Too? InterPress Service. Electronic document, http://www.juancole.com/2016/04/in-an-age-of-global-terror-do-failed-states-endanger-you-too.html.

Council of Europe (COE) 2017 Cultural Conventions. Electronic document, www.coe.int/t/dg4/cultureheritage/heritage/Resources/Conventions/conventions_en.asp

DeConto, R. M., and D. Pollard 2016 Contribution of Antarctica to Past and Future Sea-Level Rise. *Nature* 531:591–597, March 31, 2016. doi: 10.1038/nature17145.

Forrest, C. 2010 *International Law and the Protection of Cultural Heritage*. Routledge, London.

Hansen, J., M. Sato, P. Hearty, R. Ruedy, M. Kelley, V. Masson-Delmotte, G. Russell, G. Tselioudis, J. Cao, E. Rignot, I. Velicogna, B. Tormey, B. Donovan, E. Kandiano, K. von Shuckmann, P. Kharecha, A. N. Legrande, M. Bauer, and K-W. Lo 2016 Ice Melt, Sea Level Rise and Superstorms: Evidence from Paleoclimate Data, Climate Modeling, and Modern Observations That 2 Degree C. Global Warming Could Be Dangerous. *Atmospheric Chemistry and Physics* 16:3761–3812. doi: 10.5194/acp-16-3761-2016.

International Council on Monuments and Sites (ICOMOS) 2017 Charters and Other Doctrinal Texts. Electronic document, www.icomos.org/en/charters-and-texts.

———. 2013 *Heritage and Resilience: Issues and Opportunities for Reducing Disaster Risks*. ICOMOS/ICORP Global Platform for Disaster Risk Reduction. Electronic document, http://icorp.icomos.org/images/documents/Heritage%20and%20Resilience%20Book%20for%20GP2013%20Disaster%20Management.pdf.

Intergovernmental Panel on Climate Change (IPCC) 2014a *Climate Change 2014: Impacts, Adaptation, and Vulnerability, Part A: Global and Sectoral Aspects. Contribution of Working Group II to the Fifth Assessment Report of the Intergovernmental Panel on Climate Change*. Cambridge University Press, Cambridge.

———. 2014b *Climate Change 2014: Impacts, Adaptation and Vulnerability. Part B: Regional Aspects. Contribution of Working Group II to the Fifth Assessment Report of the Intergovernmental Panel on Climate Change*. Cambridge University Press, Cambridge.

———. 2014c Climate Change 2014 Synthesis Report Summary for Policymakers. Electronic document, www.ipcc.ch/report/ar5/syr/

Internal Displacement Monitoring Centre (IDMC) and Norwegian Refugee Council 2015a Global Estimates 2015: People Displaced by Disasters. Geneva. Electronic document, www.internal-displacement.org

——— 2015b Global Overview 2015: People Internally Displaced by Conflict and Violence. Geneva. Electronic document, www.internal-displacement.org

International Committee of the Red Cross (ICRC) 1977a *Protocol Additional to the Geneva Conventions of 12 August 1949, and Relating to the Protection of Victims of International Armed Conflicts (Protocol I)*. June 8, 1977, 1125 UNTS 3.

———. 1977b *Protocol Additional to the Geneva Conventions of 12 August 1949, and Relating to the Protection of Victims of Non-International Armed Conflict (Protocol II)* June 8, 1977, 1125 UNITS 609.

———. 1949 *Geneva Convention Relative to the Protection of Civilian Persons in Time of War* (Fourth Geneva Convention), August 12, 1949, 75 UNTS 287.

International Criminal Court (ICC) 2016a ICC Pre-Trial Chamber I Confirms the Charge Against Ahmad Al Faqi Al Mahdi and Commits Him to Trial. Press Release: March 24, 2016.

———. 2016b The Prosecutor v. Ahmad Al Faqi Al Mahdi. Case Information Sheet, ICC-PIDS-CIS-MAL-01–08/16 Eng. Updated: October 7, 2016.

International Institute for the Unification of Private Law 1995 *UNIDROIT Convention on Stolen or Illegally Exported Cultural Objects*. Rome, June 24, 1995.

International Organization for Migration (IOM) 2015 *World Migration Report 2015—Migrants and Cities: New Partnerships to Manage Mobility*. Geneva. Electronic document, http://publications.iom.int/books/world-migration-report-2015-migrants-and-cities-new-partnerships-manage-mobility.

Messenger, P. M., and G. S. Smith, editors 2010 *Cultural Heritage Management: A Global Perspective*. University Press of Florida, Gainesville.

Sabbioni, C., P. Brimblecombe, and M. Cassar 2012 *The Atlas of Climate Change Impact on European Cultural Heritage: Scientific Analysis and Management Strategies*. European Union. Anthem Press, London.

Union of Concerned Scientists (UCS) 2015 The Pocantico Call to Action on Climate Impacts and Cultural Heritage. Electronic document, www.ucsusa.org/global-warming/solutions/pocantico-call-action-climate-impacts-and-cultural-heritage#.VyedRmNNx6k

United Nations Educational, Scientific and Cultural Organization (UNESCO) 2017a Conventions and Recommendations. Electronic document, http://portal.unesco.org/en/ev.php-URL_ID=13649&URL_DO=DO_TOPIC&URL_SECTION=-471.html

———. 2017b Culture. Legal Instruments. Electronic document, http://portal.unesco.org/en/ev.php-URL_ID=13649&URL_DO=DO_TOPIC&URL_SECTION=471.html

———. 2015 *Policy for the Integration of a Sustainable Development Perspective into the Processes of the World Heritage Convention.* Adopted by the General Assembly of the States Parties to the Convention by its Resolution 20 GA 13.

———. 2005 *Convention on the Protection and Promotion of the Diversity of Cultural Expressions.* Paris October 20, 2005.

———. 1999 *Second Protocol to the Hague Convention of 1954 for the Protection of Cultural Property in the Event of Armed Conflict 1999.* The Hague, March 26, 1999.

———. 1972 *Convention concerning the Protection of the World Cultural and Natural Heritage.* Paris, November 16, 1972.

———. 1970 *Convention on the Means of Prohibiting and Preventing the Illicit Import, Export and Transfer of Ownership of Cultural Property.* Paris, November 14, 1970.

———. 1954a *Convention for the Protection of Cultural Property in the Event of Armed Conflict.* The Hague, May 14, 1954.

———. 1954b *Protocol for the Protection of Cultural Property in the Event of Armed Conflict.* The Hague, May 14, 1954.

United Nations Framework Convention on Climate Change 2015 *Conference of the Parties, Twenty-first session. Paris, 30 November to 11 December 2015. Adoption of the Paris Agreement.* FCCC/CP/2015/L.9.

United Nations General Assembly 1998 *Rome Statute of the International Criminal Court* (last amended 2010), July 17, 1998, ISBN No. 92-9227-227-6.

United Nations Population Fund (UNFPA) 2015 *World Population Prospects: Key Findings and Advance Tables, 2015 Revision.* United Nations, New York.

United Nations Refugee Agency (UNHCR) 2015 *Mid-Year Trends 2015.* December 18, 2015. Geneva. Electronic document, www.unhcr.org/56701b969.html

———. 2014a *Global Trends Report.* Electronic document, www.unhcr.org/2014trends

———. 2014b *Global Trends: Forced Displacement in 2014.* Electronic document, www.unhcr.org/556725e69.html

———. 1967 Text of the *1967 Protocol Relating to the Status of Refugees,* January 31, 1967. Resolution 2198 (XXI) adopted by the United Nations General Assembly. Electronic document, www.unhcr.org/3b66c2aa10.html

———. 1951 *Convention Relating to the Status of Refugees,* July 28, 1951.

Werz, M., and L. Conley 2012 *Climate Change, Migration, and Conflict: Addressing Complex Crisis Scenarios in the 21st Century.* Center for American Progress, Washington, DC.

The World Bank 2016 *Environmental and Social Framework, Standard 8—Cultural Heritage.* Electronic document, http://documents.worldbank.org/curated/en/383011492423734099/pdf/114278-WP-REVISED-PUBLIC-Environmental-and-Social-Framework-Dec18-2017.pdf

———. 2006 *Operational Policy 4.11—Physical Cultural Resources.* Electronic document, http://web.worldbank.org/archive/website01541/WEB/0_-1446.HTM

World Vision International 2016 *The Cost of Conflict for Children: Five Years of the Syria Crisis.* Electronic document, http://cdn.worldvision.org.uk/files/4914/5736/3732/Cost_of_Conflict.pdf

APPENDIX A

The Toronto Declaration on the Relevance and Application of Heritage in Contemporary Society

In October 2016, a workshop on Relevance and Application of Heritage in Contemporary Society convened at the Royal Ontario Museum in Toronto, Canada. The goal was to apply the latest theoretical and applied anthropological knowledge to develop recommendations for ensuring that cultural heritage is defined, valued, presented, and appreciated in a fair and equitable manner that enables a beneficial role for heritage in modern society.

Cultural heritage is the legacy of physical artifacts and intangible attributes of a group or society inherited from past generations, maintained in the present, and bestowed for the benefit of future generations. This includes tangible culture (e.g., buildings, monuments, landscapes, books, works of art, and artifacts), intangible culture (e.g., folklore, traditions, language and knowledge), and natural heritage (culturally significant natural features and landscapes). The workshop brought together an international group of 18 experts to discuss the importance of heritage in the modern world (relevance) and describe its role (application) in contemporary society. In the workshop, participants discussed important theoretical and applied topics relating to cultural heritage and represented a breadth of knowledge and experience in the integration of cultural heritage into various sectors of contemporary life.

Broad consultation and inclusion of stakeholders allows for co-existence of different perspectives on the past, furthering appreciation of differences and similarities among societies; an important concept in this era of widespread cultural and geopolitical conflict, transhumance, and nationalism. Recent changes in the ways that contemporary societies view, access, and value heritage present new opportunities and challenges to ensure that the heritage of a given society or group is identified, valued, and appreciated in an accurate, balanced, and respectful way. A balanced approach considers the social dynamics within and between societies, contributing to future political, economic, environmental and educational policy, planning, and implementation.

To codify these issues and beliefs, participants of the Toronto Cultural Heritage Group hereby declare the following.

> **WHEREAS**, heritage is the living expression of cultural traditions, norms, and values and is intergenerational and subject to social dynamics within and between societies, and
>
> **WHEREAS,** the strength and resiliency of nations, and communities in the world is contingent on a strong connection to cultural heritage, and respect for heritage diversity within and beyond modern political boundaries, and
>
> **WHEREAS**, contemporary values affect the significance given to tangible and intangible cultural inheritances, influencing decisions on interpretation and how heritage is presented, and it is necessary to articulate and consider the full range of values and interests with respect to local, national, and international policies, strategies, and financing, and
>
> **WHEREAS**, it is important to develop effective ways of defining and advocating the need for sustainable, responsive cultural heritage management policies to policy-makers and the public at the levels where policy-crafting, resource allocation, and planning collaboration occur, and
>
> **WHEREAS**, to ensure that heritage is defined broadly, respected and valued fairly it is essential to enlist the fiscal and human resources that include infrastructure development proponents; financial institutions; international, national, sub-national and local governments and organizations; local communities; non-governmental organizations; professional organizations; researchers; educators; the media; and the public at large, and
>
> **WHEREAS**, cultural heritage affects the quality of life for individuals, communities, and nations, and choosing not to value heritage has consequences which can be detrimental to social order, and
>
> **WHEREAS**, allowing interest in, and support for, tangible and intangible cultural heritage in a manner that can compete with other agendas in a market-driven world requires applying, legal, ethical, economic, management, community, and scientific perspectives in meeting needs with respect to two principles:

The cultural heritage agenda;

- Cultural Heritage Management (CRM) standards, including identification, documentation, protection, conservation and use
- Capacity building at local, national and international levels
- Community involvement
- Promoting cultural diversity and indigenous people's rights
- Professional training: education and curriculum development
- Establishing world-wide networks for protection, management and advocacy
- Combating antiquities theft and looting
- Data collection, management, dissemination and use
- Museums, libraries and archives, and

Integration of cultural heritage into other agendas;

- Climate change and adaptation planning
- Natural disaster planning, mitigation and response
- Contemporary social and economic planning, action and issues at local, national and international levels
- Laws and treaties
- Commerce and trade
- Population movements: migrants, refugees and displaced persons
- Cultural diversity and indigenous people's rights
- Religion: tolerance and respect
- Ethical issues
- Infrastructure development and extractive industries
- Finance: public and private
- Poverty and inequality
- Armed conflict and terrorism
- Urban issues
- Rural and agrarian issues
- Media and information dissemination;

NOW, THEREFORE, the signers of this Declaration express our intent to carry out to the best of our abilities the actions set forth below. We shall foster the relevance and valuation of cultural heritage as an important aspect of society and enlist the collaboration of individuals, groups and organizations dedicated to cultural heritage, as well as those outside the heritage field in order to have a significant impact on the valuation, identification, conservation and management of heritage. This is essential for promoting the following actions:

1. Further attention to the relevance and application of cultural heritage in contemporary society through publications, symposia, conferences, workshops and working groups at local, national and international levels.
2. Publicize best practices for management and protection of cultural heritage in the public interest through discussion and dissemination of information to ensure that individuals, communities and nations have a meaningful connection to their heritage and the full range of cultural heritage resources receives due consideration.
3. Examine, discuss, and evaluate impacts of globalization and market economies, armed conflict, climate change, migration, social and economic development, governmental policies on heritage, and formulation of sustainable long-term strategies and alliances to ensure effective application of tangible and intangible cultural heritage in contemporary society.
4. Increase public awareness of looting and destruction at cultural heritage sites and the international antiquities trade.
5. Build capacity of professionals and communities for identification, documentation, protection, management and use of cultural heritage in a manner that promotes local pride ownership and social and economic benefit.

6. Act as liaisons among governments, local communities and other stakeholders, including descendant peoples, to encourage awareness and stewardship of cultural heritage.
7. Include cultural heritage in local, national and international networks for preparedness and recovery in the event of natural disasters.
8. Develop and disseminate methods for identifying responsible parties in order to secure funds for heritage restitution and recovery actions.
9. Develop and disseminate effective educational materials, curricula and training for cultural heritage management, including an international network for distance learning on a platform that provides for exchange of information in multiple languages.
10. Develop recommendations for increased participation by descendant communities and other stakeholders in cultural heritage data generation, protection and management.
11. Support and encourage heritage programs, including museums, in local communities.

Founding Signatories

Dr. Jeffrey H. Altschul
Dr. Uzi Baram
L. Eden Burgess, Esq.
Dr. Elizabeth S. Chilton
Dr. Diane Douglas
Ms. Arlene K. Fleming
Dr. Fekri Hassan
Mr. Katsuyuki Okamura
Dr. David Pokotylo
Dr. Chen Shen
Dr. Claire Smith
Dr. George S. Smith
Dr. Hilary A. Soderland, Esq.
Dr. Jigen Tang
Dr. Peter Stone
Dr. Joe Watkins
Marion Werkheiser, Esq.
Dr. Pei-Lin Yu

APPENDIX B

Declaración de Toronto Sobre la Relevancia y Aplicación del Patrimonio en la Sociedad Contemporánea

La versión de bolsillo

Adoptada por los participantes del taller sobre la Relevancia y Aplicación del Patrimonio en la Sociedad Contemporánea, en Toronto, Ontario, Canadá, Octubre de 2016.

1. Difundir la relevancia y aplicación del patrimonio cultural en la sociedad contemporánea a través de toda la gama de publicaciones y otros métodos de comunicación.
2. Dar a conocer las mejores prácticas para la gestión del patrimonio cultural para garantizar que todos tengan una conexión significativa con su patrimonio y que se tenga debidamente en cuenta toda la gama de sitios culturales heredados, objetos y tradiciones.
3. Evaluar toda la gama de impactos contemporáneos sobre el patrimonio cultural y formular estrategias y alianzas sostenibles a largo plazo para el mejoramiento del patrimonio cultural tangible e intangible en la sociedad contemporánea.
4. Aumentar la conciencia pública sobre el saqueo y la destrucción en los sitios del patrimonio cultural y el comercio internacional de antigüedades.
5. Fortalecer la capacidad de los profesionales y las comunidades para toda la gama de acciones del patrimonio cultural para promover el orgullo local, la propiedad y el beneficio económico.
6. Actuar como enlace entre los gobiernos, las comunidades locales y otras partes interesadas, incluidos los pueblos descendientes, para fomentar la administración del patrimonio cultural.
7. Incluir el patrimonio cultural en las redes locales e internacionales para la preparación y la recuperación de los desastres naturales.
8. Desarrollar y difundir métodos para identificar a las partes responsables a fin de obtener fondos para las acciones de restitución y recuperación del patrimonio.

9. Desarrollar y difundir materiales educativos para la gestión del patrimonio cultural, a escala local e internacional, para compartir información en múltiples idiomas.
10. Formular recomendaciones para una mayor participación de las comunidades de descendientes y otras partes interesadas en la generación, protección y gestión de datos relativos al patrimonio cultural.
11. Apoyar y alentar programas de patrimonio cultural de base, incluido el establecimiento y mantenimiento de museos en las comunidades locales.

Traducción por Lilia Lizama y Luisa Cano, Arqueologos Sin Fronteras.

La versión complèta de esta Déclaration se encuentra a Capítulo Uno en este libro.

APPENDIX C

多伦多宣言：文化遗产与当代社会的相关性及其应用

袖珍版本

由2016年10月在加拿大安大略省多伦多举办的"文化遗产与当代社会的相关性及其应用"工作坊成员制定采用。

1. 传播文化遗产在当代社会的相关性及其应用，涵盖全面的出版渠道以及其他沟通方法。

2. 推广最适宜的文化遗产管理实践方式，确保每个个体与他们自己的文化遗产之间都能实现有意义的关联，确保每个文化场地、每件物品和每项传统都能得到合适的考量。

3. 评估当代社会对文化遗产的冲击，规划可持续的长期战略和同盟，以在当代社会增强物质和非物质文化遗产的影响力。

4. 增强公众对盗毁文化遗址、交易国际文物的认识

5. 增大专业人士和社区的体量，促进全面的文化遗产行动，以增进区域性自豪感、自主性和经济利益。

6. 担当政府、地方社区和其他利息相关者（包括文化遗产后裔族群）之间的纽带，

以鼓励文化遗产的管理。把文化遗产纳入地区性和国际性关联中，从而对自然灾害后的恢复工作做好充分准备。

7. 把文化遗产纳入地区性和国际性关联中，从而对自然灾害后的恢复工作做好充分备。

8. 建立和推广确认责任归属的方法，以保证文化遗产赔偿和恢复的资金来源。

9. 建立和推广文化遗产管理教育材料，在地方层面以及国际层面用多种语言共享信息。

10. 提出相关建议，以增加文化遗产后裔社区以及其他利益相关者在文化遗产数据生成、保护和管理方面的参与。

11. 支持并鼓励民间文化遗产项目，包括在地方社区中博物馆的建立和维护。

12. 提出相关建议，以增加文化遗产后裔社区以及其他利益相关者在文化遗产数据生成、保护和管理方面的参与。

阅读完整的宣言内容，请前往第1章。

APPENDIX D

Déclaration sur la Pertinence et l'Application du Patrimoine dans la Société Contemporaine

La version de poche

Adopté par les participants à l'Atelier sur la Pertinence et l'Application du Patrimoine dans la Société Contemporaine.

1. Diffuser la pertinence et l'application du patrimoine dans la société contemporaine dans la gamme complète de publications et d'autres méthodes de communication.
2. Rendre public les meilleures pratiques en matière de gestion du patrimoine culturel pour s'assurer que chacun ait un lien significatif avec son héritage, et pour s'assurer que la gamme complète des sites, objets et traditions culturels hérités est dûment prise en considération.
3. Évaluer la gamme complète des impacts contemporains sur le patrimoine culturel et formuler des stratégies et des alliances durables à long terme pour améliorer le patrimoine culturel tangible et immatériel dans la société contemporaine.
4. Accroître la sensibilisation du public au pillage et à la destruction sur les sites du patrimoine culturel et le commerce international des antiquités.
5. Renforcer la capacité des professionnels et des communautés pour mener toute la gamme des actions du patrimoine culturel pour promouvoir la fierté locale, la propriété et les avantages économiques.
6. Agir en tant que liaisons entre les gouvernements, les communautés locales et d'autres parties prenantes, en comprenant les peuples descendants, afin d'encourager l'intendance du patrimoine culturel.
7. Inclure le patrimoine culturel dans les réseaux locaux et internationaux pour la préparation et la récupération des catastrophes naturelles.
8. Élaborer et diffuser des méthodes pour identifier les parties responsables afin d'obtenir des fonds pour les actions de restitution du patrimoine et de rétablissement.

9. Élaborer et diffuser du matériel éducatif pour la gestion du patrimoine culturel, à l'échelle locale et internationale pour partager des informations dans plusieurs langues.
10. Élaborer des recommandations pour une participation accrue des communautés descendantes et d'autres parties prenantes à la protection et à la gestion des données du patrimoine culturel.
11. Appuyer et encourager les programmes du patrimoine culturel de base, y compris l'établissement et l'entretien des musées dans les communautés locales.

Pour la version complète de cette déclaration, veuillez visitez Chapitre 1.

APPENDIX E

إعلان تورنتو

لزوم التراث و تطبيقاته في المجتمع المعاصر

أكتوبر 2016

إتفق المشاركزن في ورشة العمل "لزوم التراث وتطبيقاته في المجتمع المعاصر"، التي عقدت في تورنتو، كندا، أكتوبر 2016 علي ما يلي من أنشطة لتفعيل وتنشيط عناصر التراث الحضاري في المجتمعات المعاصرة :

1. الإعلام بجدوى التراث الحضاري وعلاقته بالمجتمع المعاصر من خلال وسائل النشر والتواصل.
2. التعريف بأفضل المناهج لإدارة التراث الحضاري حتى يُتاح لكل فرد في المجتمع أن يتواصل مع تراثه، وأن تحظى المواقع الأثرية والمواريث الثقافية والعاديات المتوارثة بالإعتبار الواجب.
3. تقييم مدى تأثر التراث الحضاري بالمتغيرات المعاصرة ووضع السياسات المستدامة طويلة المدى والتحالفات لتعزيز دور التراث المادي واللامادي في المجتمع المعاصر.
4. تعميق وعي الجماهير بما يجري من نهب وتدمير لمواقع التراث الحضاري والتجارة العالمية في الآثار.
5. بناء قدرات المهنيين والمجتمعات بكل نواحي أنشطة التراث الحضاري وتعزيز الافتخار المحلي بالتراث وامتلاكه والإستفادة منه اقتصاديا.
6. العمل كوسيط بين الحكومات والجماعات المحلية وغيرهم من ذوي المصالح ومنهم سلالات الشعوب الأصليون لتنشيط رعاية التراث الحضاري.
7. دمج التراث الحضاري في الشبكات المحلية والعالمية في مجالات الإستعداد للكوارث الطبيعية و التعافي منها.
8. تجهيز وإذاعة المناهج التي تهدف إلى التعرف على الشركاء لتوفير الأموال اللازمة لاسترداد واستعادة التراث.
9. تجهيز وإذاعة (نشر) المواد التعليمية في مجال التراث الحضاري على الصعيد المحلي والدولي للمشاركة في المعلومات بلغات متعددة.
10. إعداد توصيات لدعم مشاركة المجتمعات المحلية وغيرهم في أنشطة التراث الحضاري ومنها إنتاج المعلومات وصون موارد التراث وإدارته.
11. دعم وتشجيع برامج النشاط الأهلي ويشمل تجهيز واستمرارية متاحف لأهالي الأحياء التراثية

INDEX

Advisory Council on Historic Preservation's Consulting with Indian Tribes in the Section 106 Process 106
Afghanistan 190, 191–192
American Alliance of Museums (AAM) 47–50
American Indian Religious Freedom Act 109
archaeology: armed conflict and 177–179; development in paradigms 83–85; engaged 164–166; ethics and 161–164, 179–180; human rights and 166–169; intangibles approach 100–101; role in contemporary society 81–83, 89
Archeological Resources Protection Act 109
armed conflict 11–12, 15–16, 44–45, 177–179, 190–192
Art Crime Team 47
arts and crafts 111–112
Art Theft Detail 47
Association of Art Museum Directors (AAMD) 48, 50, 51
Athens Charter 128
Australian Heritage Council 60
Australian Institute of Aboriginal and Torres Strait Islander Studies (AIATSIS) 162
authorized heritage discourse (AHD) 97–99

bi disc 38–41
Bighorn Medicine Wheel of Wyoming 108
Blue Shield 13–14, 17–19, 192

Buddhas of Bamiyan 176, 191
Bureau of Ocean Energy Management (BOEM) 108
Bureau of Reclamation 117, 119
Burra Charter 128

case studies: Grace Islet Heritage Site 23–31; highland agriculture of South America 155–156; jade *bi* disc 38–41; Sri Lanka 155
Charter for the Protection and Management of Archaeological Heritage 128
China: attitude of government toward cultural heritage 57; cultural heritage management in 56–65; Law of the People's Republic of China on Protection of Cultural Relics 57, 60, 62; National Archaeological Parks 61; new policies 60–61, 63; Principles for Conservation of Heritage Sites in China 60; principles for protecting the cultural heritage 56–57; problem of urbanization on attitudes toward cultural heritage 57–60; public attitudes toward cultural heritage 62–65; Qujiang model 63
climate change: adaptation 146; impact on cultural heritage stewardship 188–190; planning for resilience 150–152; Traditional Ecological Knowledge (TEK) and adaptation 152–156
collaboration 99–100
community development projects 143

Confederated Salish and Kootenai Tribes of the Flathead Reservation (CSKT) 117
Confederated Tribes of the Colville Reservation (CCT) 117
Convention Concerning the Protection of the World Cultural and Natural Heritage 2
Convention for the Safeguarding of Intangible Cultural Heritage 128
Convention on Stolen or Illegally Exported Cultural Property 2, 46, 191
Convention on the Means of Prohibiting and Preventing the Illicit Import, Export and Transfer of Ownership of Cultural Property 2, 46, 191
Convention on the Protection of the Underwater Cultural Heritage 2
corporate social responsibility 138–139
corporations 140–141
Cowichan Tribes 24
cultural heritage: corporate social responsibility 138–139; definition of 35, 44, 125–127; destruction of 17, 190–192; emergence of stakeholder collaborations 141–142; illegal trafficking of 44–51; impact of urbanization on attitudes toward 57–58; importance of 102–103; indigenous innovations in 115–124; innovative approaches to locational integrity 118–119; intangible 100–101, 103, 105, 111–112, 121–122, 146, 161, 167, 170, 186; international legal protections 137–138; law and ethics in management 160–180; legal regimes for protection of 135–137; management in China 56–65; programs 131–133; protecting through nongovernmental and voluntary practices 135–143; protections of 127–129; recommendations for future progress 142–143; relevance of 43; role of corporations 140–141; role of development banks/lenders 139–140; role of public–private partnerships 141–142; role of trade associations 140–141; stewardship 110–111, 186–196; tourism 15, 66–76; voluntary practices 138–139; *see also* heritage
cultural heritage management (CHM): approaches 129–131; components of 92–93; course topics 93–94; national patrimony approach 130–131; program in Egypt 85–88; social license approach 129–130
cultural landscapes 107–109

cultural property: definition of 13; four tier approach to 16–18; historical context 11–13; importance of protection 14–16; legal action for destruction of 19; military concerns for protections 15–16; reasons for damage and destruction 17; recent activity 17–19
Cultural Property (Armed Conflicts) Bill 17
Cultural Property Implemetation Act (CPIA) 49
cultural resource management (CRM) 80, 84, 105

data: collection 117; emerging challenges and benefits of the new makers 119–122; future of makers 122–123; management 117, 119; protection 118
Declaration of Principles of International Cultural Cooperation 2
Declaration on the Rights of Indigenous Peoples 170–172, 174–175
development banks/lenders 139–140

education: course topics 93–94; cultural heritage management program in Egypt 85–88; cultural heritage management programs and 91–95; heritage curriculum 86–88; in heritage management 79–83
Egypt 19, 79, 81, 85–88, 192
Emergency Protection for Iraqi Cultural Antiquities Act 50
engagement 96–103
Environmental and Social Impact Assessment (ESIA) 187
ethics 3, 161–164, 179–180
European Association of Archaeologists (EAA) 163
Executive Order 13084 Consultation and Coordination with Indian Tribal Governments 106
Executive Order 13175 Consultation and Coordination with Indian Tribal Governments 106

family camera project 42
Federal Bureau of Investigation (FBI) 47, 51
First Nations 24–25
four tier approach 17–18
French University in Egypt (UFE) 85–88

Geneva Convention 15, 190
Getty Conservation Institute 60
Glacier Ice Patch Project 120–122

212 Index

Global Heritage Fund (GHF) 128–129
Grace Islet Heritage Site case study: analysis and results 27–30; background 23–25; discussion 30–31; study methods 25–26
Grand Tour 67, 72, 75
greenhouse gas (GHG) emissions 188–190

Hague Convention on the Protection of Cultural Property in the Event of Armed Conflict (1954) 2, 11, 13, 15, 45, 190–191; Blue Shield 13–14, 17–19; Protocol 11; Second Protocol 11, 12, 13
Hague Convention with Respect to the Laws and Customs of War on Land and its annex (1899) 12
Hague Convention with Respect to the Laws and Customs of War on Land and its annex (1907) 12
heritage: climate change risks to 148–150; collaboration with public 99–100; contemporary Indian products as aspects of 111–112; defining 70; engagement of public 96–103; higher education for managers 79–89; online opinion and conservation issues 21–31; planning for resilience 150–152; plants as 110–111; political interest in 15; preservation property types 107–109; as profession 97–98; resources 147–148; stakeholders 101–102; *see also* cultural heritage; cultural property
Heritage Conservation Act (HCA) 24
heritage management: impacts of governmental policies and procedures on indigenous heritage 105–106; national historic preservation programs 106–107; preservation property types 107–109; tribal historic preservation 109–112; *see also* management
heritage tourism: benefits of 15; defining 69–70; in Early 21st Century 71–75; from the Grand Tour to 67–69, 72, 75, 81; heritage management in US and 105–113; promise of 66–67; relevance in contemporary society 75–76; value and 74–75
highland agriculture 155–156
Historic Sites Act 79
human rights 166–169

illegal antiquities: defining global problem 44–45; efforts of U.S. museums to combat 48–51; impact of armed conflict 44–45, 191–192; international efforts to fight trafficking of 45–46; U.S. efforts to combat trafficking 47

Indian Arts and Crafts Act 111
indigenous peoples: archaeologists and 83, 85; collaborative projects with 101; contemporary Indian products as aspects of 'heritage' 111–112; corporate social responsibility and 140; cultural heritage management issues 119; Grace Islet Heritage Site case study 23–30; impacts of governmental policies and procedures on indigenous heritage 105–113; international protections for cultural heritage 137–138, 170–172, 174–177; legal regimes for protection of cultural heritage 135–137; NAGPRA 118–119, 173–174; national historic preservation programs 106–107; traditional ecological knowledge 110–111; tribal cultural landscapes 108–109; tribal historic preservation 109–112
Indo-Pacific Prehistory Association (IPPA) 165
intangible cultural heritage 100–101, 103, 105, 111–112, 121–122, 146, 161, 167, 170, 186
Intellectual Properties Initiative Heritage Research (IPinCH) 112
intellectual property (IP) 167
Inter-American Development Bank (IDB) 139–140, 165–166
Intergovernmental Panel of Climate Change (IPCC) 148
International Centre for the Study of the Preservation and Restoration of Cultural Property (ICCROM) 151
International Convention on the Elimination of All Forms of Racial Discrimination 171
International Council of Museums (ICOM) 46, 163
International Council on Mining and Metals (ICMM) 138
International Council on Monuments and Sites (ICOMOS) 128, 137, 150, 163, 169, 187
International Covenant of Civil and Political Rights 2
International Covenant of Economic, Social and Cultural Rights 2
International Criminal Court (ICC) 191
International Criminal Tribunal for the Former Yugoslavia (ICTY) 191
International Federation of Red Cross (IFRC) 148
International Finance Corporation (IFC) 139, 166
International Heritage Group (IHG) 165

international humanitarian law (IHL) 15
International Institute for the Unification of Private Law (UNIDROIT) 2, 46, 191
International Labour Organization No. 169 Indigenous and Tribal Peoples Convention 171
international legal protections 137–138
International Monetary Fund (IMF) 165–166
International Organization for Migration (IOM) 192–193
International Petroleum Industry Environmental Conservation Association (IPIECA) 140–141
international protections 169–177
International Scientific Committee (ISC) for Risk Preparedness (ICORP) 150–151
International Union for the Conservation of Nature (IUCN) 137, 163, 169
Interpol 45
Iraq 11, 13, 17–18, 42–43, 45–46, 50–51, 176, 178–179, 190–192
Islamic State of Iraq and Syria (ISIS) 44, 192

Jinshixue 56

Leaders in Energy and Preservation (LEAP) 141–142
legal regimes: archaeology and 169–177; international protections 137–138; proactive and reactive. 135–137
Libya 18, 19, 176, 192
locational integrity 118–119

Mali 18, 19, 176
management: cultural heritage management approaches 129–131; cultural heritage management in China 56–65; cultural heritage management program in Egypt 85–88; cultural heritage stewardship 186–195; cultural resource management 80, 84; higher education for heritage managers 79–89; indigenous innovations in cultural heritage 115–124; law and ethics in cultural heritage 160–180; professional education in heritage management 80–83; stewardship 186–195
Middle East and North Africa (MENA) region 15
migration 192–193
Millennium Development Goals (MDGs) 166–167

Mongolian International Heritage Team (MIHT), 131–133
multilateral financial institutions (MFIs) 126, 128
museums: ban on trade in antiquities 50–51; case study of object in Royal Ontario Museum (ROM) 38–41; challenges facing 41–43; ethical responsibilities 49–50; global trade in illegal antiquities and 47–51; legal responsibilities 48–49; objects of past in 36–37; relevance of cultural heritage in 35–43; responsibilities 42–43; standards for acquiring antiquities 48, 49–50

National Environmental Policy Act 79
National Historic Landmark 108
National Historic Preservation Act 79, 105, 106, 109–110
national historic preservation programs 106–107
National Park Service: Bulletin 38 107; Director's Orders 110; funding for THPOs 110; human burials 119
national patrimony approach 130–131
National Register of Historic Places 107–109
National Stolen Property Act 47
National Trust for Historic Preservation 70
Native American Graves Protection and Repatriation Act (NAGPRA) 118–119, 173–174
New York African Burial Ground project 101
nonstate actors 177–179, 180
North Atlantic Treaty Organization (NATO) 18–19

objects: case study of jade *bi* disc 38–41; of past 36–37; as path of connection to past 36–37; as tool of communication with past 37
Of Africa project 41–42
online newspapers 22–23
Oyu Tolgoi, LLC (OT) 131–133

Paris Agreement (CMA) 188
plants 110–111
preservation property types 107–109
Presidential Memorandum on Tribal Consultation: Memorandum for the Heads of Executive Departments and Agencies 106
Protect and Preserve International Cultural Property Act 17, 47, 48

public opinion 23
public–private partnerships 141–142

reader comments 23
Reservoir Salvage Act 79
resilience 147–148, 150–152
Rio Tinto Group 140, 163–164
Roerich Pact 12
Rome Statute 16, 191
Royal Ontario Museum (ROM): Of Africa project 41–42; family camera project 42; Heritage Day 41; jade collection 38–41

social license approach 129–130
Society for American Archaeology (SAA) 140, 163, 166
Sri Lanka 155
stakeholder collaborations 4–6, 141–142
stewardship: current approaches to 186–188; global challenges and new approaches 194–196; impact of armed conflict 190–192; impact of climate change 188–190; impact of government authority and financing 193–194; impact of migration 192–193; TEK and 110–111
Syria 18, 19, 45–46, 178, 179, 192

Toronto Declaration on the Relevance and Application of Heritage in Contemporary Society 35, 116, 199–209
tourism *see* heritage tourism
trade associations 140–141
traditional cultural properties (TCPs) 107–109
traditional ecological knowledge (TEK) 110–111, 152–156
Treaty of Vienna 12
tribal historic preservation 109–112

United Nations Climate Change Commission (UNFCCC) 148
United Nations Educational, Scientific and Cultural Organisation (UNESCO): collaboration with Egypt 86; Convention Concerning the Protection of the World Cultural and Natural Heritage 72, 137–138, 175–177, 187; Convention on the Means of Prohibiting and Preventing the Illicit Import, Export and Transfer of Ownership of Cultural Property 2, 46, 191; protections of cultural heritage 128, 148; restrictions on acquisition of ancient artwork 38; scholarships for heritage management 88; training program for company commander–level officers 18; World Heritage List 147, 149
United Nations Framework Convention on Climate Change (UNFCCC) 188, 194
United Nations International Strategy for Disaster Reduction (UNISDR) 148, 150–151
United Nations Refugee Agency (UNHCR) 192–193
United Nations (UN): ban on trade in Iraqi artifacts 50; Declaration on the Rights of Indigenous Peoples 170–172, 174–175; efforts to combat global trade in illegal antiquities 45–46; heritage and human rights, 166–167; International Convention on the Elimination of All Forms of Racial Discrimination 171; Millennium Development Goals (MDGs) 166–167; Security Council Resolution 2199 50
United Nations World Tourism Organization (UNWTO) 15, 88
United States: archaeological record 102; efforts of museums to efforts to combat antiquities trafficking 48–51; efforts to combat antiquities trafficking 47; heritage tourism in 70; impacts of governmental policies and procedures on indigenous heritage 105–113; legislation for protection of cultural property 17, 46, 79–80, 136–137; national historic preservation programs 106–107; preservation property types 107–109; tribal historic preservation 109–112
Universal Declaration of Human Rights 2
urbanization: impact on attitudes toward cultural heritage 57–58; problem of 58–60
U.S. Department of Homeland Security 47
U.S. Department of the Interior Secretarial Order 3317 106
U.S. Forest Service: Departmental Regulation 1350–002 Tribal Consultation, Coordination, and Collaboration 106; innovative data collection and creation 117

values 3, 74–75
Venice 71–74
voluntary practices 138–139

World Archaeological Congress (WAC)
 161, 163
World Bank Group (WBG) 126, 139,
 165–166
World Heritage Centre (WHC) 80, 137
World Heritage Committee 137

World Heritage Convention 128
World Heritage List (WHL) 147,
 149, 187
World Heritage sites 138, 169

Yemen 18, 192